TRANSLATORS
IN MEXICO

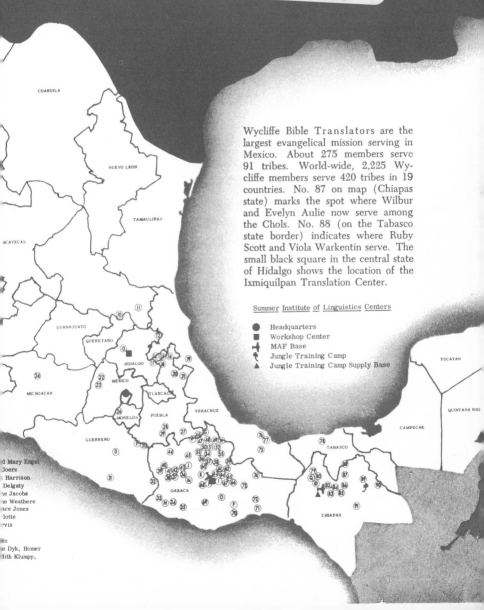

Wycliffe Bible Translators are the largest evangelical mission serving in Mexico. About 275 members serve 91 tribes. World-wide, 2,225 Wycliffe members serve 420 tribes in 19 countries. No. 87 on map (Chiapas state) marks the spot where Wilbur and Evelyn Aulie now serve among the Chols. No. 88 (on the Tabasco state border) indicates where Ruby Scott and Viola Warkentin serve. The small black square in the central state of Hidalgo shows the location of the Ixmiquilpan Translation Center.

Summer Institute of Linguistics Centers

● Headquarters
■ Workshop Center
⚓ MAF Base
Jungle Training Camp
▲ Jungle Training Camp Supply Base

PERIL
BY
CHOICE

John Beekman

PERIL
BY
CHOICE

**The Story of John and Elaine Beekman,
Wycliffe Bible Translators in Mexico**

JAMES C. HEFLEY

*Foreword by W. Cameron Townsend
Introduction by William Culbertson*

A Special Edition For
WYCLIFFE BIBLE TRANSLATORS, INC.
P.O. Box 1960, Santa Ana, California 92702

Dedicated to

the families, friends, and colleagues of John Beekman who have helped keep his heart "ticking" by their faith and prayers.

FOREWORD

Dr. Lew Wade Gosnell, formerly dean of the Day School of Moody Bible Institute, has left us his record of some words of Dr. James M. Gray, one of my predecessors in the office of president of the Institute. The words seem particularly relevant in view of this biography. Said Dr. Gray: "Gosnell, I feel that these students [at M.B.I.] are a very sacred trust. Many of them will amount to more for God and His service, than either you or I. I feel that God has set me amongst them, and has charged me strictly to do my best for them, reminding me that I shall have to give an account of my stewardship."

Dr. Gray stated a matter which is illustrated in this book: "Many of them will amount to more for God and His service, than either you or I." God has so used John and Elaine Hummel Beekman. God has raised them up, endowed them with natural and spiritual talents, called them, sustained them, blessed them and used them — and we, their friends at Moody, are humbly grateful that they passed through these halls, classrooms, offices and dormitories. John graduated from the Pastors Course in 1946, Elaine graduated from the Christian Education-Music Course in 1945 and from the Missionary Course in 1946. Little did any of us realize then, and I think especially John and Elaine, that such large usefulness in the face of so great testings lay before them. The story speaks for itself. Heart-moving experiences are set before us. But in the midst of the sorrows stands the God who causes all things to work together for good. Tears and laughter. Sorrow and joy. Trials and trust. This is life. But beyond all of the daily incidents that make up living is the glorious way God has wrought — in the testimony of life, in the call to the exacting, meticulous work of translation and language consultation, in teaching the Word of God, in the salvation of precious souls.

John Beekman worthily was Moody Bible Institute's Alumnus of the Year in 1963. He stands as an example, an inspiration and a challenge. God bless John and Elaine. Those of us at the Institute remember them as taking their place high among former students God is using so gloriously.

WILLIAM CULBERTSON
President, Moody Bible Institute

Introduction

The Apostle John foresaw " . . . a great multitude, which no man could number, of all nations, and kindreds, and people, and tongues, (who) stood before the throne, and before the Lamb, clothed with white robes, and palms in their hands" (Revelation 7:9).

But how will this be so? How will all the tribes of earth hear the Word of God when as yet it does not exist in 2,000 tongues?

John Beekman is part of the answer — an important part.

Here is survivor number three of a delicate heart valve operation; a man who is supposed to take it easy but doesn't; a man supposed to eat a banana, some prunes, or a slice of watermelon each day for his heart's sake, but can't stand them; a man who has worked hard for years helping hundreds of Bible translators put the Word into scores of languages. His ticking heart is heard around the world to the extent that his influence is felt in 420 isolated tribes of 20 nations.

Beekman started as a member of the team that translated the New Testament and some portions of the Old Testament into the Chol Indian language of southern Mexico, but he's no longer a translator. Now he's one of the indispensables we call "support personnel" who comprise about one-half of our more than 2,000 members. They include pilots, mechanics, secretaries, teachers, printers, radio technicians, electronic engineers, bookkeepers, artists, builders, executives, linguists, translation consultants, etc.

This Dutchman's support work as Wycliffe's chief Translation Consultant is something very special. This book shows it in a way that brings the technicalities of linguistics and Bible translation down to earth, weaving in the sublimity of a man's love — love toward a gifted and dedicated Irish-Dutch girl and toward his Master who said, "Go . . . to *every* creature (which naturally means in every language)."

Jim Hefley has written the story in a manner that inspires as it thrills. He has made this book a valuable contribution to the most important task that confronts all Christians — the carrying out of the Great Commission.

W. CAMERON TOWNSEND
General Director,
Wycliffe Bible Translators

Contents

Foreword (William Culbertson, President, Moody Bible Institute)

Introduction (W. Cameron Townsend, General Director,
The Wycliffe Bible Translators)

Prologue *The Sword and the Cross*

ON THE MISTY morning of March 3, 1517, an Indian sentry guarding the northern coast of Yucatan spied three dark objects riding the waves. He watched first with curiosity, then with alarm as the wind blew them nearer the rocky shore. Then he turned and raced across the rocks to alert his chief in a town nearby.

The Spaniards on board the sailing vessels wiped their red eyes and shouted with relief at the sight of land. On a slave-hunting expedition to some newly discovered islands between Cuba and Honduras, a tropical storm had blown them far off course.

Fernandez de Cordoba, their commander, strained to see the rock-strewn beach which faded into a grassy savannah. "This is an unknown land," he remarked soberly to his crewmen. "It is not on our charts."

Suddenly the Spaniards beheld a strange sight rising out of the misty mainland. As the vessels drifted nearer, they could make out a high limestone wall, and above it a series of terraced pyramids and strange buildings. The explorers rubbed their sleepless eyes and questioned each other's sight. It was no mirage. They called it Great Cairo.

They dropped anchor and decided to wait a day before advancing. At dawn the next morning they woke to see a procession of ten long boats, manned by up to forty Indians apiece filing toward them.

The Indians were neatly dressed in cotton shirts and breechclouts. They babbled an unknown language to the Spaniards who sought to express interest in the new land with signs. When the Indians were given strings of glass beads, they turned the boats around and rowed away.

The next morning the natives returned towing several empty boats. Cordoba ignored better judgment and ordered his men to go ashore.

The Spaniards landed and cautiously followed the procession inland toward the town. A short way from the beach they entered an area of grassy mounds. Suddenly loud shrieks split the air and painted warriors lying in ambush behind the mounds began pouring arrows upon the foreigners.

Fifteen Spaniards fell wounded. The rest dove behind mounds and rocks and blazed away with their muskets. The Indians who had never seen such smoking sticks dropped and scattered in disarray. Those able to run fled in terror away from their walled city.

Cordoba's men cared for the wounded, then advanced on "Great

Cairo." The temptation to explore the mysterious city was stronger than the apprehension that they might be walking into a trap.

They entered through a narrow doorway and stood in awe. Before them stood huge buildings formed of stones laid perfectly together and decorated with great sculptured heads of serpents, jaguars, and demon-like creatures. Along the back walls of the temples they found massive stone altars covered with carvings of costumed chieftains, priests, and human heads joined to animal or serpentine bodies.

Incense still perfumed the air, evidence that the buildings had been deserted only moments before. The Spaniards put aside the worry of a counterattack and dug greedily into the wooden chests on the altars. They scooped up handfuls of golden figurines of animals. Then they raced for the beach and their waiting ships. Later, they assured themselves, they would return and secure a king's ransom.

Fifteen years before, Christopher Columbus had gone ashore at one of the Bay Islands off the coast of Honduras and met an Indian trading party in a long dugout canoe. The Indians had pointed north and said, "Maiam. Maiam." This was the strange land Cordoba had discovered.

Cordoba had unknowingly executed a turning point in history. On the rocky sands of Yucatan, warriors from opposite worlds had met in a clash of arms. The white giants with smoking sticks had tasted the heady wine of strange treasure. This, they thought, might be the lengendary El Dorado, that mysterious kingdom of untold wealth which had lured adventurers across the uncharted Western Sea. It was reputed to be a paradise "where the sands sparkled with gems, and golden pebbles as large as birds' eggs were dragged in nets out of the rivers." They were determined to conquer the new land with the cross and the sword at all costs. The tragedy of the conquest of a new continent had begun.[1]

After 15 days of sailing along the coast, Cordoba's party went ashore again and visited another Mayan city without mishap. But the third time they disembarked, warriors swarmed onto the beach and surrounded them. Outnumbered 200 to 1, the Spaniards built barricades and forced the Indians back by fire power. Cordoba, suffering from ten wounds, led his men to their boats. They escaped across the water with arrows and lances showering the air behind

[1] In 1511, four years before Cordoba landed on the coast of Yucatan, Captain Valdiva and 20 men drifted onto Cozumel Island and within sight of Yucatan. The Maya natives killed all except two and traded these as slaves to the Lord of Xamanzana on the Yucatan mainland. Cordoba's men fought the Mayans in the first mainland battle between Europeans and American Indians.

them. Days later they limped into Cuba where Cordoba died of his wounds.

Survivors' tales incited a second expedition to the Maya lands under the command of Juan de Grijalva. He also met a hostile welcome, but subsequently managed a peaceful meeting with a powerful Mayan chieftain. The chief presented Grijalva with jewels and other articles of gold, then declared that in the direction of the sunset there was much more. Pointing, the chief said, "Colua, Colua, Mejico, Mejico."

Inflamed with the fever of conquest, Grijalva led his fleet along the shoreline that curved in a westerly direction. In a few days they sighted the present state of Veracruz where hordes of plumed warriors waited on the beach.

Unknown to Grijalva, news of Cordoba's earlier expedition had reached Montezuma, the king of the Aztecs. He proclaimed the fulfillment of an ancient prophecy which said that a long banished god, Quetzalcoatl, would return from "the direction of the sunrise" to lead the people in a new order. Montezuma believed that the appearance of the strange ships and the bearded men marked the arrival of his kingly successor.

Grijalva, however, merely disembarked briefly on the coast to trade for gold. Then his ships returned to Cuba.

It remained for Hernando Cortez to return the following year and subdue the Aztec empire, just as Montezuma's prophets had predicted. Cortez brought the Spanish greed for gold, the religious intolerance of the Inquisition, and the slavery of feudalism to the Indians of New Spain.

After the Aztecs, it was the Mayans turn to be conquered. But their subjugation was not so rapid. They beat back a Spanish effort to establish a colony at Chichen Itza, now a famous archaeological site. Not until 1541 did the Spaniards break the fighting spirit of the Mayans at their city of T'ho. The Spanish commander renamed it Merida. From that time the once glorious Mayan empire began sliding toward oblivion.

The padres followed the soldiers, some bad, some good, all hungry for souls to build the Catholic church. The priests took over from the military commanders and set about baptizing and systematically destroying the Mayan culture and building a system based upon European values. In their fanatical frenzy to erase all traces of heathenism, they destroyed almost all of the Mayan written records that had survived the battles — thus crippling the work of future scholars who would seek to reconstruct a history of a civilization more advanced than any Europeans had ever dreamed possible in New Spain. A few priestly writers were able to compile an informal Mayan history for the Spanish court, but these accounts were not published until three centuries later.

After the priests came the Spanish colonists, washed ashore by westerly winds. They came allured by the promise of land and free Indian labor. Indians that attempted to run away, they hunted down mercilessly with bloodhounds and either hung or roasted alive as examples to other would-be escapees.

One lone voice was heard above the crack of slave whips and the moans of suffering Indians. Bartolme de Las Casas, a conquistadore turned monk and later a bishop, trumpeted against the injustice that was making Spain wealthy and powerful in its new possessions. He reminded Charles V that emperors whose orders go against the common good cease to be princes in God's sight. If the Indians must suffer as they were suffering to become Christians, Las Casas argued, better for them to remain heathen. Though hated by both conquistadores and religious colleagues, the reform-minded bishop managed to get laws passed abolishing slavery. But the laws were later repealed and Las Casas spent the last years of his long life (1474-1566) in Spain publicizing the wrongs inflicted upon the Indians. Today he is a hero in Mexico. The market center in the State of Chiapas that bears his name is known as the Indian capital of the world.

In the years following the conquest, the foreign colonists forcibly removed thousands of Mayans from ancestral villages to their estates. A sad recounting of this deportation was found in a Mayan chronicle written shortly after the conquest: ". . . it was the beginning of tribute, church dues, strife with guns, trampling of people, robbery with violence, debts enforced by false testimony — the beginning of vexation."

So a once proud people bowed to their light-skinned masters and gave lip service to the dogmas of Spanish Catholicism. Their great cities slowly but surely melted into the obscurity of the jungles of what is now southern Mexico and Guatemala. But even after their altars were gone — often crushed under the foundation of Spanish churches — the Mayans still retained belief in their ancient deities. They continued secretly to implore the deities of the solar heavens when planting their fields. As year after year of oppression passed, the descendants of the Mayans held on to their pagan beliefs and their language which in time splintered into a maze of mutually unintelligible dialects.

For over two centuries the Mayans continued to be an obscure people, considered fit only to be slaves of civilized men. Then in 1773 the ruins of their greatest city, Palenque, were unveiled and publicized. Expeditions of scholars began invading the green jungles, seeking more information about the lost civilization. Theories abounded about their origin. One opinion had them descending from the Lost Tribes of Israel; another from the pyramid-building Egyptians. Scholars proposing the latter origin pointed to the huge stone pyramids, hieroglyphic writing, and relief sculpture discovered in the jungles. Another theory suggested that the legendary lost island of Atlantis had been the common ancestral home of both Egyptians and Americans. Still another suggested Noah's ark had come to rest in America and the Indians were his descendants.

In 1840, John Lloyd Stephens, a well-traveled New York lawyer who had seen Roman and Egyptian ruins, came with an artist friend to the Mid-America jungles. They proved that the pre-conquest Mayans had an amazing intelligence, having developed mathematics, astronomy, and chronology centuries before such abstract science was known anywhere else.

More ruins have since been uncovered bringing hordes of curious tourists to the jungles where three or more million people once lived. Today the ruins at Palenque, Chichen Itza, and other sites are major tourist attractions. The National Anthropological Museum in Mexico City is filled with Mayan artifacts.

Hundreds of books have been written about the history and civilization of the Mayans. Latest speculation links the Mayan and other Mid-American Indians to the ancient Olmecs ("rubber people") who lived in Mid-America when the Israelites were delivered from Egypt. The popular view is that the ancestors of the Olmecs came from the Orient via the Bering Strait and through Alaska to Indianize the hemisphere. The Mayan calendar, which is more accurate than the one we use, begins for unknown reasons in the year 3113 B.C. However, in December 1967, Mexican scholars announced the finding and dating of identifiable human remains near Mexico City that they believe to be 24,000 years old.

But what of the descendants of the Mayan peoples whose architects, mathematicians, and sculptors ranked with the most erudite civilizations of ancient times? As Spanish civilization advanced in the New World they divided into over a score of tribes, retreating west and south into present Central America (mainly Guatemala) and the Mexican state of Chiapas. Remote Chiapas, where jaguars still devour children, is still ninety per cent Mayan, peopled by the Chols, the Tzeltals, the Lacondons, the Tzoltils, the Chamulas, and ten other tribes who share a common ancestry.

Their national pride has shriveled since the conquistadores landed. Instead of great cities and monuments of art, most now build only crude stick and thatch houses. They practice slash-and-burn agriculture, using only the machete and the primitive dibble stick. They are economically dependent upon the minority Spanish-speaking propertied class, to whom they sell their products, for whom they toil in fields and factories, and from whom they buy liquor and other commodities. Illiterate and naive, many remain perpetually in debt to the *ladino* or Spanish speaking class.

Their religious beliefs and practices vary from tribe to tribe, but may be classified as Christo-Mayan. They have outwardly adopted the trappings of Spanish Catholicism — the saints, the feast days, and some of the ceremonies. But they still worship the sun and the moon and other terrestrial deities. They grudgingly obey the Spanish-speaking priest who may visit a tribal church once a year, but in day-to-day life they fear the witch doctors. Before modern reforms began to sweep the Catholic Church, they were counted as Catholics. Now there are voices within Catholicism that classify them pagan.

Until recent years the Indians of Chiapas were ignored and allowed to exist in servility, poverty, and superstition, while throngs of scholars and tourists paid homage to the cities and temples of their Mayan ancestors. But the winds of revolutionary change are now sweeping these Indians into a new order.

These winds of change have been principally put in motion by two humanitarian forces, one political and one religious. The political force has been the progressive revolutionary government of modern Mexico which has broken up many huge feudal estates and made land available to the landless. The major religious force has been the Wycliffe Bible Translators, who, motivated by God's love for the lost tribes and armed with the tools of modern linguistics, have marched into the most remote villages of Chiapas. Named for the first translator of the whole English Bible, the "linguisticos" have sparked a spiritual revolution among the Indians. For this they have been praised by Mexicans of all stripes. (Example: In 1961 the President of Mexico, Adolfo Lopez Mateos, said, "Their work has achieved notable success and my government will continue to back such a transcendental task.")

The fruits of Bible translation are now to be seen among the tribes of wild tropical Chiapas. The truth of the Scriptures in "every man's" tongue has unlocked for thousands the doors to spiritual, moral, economic, and social freedom. The evangelical church has grown enormously with Presbyterian membership alone more than doubling in Chiapas between 1950 and 1960.[2]

Here is ample proof that the "Sword of the Spirit" has a cutting social edge. Economic slaves have become land owners. Indeed, whole new Christian communities have sprung up. Victims of witchcraft and horribly inadequate hygenic practices now treat their own neighbors with modern medicine. Pride has replaced servility — the Indian now looks the man of Spanish culture in the eye when he meets him on the trail. Bible teaching has stamped sanctity upon life, for example, removing the cruel practice of killing the weakest newborn twin.

Here unfolds the story of one translator couple who came four centuries after the Spaniards, not to exploit, but to exemplify a new way of life; not to subdue but to serve in the name of One who "went about doing good"; not to destroy but to restore and dignify the native language and its best culture.

The heroic efforts of John and Elaine Beekman and their colleagues produced the Chol New Testament, which in turn became the Charter of a virile church whose history reads like a chapter from the Acts of the Apostles.

Here is a declaration in experience that the Bible can produce the answers to the multiple problems of the world's suffering millions.

Here is a testimonial that human frailty dedicated to God can accomplish what armies can never do.

Here is sacrifice, heartbreak, suffering, persecution, and above all, triumphant love that conquered the powers of darkness.

Here is a powerful drama, not because of the skill of the writer, but because of the witness of the participants who made peril their choice.

[2]Official government census figures show that Protestant population in Chiapas grew from 19,292 to 50,877, an increase of 164% during this ten-year period. No other state in Mexico showed such an increase. At least 25,000 of this increase came from the Chol and Tzeltal tribes where Wycliffe Translators have produced New Testaments.

1. Stubborn Dutch Boy

THE LAST MAN was out on the sandlot. "Goin' to the 'Y,' Beekie?" the freckled first baseman asked.

John Beekman slapped the dust with his bat and tried to sound casual. "Naw. Goin' home to work on my racer."

The boys sped away on their bikes. John, blond and skinny, shuffled home on foot. It was time for lunch when he reached the vine-covered gray stucco house at the corner of Prospect and Glen. Too tired to eat, he flopped in the cool shade of the silver maple in his side yard.

The thin boy lay there in his patched denims, chest heaving, trying to recover his strength. He had never told his friends after a game the real reason why he couldn't go to the 'Y' for more fun and games. He hoped no one would ever know besides his parents and doctor.

A routine school exam had moved John's parents to take him to a heart specialist. "The boy has a murmur," the doctor pronounced. "It will probably get worse unless he stays quiet." Looking into John's serious blue eyes, the medic said, "Better tiddleywinks and marbles instead of baseball and football if you want to live a long time."

But John couldn't sacrifice the active games he loved so well, not even if they left him exhausted after an hour of play. Now as he lay in the cool grass, he wondered just how he could continue to compete in a normal world.

He turned his face in the Bermuda grass and spied a wooly caterpillar creeping toward the base of the maple. He watched as it crawled to the tree and began inching upward. A resolution formed in the boy's mind: "I can be like that caterpillar; *I can crawl and climb.*"

The Beekmans were Dutch — stubborn, loyal, and close as a

20

family. Garret John[1] was the eldest, Richard three years younger, and little Jean the youngest. Their parents, Thomas and Bella, had been born in Holland and brought to New Jersey as toddlers. Thomas' family spoke the *Amsterdam* Dutch dialect, Bella's family the *Friesian* dialect. They talked Dutch at home only when discussing a surprise planned for the children.

Thomas Beekman's gardener father settled in Midland Park, 25 miles north of Newark and inland 20 miles from the Hudson River. Bella's parents had a dairy farm nearby in Prospect Park. Bella and Tom met at a Dutch baker's house and ever after the big blond Dutchman bragged about "the prize I found in a baker's shop."

John was born in a rented two-story frame house on Cottage Street in Midland Park. One fine day he waddled outside and stripped the landlord's flowers from their stems. The Beekmans quickly received moving orders. Fortunately they found a house a mile away that they could buy with a small down payment.

Bad winds blew in 1929 when John was 10. Jovial, easy-going Tom Beekman became ill and could not ply his mason's trade. Baby Jean, only four weeks old, kept Bella home. John and Richard's paper route did not bring in enough money for living expenses Something more had to be done.

Flower making and selling became a family affair. Tom snipped and twisted wires. Bella cut artificial petals from crepe paper. John and Richard used their express wagon as a delivery truck for door to door selling. Sometimes when the weather was warm they took baby Jean along for the ride.

Bella Beekman made the boys' clothes. An old man's overcoat, for example, she ripped apart and dyed to furnish them new coats. She also took in sewing and when Jean was older, Bella worked in a silk mill for $13.00 a week.

Still financial ends did not meet. The house payments dropped further and further behind, until a foreclosure notice arrived. Tom looked on helpless from his sickbed as Bella wrung her hands in despair. John sized up the gloomy situation. Grasping his little brother by the hand, he said, "We're going to see the man."

The boys trudged to the mortgage holder's house. They were a pathetic pair in their handmade, well-worn clothes, and scuffed shoes. "We can't pay the back payments," John explained, "but,

[1]Named for his paternal grandfather, John uses the name Garret only in documents.

please, couldn't we stay on and pay rent? We'll all work as hard as we can."

The man looked at the two boys who were close to tears. He nodded in assent. The boys raced away to tell their parents. The family continued to live in the house at Prospect and Glen.

Thomas Beekman recovered and the financial cloud lifted a bit. John could even have an occasional treat of his favorite dessert, graham cracker cream pie. Still the budget was too tight for the Beekman boys to attend the Dutch parochial school with their cousins.

Contrary to the heart specialist's advice, Tom and Bella allowed John to lead, as nearly as possible, a normal life. Sandlot baseball, touch football, and ping pong were his favorite sports. Because he fatigued easily, he spent many hours in the garage, building soap box racers from materials thrown away by residents of adjoining upper-class Ridgewood. Then (and today) most Midland Park folks were tradesmen who worked for the Ridgewood managers and executives who commuted to offices in New York City.

John never won any awards in soap box racing, but he and Richard did attract the notice of the Midland Park police by a more dangerous winter sport.

Their trick was to run alongside the rear of the municipal bus as it slowed to turn the slippery corner at Prospect and Glen, then grab hold of the bumper and flop on their sled when the bus started uphill. At the top of the hill, the boys turned loose and slid back home. Once when their mother was in bed with a broken hip, a policeman came to the house. Shaking his finger in John's face, he said, "I've warned you boys for the last time." Bella Beekman called from her bed, "Take them with you, Officer. I can't make them mind." The boys stood shaking until the policeman finally said, "O.K., one more chance."

Another time Tom Beekman smelled smoke in the garage. He raced in to find both sons drawing on corncob pipes, unaware that their new Christmas coats were burning. This shennanigan called for application of the razor strap to their posteriors. Richard, the younger brother, wailed and cried. John clamped his jaws together and silently bore his punishment.

"That was John," his mother now recalls. "You could beat him half to death and he wouldn't cry. But hurt his feelings with a sharp word and the tears would flow."

And Jean, now married to Dutch homebuilder Peter Braunius, says,

"John was like our father, uncomplaining when in pain, very stubborn, soft spoken, and always looking for a laugh."

The straight-laced and devout Beekman family attended the First Reformed Church on Center street. They went there three times a week. The Church dates its history back to 1872. Across the Hudson on the tip of what is now called Manhattan, the first Reformed Church in America was organized in 1628. On nearby Staten Island the "Voorlezer's House," a Dutch School built before 1696, still stands. It is claimed to be the oldest elementary school building in the United States.

The Reformed church of John's boyhood proudly practiced three C's: conservative in theology, crusty in tradition, and clannish in togetherness. Marriages to non-Dutch were taboo. Bowling, skating, and other commercial amusements were thought "worldly."

John had a mischievous streak in him that exasperated the church elders. He sat in the balcony and flipped paper wads on bald heads. Once, Pastor Poole interrupted his sermon to shout, "Johnny Beekman, behave yourself!" He cheated on his catechism lesson, sometimes fleeing before the last question was asked. Once, the Dominie chased him out of the class and up a tree. Afterwards the balding minister shook his head and wailed, "The Lord only knows what is to become of that boy." But Mrs. Poole was not so pessimistic. "The Lord will make something out of Johnny Beekman," she predicted. "I just know He will."

John's antics were especially annoying in his Uncle Gary's Sunday school class. After services, Uncle Gary came to the house and begged, "Please tend to John. He's ruining my class." Down came the razor strap for the proper punishment.

After several strappings for this problem, Bella Beekman asked Uncle Gary, "How can one boy do so much mischief? Mustn't he have some helpers?" Uncle Gary allowed he did, but John was the chief culprit among several involved. John got no more whippings for mischief in Sunday school.

Some church teaching did reach John. Once in the ninth grade he was kept late after school for several consecutive days. When his mother asked him why, he said, "Well, the teacher keeps saying we come from monkeys, and I keep saying it isn't so."

During his early teen years, John attended a weekday Bible class taught by church elder Jake Vandermeer, a bakery truck driver and lay minister. For several months the lessons centered on Old Testament characters — Enoch, Noah, Abraham, and others. John came faithfully but according to the memory of the teacher showed little interest.

Besides John, at least three more of Jake Vandermeer's students have left memorable impressions in the Christian world: Al Smith, the song writer, John Stam, and Bill Sirag, who both became missionary martyrs in the Orient.

In May 1936, John graduated from nearby Pompton Lakes High School. Midland Park then supported only elementary schools. He ranked well in the middle of a class of 300. His favorite subject was commercial arithmetic.

A few days later he hitchhiked into New York City to go job hunting. After several fruitless days, he walked into the telephone company's personnel office on Broadway. Fearful of being shooed out by the receptionist because he had only a high school diploma, he sneaked down to a room where ten young men were taking a job test for a clerk's job in the accounting department.

"How'd you get in here? Who recommended you?" the supervisor asked after John sat down.

"Nobody," John replied smartly. "I came to take the test."

"You've got nerve," the supervisor said. "Here, see what you can do."

The other applicants were all college night students. But John got the job.

John's bent for numbers and systems led him to try horse betting. He worked out a system where he was prepared to lose the first 10 or 12 small bets until he won on a horse that paid enough to recoup his losses. When by chance he won early, he came out ahead. "I was never a compulsive gambler and usually only broke even," he recalls. "Occasionally I won enough to buy a gift for the folks which they thought came from job earnings."

On the commuter he maneuvered a bridge friendship with a high company official who rode the same train and played in company bridge tournaments. When the official needed a partner in an important tournament, he remembered John. The report of their winning appeared in the company news magazine. Shortly, John was promoted to assistant office manager.

Gossip reached the elder Beekmans that John had become "some kind of atheist." They knew nothing of his activities outside the home and passed it off as idle talk. Then the new pastor, Rev. William DeJong, came to talk to John about church membership.

"You have always loyally attended our church," the pastor commended. "Now it is time that you confess your faith before the elders. Remember that Christ said, 'If you confess me before men, I will confess you before my Father.'"

John sat a few feet away twirling a yoyo. Suddenly he swung it toward the pastor, flipping the spool an inch from the pastor's nose and the pastor pretended it was an accident.

"Are there any reasons for you not to make your confession?" the pastor asked.

John retrieved the yoyo, cupped it in his hand, and set his chin. "Yes. I don't believe in the Bible. I think the miracles are all made-up stories. I even doubt there is a God."

His devout parents sitting nearby froze in shock.

"You're not funny at all, young man," the pastor retorted.

Again swinging the yoyo toward the pastor, John said, indifferently, "That's how I feel."

The pastor tried to present arguments supporting the Bible. John curled his lip in defiance and continued to swing the yoyo. Finally the pastor gave up trying and left.

Afterwards John told his parents, "I don't want to talk about religion. I'll go to church with you on Sunday morning, but not at night. I've got an extra job keeping books for a service station manager."

They consented to the compromise. But the following Sunday evening they left Jean and Richard at the church service and hurried home to check. When they saw John seated at his desk in a corner of the dining room dutifully writing in a ledger, they returned to church.

John soon realized that without more education his chances for further advancement with the telephone company were poor. He enrolled for an accounting course with the LaSalle Correspondence schools.

One evening he went to the Midland Park public library to do research. While looking for a book, he noticed a small green book stuck between two larger ones. The size suggested it was obviously in the wrong place. Having a penchant for order, he removed the book to give it to the librarian.

He glanced at the title, *The Wonders of Prophecy*.[2] Mildly curious, he flipped the fly leaf and read the subtitle: "What Are We To Believe?" Underneath that he read a statement by the famous mathematician, Pascal: "Under the Christian religion I find actual prophecy and I find it in no other."

He read further into the first chapter, all the while scolding the author for bias toward the Bible. With gathering interest, he reached the third chapter that dealt with the doom of ancient Tyre and Sidon. Then on impulse he reached for pencil and notebook and jotted down Bible prophecies which the author claimed came true in later history. His eyebrows lifted at the claim that Ezekiel 7:12, "and they shall lay thy stones, and thy timber, and thy dust in the midst of the waters," had been literally fulfilled two centuries later when Alexander the Great conquered Tyre.

Suddenly John became concerned at the implications the book posed for himself: If verifiable proof existed that many ancient Bible prophecies had come true after they were written, then he had only deceived himself. He decided to check the author's statements against reliable secular sources.

At first opportunity he strode into the mammoth New York Public Library, notebook and pencil in hand. With meticulous care he began checking the fate of a list of ancient cities and nations whose downfall had been foretold in the Bible. An hour later he sat stunned at the amazing testimonies of history. Further study of Messianic prophecies convinced him that the Bible must be divine in origin and Christ the Son of God.

As he rode home on the commuter, questions haunted his mind: What will you do? Will you admit what you know is the truth? Will you now stand up for the Bible?

As John remembers, "I felt the Bible was true and Christ the Son of God who died and was resurrected. I had to make a commitment — to decide to go in the opposite direction from which I had been going. From this time forward, I knew I must acknowledge Christ as my Saviour and do God's will."

The following Wednesday evening John went to prayer meeting for the first time in several years. He sat quietly until the pastor asked for volunteers to pray. When he stood and prayed aloud the

[2]Urquhart, John, *The Wonders of Prophecy*, Christian Publications, Harrisburg, Pa.

elders and minister gaped in surprise. For them, more surprises were yet to come.

Jake Vandermeer grasped John's hand at the close of the prayer meeting. "You've come through, boy," he shouted with unrestrained joy. "Praise the Lord!"

John smiled back at the bakery salesman whom he had long admired and respected. Besides the Bible class, they had been on many fishing trips together. Not once had Jake tried to pressure John.

Vandermeer and another elder, Elmer Van Dyke, started taking John along to rescue missions and street meetings. One evening John gave his testimony in a meeting. Afterward, a colorful character known as "Coffee Pot" Jake came to him and said, "Young man, don't change your message. Keep telling 'em about salvation through Christ."

In the days ahead John became better acquainted with Jake, an ex-drunkard who ran a diner in nearby Paterson. "I didn't come to Christ until past 50," Jake often reminded him. "You've got a whole lifetime to serve Christ."

Jake also frequently told John over coffee and doughnuts, "I serve food for the body. Food for the soul is more important." When John learned that the nearby Hawthorne Bible Church had an evening Bible school, he enrolled. Here he discovered that the Hawthorne youth department had placed in the library the book on Bible prophecy that had led to his conversion.

John itched to organize the young people in his own church for service. Rev. Anton Schermer, the new pastor, encouraged him to begin a Christian Endeavor program. Soon John had a crowd of youth participating in Bible study and group recreation.

The church elders liked the Bible studies but not the recreation. "He's throwing the ball in the barn," one said, referring to the bowling parties. "Leading our youth astray."

Complaints reached Pastor Schermer who diplomatically suggested that the youth disassociate their recreational activities from the church with the pastor attending as an interested friend. This satisfied the critics.

Soon after Pearl Harbor Richard enlisted in the Air Force and became chauffeur-pilot for a general. John tried to enlist in hope of becoming a chaplain's assistant, but was rejected because of his heart murmur.

The idea of climbing the corporate ladder with the telephone company became less appealing. John wanted to serve God full time. But at 25 he felt four years of college and three of seminary was too long to prepare. Elmer Van Dyke suggested the Moody Bible Institute which offered a three-year pastor's course. John decided to apply to the Chicago school.

While waiting approval of his application, John began thinking and praying about a wife. He had been dating three girls, one for several years. He tried to project his long-time girl friend as a minister's wife. The image looked fuzzy. One day he quietly told her of his doubts and hinted that she should date other boys.

A letter came saying that his application had been accepted by Moody for enrollment in the fall semester of 1943. He resigned from the telephone company and boarded a train for the Windy City.

John moved into room 73 in the boys' dorm at 153 Institute Place and signed up for a heavy schedule of courses that included Greek. He wrote home, "Like a starved boy gulping a piece of bread I have plunged into my studies."

Tall and sporting wavy blond hair, the twinkle-eyed Dutch boy attracted more than a few glances from girls who noticed that he never dated. Only a few close friends in the dorm knew the reason for his resolution not to date. Because he did not expect to attend seminary, he was determined to spend his time getting all the training he could pack into three years.

But he couldn't escape sitting next to girls in class and mingling with them in the Institute dining room and in social activities. His resolution weakened. He decided to list several girls who appeared attractive and investigate their qualifications.

A pastor's wife should, he concluded, be a devoted Christian, neat in appearance and handwriting, be musically talented, and pleasant to look at. Blond, hazel-eyed Elaine Hummel met the last qualification on his carefully drawn chart. He would check on the rest. If she didn't pass, he would investigate the next girl on his list.

John was working his way through school and at that time operating the elevator part time in Crowell Hall. His ups and downs took him past the registrar's office where he had a smiling friend. One afternoon he asked a special favor: Would she check Elaine Hummel's grades for him?

The girl's reluctance melted under John's smile. Such a nice fellow could not possibly take advantage of a girl. She would look in the files.

The verdict: Excellent grades in both Bible and music. Beautiful handwriting.

Next on the Beekman agenda: An introduction, and hopefully a date. Then he would begin rating her on his chart.

2. *Hearts and Hopes Together*

JOHN LEARNED THAT Elaine would be serving at the upcoming Senior banquet in April. He went straight to the clean-up supervisor and said, "I'll work in your crew if you'll put me at Elaine Hummel's table."

The deal was arranged. Gwen Hummel, an M.K. (missionary's kid) and Elaine's girl friend but no relation, made the formal introduction.

After the dishes were cleaned, John popped the question, "How about going with me Sunday night to hear Dr. Christiansen at Swedish Covenant? He just returned from Africa and should be interesting."

Elaine's face colored. She had seen John in a crowd and thought him "dreamy," but this was so quick and forward. "I guess so," she finally said, breaking the stiff silence.

Later she had second thoughts and wrote a note to John declining the date. She walked around with it for a day, finally deciding against putting it in his mail box. What John did not know was that she, too, was off the opposite sex but for a different reason.

Elaine had been popular at Clearfield High School in the Pennsylvania Dutch country where she reigned as May Queen during her senior year. Several boys rushed her and one became a steady date. But after she sat with another boy on a bus trip he became angry and began dating another girl.

Forth came a young evangelist to lead a revival crusade in her Evangelical United Brethren church. He called at the principal's office where Elaine was the secretary to inquire about speaking in school assembly. Jerry (not his real name) was all that some other boys she knew were not: courtly, poised, flattering, and most important, an apparently dedicated Christian. She fell easily for him.

Jerry wrote long, sentimental and newsy letters as he moved on to other churches. When he held meetings in nearby towns, Elaine attended and he proudly introduced her as "my girl." Jerry was an alumnus of Moody and convinced Elaine she could best develop her musical talents there. He helped by writing a letter of recommendation to the music faculty.

When Elaine arrived in Chicago, she found Jerry was well known by other Moody girls — too well known. Her heart dropped as she heard her own story repeated by various girls whom Jerry had rushed. When Jerry arrived he pledged his undying love, declaring that past romances were history and nothing more. Elaine, disillusioned and wary, was unwilling to take another chance.

Sunday evening after the senior banquet John came to take Elaine to the Swedish church. He surprised her by suggesting they pray together before leaving the dorm. Not even Jerry had done that. Then with prayers said, they walked along the street in the gathering dusk and talked about school life. When the talk switched to families. John thought they had some ancestry in common. Elaine's Irish mother was married to a Pennsylvania Dutchman. But John learned later to his chagrin that the Pennsylvania Dutch are German in origin.

After the service, John said, "I propose . . ." and then paused. Despair swept over Elaine. "Oh no, not another!" she almost moaned aloud. Then John tossed off a teasing smile and added ". . . that we do this again." Elaine laughed nervously and said, "Yes, perhaps we should."

They did. Usually they went to church or a musical program. One Saturday afternoon they enjoyed horseback riding in Lincoln Park with John teasing Elaine about trying to mount on the wrong side of the horse. Then as they were walking home and discussing a problem at school, John suggested quietly, "Let's pray about it as we walk."

"The idea of prayer on a public street shocked me," Elaine now says. "But I soon learned that breaking convention was second nature to John. He seemed to take an impish delight in pulling me out of my straightjacket of formality."

Sunday mornings they usually went to their respective Christian work assignments. Sunday evenings, they attended together the Moody Memorial Church eight blocks north of the Institute on

LaSalle Street where missionaries and nationally known Bible expositors frequently spoke from the pulpit of famed Dr. Harry Ironside. Once when Dr. Ironside's son, the assistant dean of men at Moody, had a heart attack and his wife was in the hospital, the father asked John to fire the son's furnace. For this Dr. Ironside called John into his office and presented him 30 of his own books.

At the Moody Church and around the Institute John sensed the influence of the unconventional founder, Dwight L. Moody. The courses were practical, geared to prepare Christian workers with practical skills to use at home and abroad in pastoring, Christian education, music, script writing, radio announcing, and even flying.

John frequently chuckled over familiar sayings and actions of the irrepressible Moody who had directed in a Chicago slum the only Sunday school Abraham Lincoln ever visited.

He liked such Moodyisms as: "I want a faith that's got legs and can run." And, when a man was orating a long prayer, "Let's sing a hymn while our brother is finishing his prayer."

John, like Moody, saw no value in a dreary, boring piety that made prayer and formal church services ends in themselves. Like Moody, he wanted a faith that had "legs" and could "run." To have this kind of faith, he organized his time alloting specific slots to study, prayer, darning socks and other activities. In apologizing for sending mimeographed letters to friends in Midland Park, he listed this weekly schedule:

50 hours	Scheduled studies per week
10 hours	Home prayer leadership
5 hours	Group devotions
5 hours	Prayer sessions
10 hours	Chicago Detention Home
10 hours	Leader of Hospital Visitation
90 hours	

The schedule did not include part-time work to apply on school expenses. One of his jobs was washing the windows of Crowell Hall that towered above the street. "Red" Brown, a radio technician with Missionary Aviation Fellowship who later installed a radio transmitter for the Beekmans in their tribe, recalls John from Moody days as "a skinny, blond fellow hanging from a safety belt far above the street like a human fly."

John's faith with "legs" gave him many opportunities to share

Christ with others in Chicago. In a hospital he found a 13-year-old boy who had been hit by a train. John wrote home, "George thought Jesus only a good man. I presented the simple plan of salvation and he accepted Jesus as his Saviour. When I was about ready to leave, he started to cry softly because of the pain. I asked if he knew the song, 'Jesus Loves Me.' He did not so I sang it for him. He memorized several verses while in the hospital and was released just last week."

A Jewish girl who John met on a train was not so receptive. He wrote, "She talked freely of her drinking escapades, wild parties, and other sinful habits. I showed her the love of Jesus from the Old Testament but she preferred to continue her irresponsible life."

John's passion for personal evangelism did not intrude into his habits of study. His forte was Greek and he studied under Dr. Kenneth Wuest and Dr. John Cable, both now deceased. "Unlike Latin in high school," he remembers, "I saw a purpose in Greek." Even then, when he had no thought of becoming a Bible translator, John was impatient for a fresh translation. As he puts it now, "I felt something true to the original was needed in the idiom of modern Americans. Though a poor translator, I started with the Epistle of James. What I wanted to do was something like that completed by Kenneth Taylor in his *Living New Testament*."

John earned "A's" in all courses except music notation and voice. In the latter he was probably diverted by Elaine who had the same teacher just before his class. Between bells they stood in the hall and talked.

During his second year John made a second "proposal" to Elaine — that they date each other exclusively. Elaine wanted to say "Yes," but a deeper commitment made her cautious and concerned about getting too serious.

Evangelical zeal was in her family. Her paternal grandfather, known far and wide in Pennsylvania Dutch country as "Uncle Ben," had been a United Brethren pastor since before Elaine's birth. Her father was a lay minister. He frequently took Elaine with him on preaching assignments and in the car they discussed what he would say. Two younger brothers, Ben and Dan, stayed home and attended church with their mother. Her maternal grandmother kept her spellbound with stories about missionaries as they washed dishes together. One day she gave Elaine a printed story of Joan of Arc. Elaine spent hours contemplating a painting of Joan being burned at the stake.

At the age of 11 she heard a woman missionary from Africa and whispered to her mother, "That's what I want to be." To which her mother sighed, "Oh, Elaine, anything but that."

Not until she was 20 and at Moody did she make a determined commitment to serve on the mission field.

One day John asked her casually, "What are you going to do after graduation? Everybody says you have a beautiful voice. Your talents could really count for the Lord as a pastor's wife."

Elaine blushed. "Well, I've trained mainly for choir and youth work. But I've been reading the life of Samuel Morris who served in Africa. I was impressed by the conversion and spirit-filled life of this African boy who was truly a diamond in the rough. The Lord has challenged me with Psalm 2:8, 'Ask of me and I will give you the treasures of darkness.'"

John looked at her in mild alarm. "A foreign missionary? Is that what you're going to be?"

Elaine nodded with a catch in her throat.

John looked away so she wouldn't see the disappointment in his eyes. "I would like to be a missionary very much. But I've figured 4-F for the Army, 4-F for the mission field. I can only hope for a safe pastorate at home."

She placed her hand on John's arm. "I like you very much. I —" and she paused, biting her lips. "But no matter what it means to us, I really feel called to the mission field."

They sat without speaking for a moment. Finally Elaine brightened. "You have the best bad heart I've ever heard about. You can do almost anything — skate, bowl, even hang from tall buildings. Maybe you could pass a medical."

Haltingly, John recalled to her what the specialist had said when he was 12. "I haven't followed doctor's orders as it is," he added.

She pressed his arm. "There would be nothing wrong with another checkup, would there?"

John, too, felt there wouldn't and made an appointment with the school physician. Dr. Titus Johnson had been a medical missionary until called home by serious family illness. He could give an examination and the needed advice.

Dr. Johnson carefully checked John's heart and circulatory system. "You've got a problem here," he said soberly. "There's a distinct murmur and you have poor circulation. I'm not a specialist, but I'd say you have less than a normal life to live. You might not live past 40."

John threw the big question at the doctor. "Would you advise me to consider missionary service?"

The doctor looked away. The time it took him to answer seemed like an eternity for John.

"Put it this way, John. If I were you, I would rather give less years of my life to those who have never heard the Gospel than more years to those who have heard."

John's face broke into a smile. "That's what I wanted to hear, Dr. Johnson. Thanks. Thanks a lot!"

He hurried to tell Elaine. She squeezed his hand and said, "That's great!"

"Yes," John said huskily, "but it may be tough to find a mission board that will take me."

Now John felt free to join the student Missionary Union and participate in its activities. When he told his mother, she gasped in shock, "No, John. Remember your heart. Stay home and serve God a long time."

John tried to assure her of God's call. Finally she relented and said, "I don't want you to go. But don't stay home for my sake."

That fall John was elected president of the Missionary Union. He planned some programs that were not soon forgotten.

For one, he rented a monkey from a pet dealer to make more realistic a skit on jungle missions. While the program unfolded two boys beat drums in the background. John got instant attention when he said, "Every drum beat signals the dropping of a lost African into eternity."

Another program dealt with the doctrines of Mormonism. John spoke, pretending that he himself had been a Mormon. Straightforwardly, he recounted his life from the time when he had difficulty in distinguishing which of his father's two wives was his mother, to the day he married two of his girl friends.

Some late arrivals were not aware that John was only giving a simulated testimony. These girls rushed to Elaine asking what she thought of her boy friend's previous marriages. They also wanted to know what John had done with his former wives.

In January 1946 John was invited to become student pastor of the Missionary Bible Church in suburban River Grove near the present site of O'Hare International Airport. The group had split from a Baptist church and were meeting in a store building.

He purchased a 1930 Pontiac to transport Moody students to help in a community survey and to pick up children for Sunday school. The car, he bragged to Elaine, "travels at the daring speed of 30 mph — 10 miles up and down and 20 miles forward."

Bad weather did not keep the young militants from doing visitation. John recorded: "One rainy Sunday afternoon the man of the house answered our knock but gave us no invitation to enter. Together we stood in the rain and explained the way of salvation. Elaine's hair lost its curl, but after a brief retreat for fixing, we were off again in house-to-house calling."

And again, "We opened up the Word of God to a university student and he gave up his belief in Buddha. He is still unwilling to accept Christ. I'll be seeing him again this Sunday."

Valentine's Day, 1946, was not just another class day. Early in the evening John called at Elaine's apartment with a corsage of violets to take her to dinner at the Palmer House's Coral Room. For this John had received special permission from the Moody Dean of Men, Frank Broman.

The evening passed too swiftly. As they alighted from the street car near Elaine's apartment, neither complained that the slush had frozen hard in the falling temperatures. John squeezed Elaine's hand tight, guided her over the slick spots, and tried to make small talk. Obviously, this time at least, he felt at a loss for words.

They walked back to her apartment and paused at the door. "You'd think there would be some place around here where we could be alone," he grumbled.

Elaine smiled and replied coyly, "What did you have in mind?"

"Remember those two proposals I made, the first to have another date, and the second to date each other exclusively? Well, I have a third."

Elaine knew she should not feel surprised. But still her heart pounded.

"I propose," John said in the bravest tone he could summon, "that you marry me. I even have a scripture, Song of Solomon 5:16 which I will slightly misquote, 'You are altogether lovely. You are my beloved.' "

Elaine squeezed his hand tightly. "I accept that proposal."

Unfailingly courteous, John bent toward her and whispered huskily, "May I kiss the prettiest and sweetest girl in the world?"

Elaine did not need to reply in words as she lifted her face toward his.

Elaine selected a knife-edged white gold band with a small solitaire in a Loop jewelry store. John wrote home, "During my first term I resolved not to date any girls. Studies alone and altogether was my motto. This is one resolution I have no regrets for having broken. I break out with a glad 'Blessed be the Lord!'"

After Elaine graduated in May, 1945 from the Christian Ed. Music Course, she moved into an apartment with a girl friend, Virginia Jackson. In May, 1946, she finished the Missionary course. John still lacked another term in the Pastor's course and wasn't due to graduate until August 2. They planned an August 8th, Thursday evening wedding in Elaine's home church.

They were then thinking of serving in Indo-China under a mission board that had work there. But John learned of a point of board doctrine he could not accept. He discussed his reservations with a veteran missionary of this group.

"I don't believe that either," the missionary said. "You'll have to sign the statement of beliefs with mental reservations."

John stubbornly set his jaws. "No. I won't sign what I can't accept."

It soon became evident to John and Elaine that they would probably have to serve with a "faith" mission, one that required them to raise and maintain their own support. Denominational boards generally insisted upon college and seminary for men candidates, except for unusual exceptions. And there was John's murmuring heart.

Elaine worried about their future support. "I just can't go to people and ask for money," she told John. "I'd be embarrassed to tears."

To which John said, "I'm sorry you feel that way. The Lord will have to deal with you about that."

A few weeks later Elaine and her roommate planned a Saturday night dinner for four in their third-floor apartment. Late in the afternoon Elaine was returning from grocery shopping and heard fire sirens. As she turned the corner to her street, she saw the fire equipment in front of her apartment building from which black smoke was billowing.

She ran up the sidewalk to tell the firemen that her roommate was in the apartment. But Virginia was standing in the crowd on the sidewalk.

All of Elaine's and Virginia's belongings were lost in the blaze. They salvaged the rest of the evening by going to dinner with John and Virginia's friend. Then the two homeless girls accepted a friend's request to stay in her apartment.

Elaine worried about what some members of her family might say about the fire. They had wanted her to attend a denominational college instead of Moody. That night she slept fitfully, asking over and over for more faith. The verse, "Think it not strange concerning the fiery trial which is to try you . . . but rejoice"[1] encouraged her.

The next morning she opened her mailbox and found it crammed with dollar bills! News of the fire had spread among students and the money was the result of a whirlwind fund-raising campaign. Her's and Virginia's plight was announced over the Moody radio station, WMBI, and the next mail brought more dollars.

After replacing her Bible lost in the fire, she told John, "I believe I can trust Him to provide for us through the gifts of those who love Him."

As their marriage date approached, a new fear seized Elaine. Her innovating fiance had insisted they write and memorize their own ceremony in which each would give a brief testimony. She was fearful of forgetting.

Promptly at seven p.m. on their wedding day, Pastor Gauntt, John, Richard (the best man), and the ushers took their places before the audience of family and friends. The front of the church was decked with palms, ferns, white gladiola and four white candelabra with burning tapers. The pianist and vibraharpist began a soft medley of wedding music.

After a long ten minutes, Jean Beekman, the first of Elaine's three attendants came down the aisle. The bridal party had been held up by a freight train. When the bride's attendants were in place, the soloist sang, "I Love Thee, Dear." Then the bride, dazzling in a floor-length satin brocade and chiffon dress and carrying a bouquet of white roses and gardenias, swept down the aisle on the arm of her father.

Pastor Gauntt gave his usual opening remarks, then announced that John and Elaine would pronounce their vows. John spoke first.

"Elaine, six years ago I accepted Jesus as my Saviour. He promises never to leave or forsake me. So I can promise to always be a Christian husband to you.

[1] I Peter 4:12.

"As a Christian husband, I promise to be obedient to Christ. He has called me to serve Him as a missionary. Wherever He leads, even to the ends of the earth, I promise to go. I promise to obey those instructions which Christ has given in His Word for husbands. Elaine, you are my best earthly friend. I promise to love and protect you, to be considerate of your happiness, and in all things seek your welfare. I promise to live, by the grace of our Saviour, according to the principles of the Gospel as long as God shall give me life."

John gave his ring in token of his pledge. Then Elaine spoke her pledge.

"John, Ephesians 5:24 says, . . . as the church is subject to Christ, so let the wives be to their husbands . . . .' This verse tells me that my relation to Jesus must also be my relation to you.

"I love and trust Jesus because He first loved me and gave Himself a ransom for me. I want to obey Him and please Him in everything. John, you are my best earthly friend. I promise to love, comfort, and assist you in the Lord's work and in all things to esteem your happiness as my own. I promise to live, by the grace of our Saviour, according to the principles of the Gospel as long as God shall give me life."

Elaine slipped her ring on John's finger. The soloist sang, "Because." They knelt before the pastor who prayed, "Thou hast heard the promises of these Thy servants. Let there ever be the most perfect confidence and love between them. May their love know no doubt, but cause it to grow in purity and sweetness with the number of their years . . . ."

He pronounced them man and wife, and they left after the reception for a week's camp-out honeymoon at Lake George in the Adirondacks. Elaine's parents loaned them their family car.

They spent their wedding night in a motel enroute, supremely happy in the union of sacred love. Ahead lay an unknown course in which their love would be strengthened by both heartbreak and happiness.

3. Charting the Course

THE NEWLYWEDS WERE, in the bride's words, "snug as two bugs in a rug" in their two-room furnished apartment at 1517 N. LaSalle in Chicago. They were also busy bugs. Elaine was working as an office clerk, and John was pastoring the Missionary Bible Church in River Grove and learning how to fly at the Moody aviation school. One quarter he filled in for an absent prof and taught an accounting class at Moody.

John didn't expect to qualify as a full-time missionary pilot, but he reasoned that he could cover more ground in a primitive area by flying his own small plane.

As their first Christmas together approached, John began washing windows in high buildings to earn extra money. One cold December evening he came home and flopped exhausted on the bed. About midnight Elaine noticed that he was having difficulty breathing.

Alarmed and worried, she pushed two pillows under his head and opened a window. "I can't feel in my feet and fingers," he whispered between labored breaths.

Elaine ran to call their landlady. She suggested, "Put ice to his heart, and hurry!"

Elaine quickly prepared an ice pack and pressed it against John's heart. Her own heart pounded in anxiety as she timed his slowing pulse – 40, 30, then dropping to 20 beats per minute before finally picking up. But the doctor they consulted the next day did not show concern. "You've been working too hard and suffered a heart block," he said. "Take it easy for awhile."

The winter snows melted and spring turned the corner. Attendance doubled in the church, moving past 100 on special occasions. Older members even began talking about a reconciliation with the

40

Baptist congregation from which they had separated. Restoration, however, did not come until after John and Elaine left. According to one of the long-time members of the present River Grove Bible Church, "the service of John and Elaine helped heal the breach."

John continued flying lessons and also studied phonetics. "We're learning a new alphabet," he wrote his parents. "Any sound or combination of sounds in any language never before heard can be written with the use of this alphabet . . . even the sound of a kiss."

At the urging of the phonetics teacher, Miss Edna Fritch, they decided to attend the 11-week linguistic school conducted by the Wycliffe Bible Translators at the University of Oklahoma. "The training will give you a good foundation for later learning a foreign language," she said.

John and Elaine arrived in Norman, Oklahoma in early June and immediately plunged into a world of strange speeches and sounds. Besides attending lectures, they spent one hour a day listening to recorded sounds from tribes all over the world. The concept that each language had its own pattern began to grip John.

They heard Dr. Kenneth L. Pike,[1] soon to become one of the world's most outstanding linguists, says: "Just as each human being or tribe must follow a pattern for doing certain things — eating, sleeping and so forth — so each tribe must have a pattern in its language. The linguist must learn the methods of *searching for a pattern* in the welter of sounds that will strike his ear when he reaches the tribe."

And they knew that no missionary could succeed without entering through the language gate into native thought forms and beliefs.

The striking peculiarities of tribal languages fascinated the young couple. They heard words of amazing length, like *tsiyatamparshataniya*, which means to the Candoshi Indian of South America, "we did not talk enthusiastically then." They listened to a veteran translator explain how one verb could be written in over 100,000 different forms in his tribe's dialect. They learned that there are subtle but important differences in sounds spelled the same way, like "chaa" in the Mixtec language of Mexico, which can mean "come," "man," or "will smoke a cigarette," depending on how its pitch is intoned.

One hot afternoon following Dr. Pike's class, John voiced growing conviction to Elaine. "For a long time I've felt the importance of Scripture being put in the idiom of the man on the street here in

[1]Dr. Pike now heads the Department of Linguistics at the University of Michigan and also serves as Linguistic and Anthropological Coordinator for Wycliffe.

the United States. How much more important is this for the tribesman. You can't just match words and string them together to make
a sentence. Why, how would a translator render 'shepherd' for a
tribe that had never seen sheep? He'd have to use a descriptive
equivalent that his people understood.

✓ "A translator can be very easily misunderstood by literal-minded
Christians," John continued. "But if you study Scripture in the light
of the times when it was written, you realize that the Holy Spirit
inspired godly men to set down the originals in their own languages
and to use their own idioms."

"So you want to be a Bible translator," Elaine broke in. She did
not add her feelings that her Christian education and music training
would be of little value in a primitive tribe.

"Frankly, I'm not sure that I'm qualified. But the burden of
Wycliffe is beginning to get to me."

"Me, too," Elaine admitted.

"I never knew before that more than a thousand tribes[2] do not
have a single verse of Scripture in their language. And that some
of these tribes are disappearing as civilization moves toward them.
Think of all the Bibles we have in this country, and think of those
who do not have a verse. If I could, I'd like to do something about
this."

Both John and Elaine felt the pulsating spirit of the mission, named
for the first translator of the whole Bible into English. They noted
that Wycliffe members came from many denominational and occu-
pational backgrounds and stood united in marching toward the goal
of Scripture translation for all the lost tribes. This meant leaving
the ninety and nine at home and going into inhospitable jungles and
deserts.

They heard about the founding of Wycliffe by William Cameron
Townsend. As a thin, frail 21-year-old college student, Townsend
had gone to Guatemala in 1917 to sell Spanish Bibles and discovered
that 150,000 Cakchiquel Indians were trapped in an unwritten language. He gave ten difficult, pioneering years to deciphering the
language and translating the New Testament into Cakchiquel. He
left a thriving Cakchiquel church and a host of new readers, and
returned home to recruit and train linguistic soldiers.

Townsend and L. L. Letgers, another missionary who shared his

[2]Latest surveys show that more than 3,000 languages and dialects are spoken
in primitive areas, with more than 2,000 awaiting Bible translation.

concern, enlisted only two men for a chicken shed linguistic school in the Arkansas Ozarks. Letgers died and Townsend came down with tuberculosis, but the vision did not fade. Townsend recovered and entered Mexico in 1935 with a half dozen recruits.

They went as "scientific investigators," for missionaries were not being allowed in by the Mexican government. Townsend convinced a few reluctant Mexican educators that Mexico's many Indian tribes needed to become literate in their own languages before they could develop as productive citizens. "We will decipher their languages and teach them to read and write," he offered, "if you will permit us to translate the Bible." The Mexican government accepted this proposal.

By the time John and Elaine came to Norman in 1948, over 150 translators had entered Mexico and dispersed into the Indian villages.

"I'd really like to be a translator in Mexico," John told Elaine again, "but I don't think I'm qualified with only a Bible school education."

However, John found getting off the Wycliffe hook wasn't that easy. Back-up men were needed — support personnel ranging from office managers to literacy workers. The office work didn't appeal to John. He had left that for a more direct ministry. But literacy did, especially after he and Elaine met Ethel Wallis.

"I trained to be a journalism teacher at the University of California," the tall brunette with sparkling eyes told them. "Then I heard about the tribes. For five years I've been serving the Otomis of Central Mexico." She paused and looked at John. "You're of the Reformed Church, aren't you?"

John nodded.

"Your denomination has missionaries in the State of Chiapas where there are several large Indian tribes of Mayan descent. But they work with Mexicans and the few Indians who can speak Spanish. They would welcome some more help with the Indians. Marianna Slocum is already there translating among the Tzeltals, and Florence Gerdel, a nurse, is going this summer to help her. They cooperate with the Reformed Mission."

John broke in. "But I'm not qualified to be a translator."

"Well, why don't you consider doing literacy work among the Chols, right next to the Tzeltals? That's a necessary follow-up to translation. Evelyn Woodward started there in 1941. She reduced one of the Chol dialects to writing and has translated Mark.

Marianna worked there for awhile, before her Bill died. By the way, have you heard about Bill?"

The Beekmans hadn't.

"He was at Moody a few years before you. He went to Chiapas in 1938 and lived among the Tzeltals for two years. While there he met and fell in love with Marianna who, as I said, was working with Evelyn among the Chols. They became engaged on Valentine's Day and planned to be married in the spring of 1941. Six days before the wedding Bill was found dead in bed from a heart attack. It was so sad. They had planned to translate the Tzeltal New Testament together."

Elaine daubed at her eyes with a handkerchief. John sniffed and looked down. They, too, had become engaged on Valentine's Day.

"Marianna," Ethel continued, "is there now finishing the work she and Bill had planned to do together. Evelyn and her new husband, Wilbur Aulie, are the only workers among the Chols."

As John and Elaine prayed and talked, their hearts kept pulling them toward Chiapas. They talked with Dr. Eugene Nida,[3] one of the Wycliffe faculty at Norman. Nida had served a tribe in Mexico. He shared Ethel Wallis' enthusiasm.

"It would be ideal having you two in Chiapas. Wycliffe and the Reformed mission haven't always seen eye to eye on the importance of work in the Indian languages. You, John, could help build a bridge of understanding."

It was hard to ignore the interest of two dedicated people like Ethel Wallis and Eugene Nida. John wanted to be related to his denomination. He wanted to do tribal work. In Chiapas they could do both.

They checked into Wycliffe's organizational policies and found them quite similar to other faith missions except for one basic difference: Control of field policies was in the hands of the missionaries instead of with the home office in the United States. Cameron Townsend had felt that the missionaries knew best how to make their own decisions.

They dug up all the information they could find about Chiapas. It was the southernmost Mexican state, shaped like, but a little larger than, Ohio and bordered on Guatemala and the Pacific Ocean. Chiapas meant "plant-in-water" and was split by swift rivers running

[3]Dr. Nida, the author of several books on linguistics and anthropology, is now Translations Secretary for the American Bible Society.

between precipitous gorges that divided the steep mountain ranges. The few travelers who had ventured outside the state capital of Tuxtla Gutierrez described it as one of the wildest areas of the world.

The population was then slightly over 900,000, 90% Indian, but historians estimated it had been one of the most thickly populated areas of the world before the Spanish conquest. Warfare, slavery, and disease had taken heavy tolls among the 14 tribes of Mayan descent who still used sticks as hoes to raise corn and toiled for the Mexican coffee ranchers.

John and Elaine made formal application for membership in Wycliffe and literacy work among the Chols. A local physician examined them and certified their health. How John's murmuring heart got by the doctor is still a mystery. Medical examinations for Wycliffe personnel are now handled by a Wycliffe doctor, and it is commonly agreed that a heart ailment would not go unnoticed.

On July 28 word came that they were accepted as members with the understanding that they would return from Mexico the following summer for another session of study at Norman.

Turning the old '30 Pontiac northeastward, they made quick visits to Chicago, Clearfield, and Midland Park. The River Grove Church and both their home churches gave them send-offs and pledged financial support. They also spent time in New York City, at the headquarters of the Laubach Literacy Crusade. On November 4th they headed for Mexico. The four months had passed at a dizzying pace.

At the Laredo border crossing they met translator Otis Leal and six new single girl recruits. John arranged for his and Elaine's visas only after five trips across the bridge. He sold the old Pontiac with trailer for $150 and put 43 boxes of belongings on a train for Mexico City. Amazingly, he was not required to pay a peso of duty.

Then they boarded a bus for the capital and began observing the life of exotic Mexico like two wide-eyed children. Elaine recorded their impressions:

"The barren cactus and sagebrush stretched into the mountains with their horseshoe turns and constant ascents. We saw homes along the way made with cactus walls, others were brick, others with mud plastered over sticks. People were always carrying something: Babies both fore and aft; baskets and jars on their heads; huge cans of water hung from sticks, balanced across their shoulders; wood piled high on bent forms; cornstalks 10 feet high moving along with a man somewhere underneath; then a funeral procession led by four barefooted men carrying a casket. These physical burdens made us think of their spiritual burdens, and again we gave praise to God for the gift of salvation and the privilege of being His ambassadors."

After 26 hours on the bus, the "ambassadors" reached Mexico City. Translator Otis Leal had accompanied them from the border and herded them off in taxis to Wycliffe headquarters. Four of the single girls later went to Peru.

They stopped in front of an aging two-story stone building, and Leal said, "This, my friend, is 'The Kettle.' We don't boil you alive in it. It used to be a hotel called "El Palacio de Quetzalcoatl," in honor of an Aztec god. The tourists couldn't pronounce the god's name right and started calling it 'The Kettle,' and it has remained that since we bought it."

John and Elaine moved into a one-room apartment. They found "The Kettle" jammed with translators, children, a variety of bare-footed Indians who had come to check manuscripts before publication, and roaches and rats. Several years later Billy Graham visited "The Kettle" and came home to tell his "Hour of Decision" radio audiences about the young scholars who had sacrificed comfort in the U. S. to live in the cramped, tiny, one-room apartments.

The new missionaries adjusted to the mile-and-a-half altitude of the capital and began studying rudimentary Spanish and Chol, the latter from a dictionary prepared by Evelyn Woodward Aulie. They felt glad that they didn't have to start from scratch as had Evelyn and looked forward to entering Chol country in January.

The mild days and cool nights felt invigorating. John chuckled at what the weather must be like in New Jersey and wrote, "I hear you've been having some cold weather. Here the other night there were two feet of ice. I'm not kidding — just that. They were Elaine's."

And he had a comment about the beggar who thought of "The Kettle" as a rest home for American millionaires. "One young beggar said, 'My mother and father are dead and they'll both beat me if I come home with nothing.'"

But Christmas Eve a not-so-funny joke was on John. While visiting another missionary couple, he became thirsty and grabbed a glass of hypo-eliminator used in film developing. He stopped on the second gulp, feeling like a "smoking volcano." Soda, egg nog, and real water couldn't induce a "coming up party." When he showed no ill affects from the beverage, Elaine commented, "You must have a stomach made of iron."

In December John left by bus for Chol country. He was so excited that even leaving Elaine for the first time in many months didn't dim the sparkle in his eye. She had originally planned to ride the bus down with him, but a trip to the doctor had necessitated a change of plans.

The new year welcomed Elaine with a mild earthquake, alarming to her, but of no great concern to Mexico City residents who are accustomed to tremors. She flew to Chiapas a week after John left and was welcomed by Mrs. John Kempers in Tuxtla, the State capital. John and Dr. Kempers, the veteran Reformed Church missionary who had served in Chiapas since 1926 and was known to fellow missionaries as "Kemp," had already left for a survey trip in Chol country.

Elaine thought of their monthly wedding anniversary on January 8th and wondered if John had remembered. He had. In her room at the Kempers' home, she found 17 very red roses; one for each month of their marriage; and in the center, a tiny, white bud that reminded her of the budding little life within. It was she, not John, who had insisted that "it is high time we get one of those cuddly little ones at our house."

While Elaine was admiring the roses, John and Kemp were slushing through mud and slipping on rocks in Chol country. John was certain it was the wildest land he had ever seen. They plunged through jungle so thick he could hardly see three feet on either side. They took turns riding their single horse, but when the trail skirted a steep precipice, John insisted on skipping his turn. He had washed windows at dizzying heights in Chicago, but there he had a safety belt.

John kept lagging behind when it was his turn to walk. He could feel fatigue that he knew was caused by poor circulation, creeping over his body. Each time Kemp graciously waited for him to catch up, never scolding. Not until almost ten years later did Dr. Kempers learn about John's bad heart.

Along easier stretches Kemp told John what he knew about the history of mission work among the Chols.

Leonard Ingram,[4] an English Plymouth Brethren missionary, had

---

[4]Ingram, now in his 90's, lives in Mexico City and continues to carry on a colporteur ministry. He estimates having printed and sold 1,680,000 evangelical booklets in Mexico.

sold Spanish Bibles in Chiapas as early as 1902. He found few Indians that spoke any Spanish. Once he asked a Chamula Indian for a word that meant great joy. The Chamula blurted a word that meant "to get blind drunk."

In the early 1920's, a Presbyterian Mexican coffee rancher living near the Chol village of Tumbala invited a Mexican pastor to conduct services on his ranch. A few Chol work hands who could understand some Spanish attended and declared themselves believers. When John Kempers arrived in Tuxtla in 1926, fresh from Princeton Seminary, there was a small Chol church meeting in Tumbala with a Spanish speaking lay pastor.

When the Tumbala lay pastor died, a member walked the six days' journey to Tuxtla and asked Kempers for help. Kempers sent in Santiago Gonzalez, a Mexican pastor paid by the Reformed mission. By 1940, when Evelyn Woodward arrived, there were two Chol congregations and some isolated believers in other villages. By 1948, when John and Kemp took their survey trip, about 800 Chols were counted as believers. Mark and few hymns had been translated into Chol by Evelyn and her new husband, Wilbur Aulie, who had settled at Hidalgo on the southern edge of Chol territory. There was obviously much work still to be done.

There was a pathetic sameness about each village John and Kemp passed through. Half-naked children in tattered, dirty clothes peered at them from inside smoky one-room pole huts. Frequently they saw men lying in a drunken stupor between and around the huts. The sober Indians whom they met were slumped in posture and stared at the ground, speaking only when addressed. Centuries of subjugation and poverty had bent them into a pitiful servility.

"They're caught in a vise of degradation," Kemp explained. "They work for the coffee ranchers who pay a starvation wage. Then they spend most of the money at a ranch store to get drunk. Whatever is left, the witch doctor usually gets."

"Are any of the Chols land owners?" John asked.

"Some of them live on land given to them many years ago by the Federal government. They could get up to 25 acres for each family through the government's reform ejido system just by going to Tuxtla and making application.[5] They couldn't sell this land or

[5]After the 1910 Revolution, the Mexican government broke up the huge feudal estates on which peasants had toiled as virtual slaves, and divided the land into 25-acre tracts. The government decided to keep title to keep exploiters from buying back the land and re-forming the estates.

be cheated out of it. The government holds the title. But the family could possess it as long as they cultivated it."

John looked puzzled. "Why don't they apply?"

"Fear. They've been cheated too many times in the past to trust anyone. But probably they are most afraid of some ranchers who want to keep the Indians working at low wages. I heard about one man who tried to organize his village so they could all get more land and operate a community coffee ranch. This fellow was caught by the ranchers, stripped naked, and chained to an ant hill."

John shuddered. "Why doesn't the government act?"

Kemp stopped and looked at the younger man. "My boy, there are Mexican leaders in Tuxtla and Mexico City who would like to do something. But back here the local politicians call the shots. They think it best to keep the Indians in their place."

After a toilsome climb John and Kemp reached the top of a high mountain that looked out over a deep canyon. John rode and Kemp walked along the rim of a land table which dropped off to a sheer cliff only a few yards from the trail. A few miles further on they neared Tumbala, one of the oldest Indian towns in Chiapas. John squinted to see huts scattered among high rocks that appeared to have once formed the crater of a volcano.

They walked into the village plaza and stood alongside a layer of rock where Chol women displayed a few vegetables for sale. John saw the big stone Catholic church that appeared incongruous among the scraggly huts and lesser buildings. Kemp had already mentioned that most of the Indians followed a strange hybrid religion of Catholic and native beliefs. The *conquistadores* had forced the Indians to adopt the shell of the foreign religion. They had not been able to tear away the Indians' cultural armor that encompassed beliefs hardened by centuries of tradition.

Darkness was coming on, so they stopped for the night at a ranch where Kemp was acquainted. The next morning they hired a fresh horse and pushed on.

A short distance from Tumbala they came upon the ruins of an old church beside an awesome gorge thousands of feet deep. Kemp explained that 13 crosses had once stood near the old church, staked over the bodies of Indians killed for seizing a Spanish priest, tying his hands and feet, and throwing him over the precipice.

The trail toward the village of Amado Nervo,[6] their destination,

[6]Named for a distinguished Mexican poet.

was worse than John had imagined. It wound down one forested slope, then another, passing through a narrow cleft in a huge mass of rock and by dark caves. Often they had to lead the horses over masses of tree roots and leaves which hid deep holes. Later John heard Indians say that jaguars used the holes for dens.

Late in the afternoon they crossed a deep river in which the water almost ran over the horses' backs. They soon began climbing a trail so rocky and steep that both had to dismount and let the horses lead, holding onto their tails for added lift.

At six o'clock, chests heaving and soaked with sweat, they came into Amado Nervo. They had not eaten since breakfast. Here, Kemp thought, might be a good spot for Elaine and John to live. There were believers, and they had built a small white-washed mud church on the side of the mountain overlooking the village. John could find language informants among them and begin work.

A light rain began falling as John looked beyond the ragged Indians clustering around them. The huts of Amado Nervo were spread along the sides of a natural land bowl that cupped into the side of the mountain and opened over a high precipice that plunged down to a rushing stream. A shimmering waterfall tossed up spray a little way below the village.

The village elders arrived, and Kemp explained in Spanish why the Beekmans wanted to live in Amado Nervo. Some nodded, others shook their heads. They promised to take the matter under consideration.

Kemp motioned to John to stand back while the leaders huddled. Finally they returned to report. Most wanted the foreign brother and his wife and were willing to build them a hut. But some of those opposed had expressed themselves strongly. The foreign brother would have to decide.

That night John and Kemp slept on strips of boards in the mud church. The next morning they started the long ride to Yajalon, the Mexican market town where Elaine was to arrive by plane from Tuxtla. As their horses climbed upward along the trail overgrown with ferns, John wondered how Elaine, three months with child, would manage the trip into Amado Nervo. The doctor in Mexico City had warned against horseback riding.

"There is only one way," Kemp said. "She will have to be carried in a chair on the back of porters."

FROM DARKNESS TO LIGHT

The chart at the right depicts the fascinating history of the people which John and Elaine Beekman served.

Radioactive dating of bones discovered near Mexico City put humans in America 24,000 years ago. Scholars generally think the first Americans came from the Orient and across the Bering Strait, then migrated south through the hemisphere. Other theories have them coming from Noah's family, the Lost Ten Tribes of Israel, Egypt, and the legendary Atlantis.

The Mayans as a distinct people emerged about 1,500 B.C., near the time when the Israelites departed from Egypt, and perhaps from the more ancient Olmecs. They reached their greatest genius about A.D. 800, and were decisively defeated by the Spaniards in 1541. Their monuments (see some on following pages) show them to be the most brilliant of all American Indian civilizations and in some instances superior to the rest of the world. They were masters at writing, astronomy, arithmetic, calendric development, chronology, and recording history. They excelled in architecture, sculpture, and painting.

Following the Spanish Conquest they dispersed throughout southern Mexico and Central America. Their language splintered into more than 20 mutually unintelligible dialects. In 1917 W. Cameron Townsend began Bible translation for the Mayan Cakchiquels in Guatemala, marking the beginning of a new era. Since then Wycliffe Bible Translators have begun work in all major Mayan dialects. One is Chol, native to the Mexican state of Chiapas, which itself has divided into sub-dialects, Tumbala Chol and Tila Chol. The subjects of this book worked in the Tumbala dialect.

First Americans	22,000 B.C.
Olmecs	2000 B.C.?
Mayans	1500 B.C.?
Spanish Victory	A.D. 1541
Bible Translation Begun in Neighbor Tribe	1917
Evelyn Aulie Begins Chol Study	1941
Beekmans Arrive	1947

Upper left: The Toltec capital at Tula, about 50 miles north of Mexico City, and built about A.D. 900. The Toltecs migrated to the Mayan area about A.D. 1,000. Standing beside the giant Atlantis is Wycliffe Translator Dr. Burton Bascom and a modern descendant of the Toltecs.

Upper right: This huge pyramid of the sun was built about 500 years earlier by the ancestors of the Toltecs. Standing 216 ft. high and covering 10 acres at its base, the pyramid is the crowning tourist attraction in the ceremonial city of Teotihuacan. This was probably the largest city (est. 500,000 pop.) in ancient America and only 30 miles from Mexico City.

Lower right: Mayan archaeological history begins here in the ancient and mysterious city of Palenque. It was abandoned for some unknown reason in the 9th century A.D. and not discovered until 1773. Now a tourist site, Palenque is on the edge of Chol territory where John and Elaine Beekman served.

A stairway of 67 steps was discovered leading downward to a crypt within this sacred pyramid in Palenque. On Nov. 27, 1952, a solid stone slab was lifted to expose the skeleton of a Mayan King-High Priest. A jade mask of 200 pieces covered his face. Jade rings, necklace, and bracelet were on his body. Inscriptions show the tomb was dedicated Jan. 27, 633 A.D.

The face at lower left is one of two marvelous stucco sculptures found beneath the columns of the crypt. It is ornamented with sacred Quetzal plumes and a crown of flowers.

The man is the first Chol Elaine Beekman saw upon arriving in Chol country. Note the facial similarities (broad head, etc.) between him and his ancestor at left.

On March 3, 1517, Spanish explorers anchored near this spot on the coast of Yucatan. The Spaniards beheld a strange city rising out of the misty mainland which they called "Great Cairo." They went ashore the next day and were ambushed, marking the first land battle between American and European warriors.

The ruins of the Temple of the Warriors at the great Mayan city of Chichen Itza in Yucatan, so called because of the hundreds of columns with carved warriors. The temple is almost a copy of the Toltec temple at Tula, 800 miles northwest of Yucatan, and shown on a previous page. This and other evidence indicates that the Toltecs migrated to Yucatan and subdued or merged with the Mayans before the 10th century A.D.

The pyramid temple of Kukulcan, the plumed serpent god, at Chichen Itza. While restoring the ruins in 1937, archaeologists found a core temple underneath. A secret stairway led to a throne room. Here a life-sized effigy of an open-mouthed red jaguar stood guard, spotted with 73 round disks of polished jade.

An example of Mayan architecture at Chichen Itza. The Mayans were truly the Greeks of the new world. Evidence of their skills in sculpture are found throughout southern Mexico and Central America. John and Elaine Beekman found their descendants living in pole and thatch huts, never thinking of building monuments.

The astronomical observatory at Chichen Itza where the Mayans studiously examined the heavens. They believed in a form of heaven and hell and even had a flood tradition which the Beekmans found still existing among the Chols. The Mayan calendar was more accurate than the one used in the Roman Empire. Their calendar was based on a solar year of 365.24 days and a lunar month of 29.5 days, the fractions taking care of the extra day we add to February every fourth year. The Beekmans found the poor Chols, descendants of the Mayans, unconcerned about dates. Parents did not even know the ages of children.

Note the size of the serpent heads beside this modern Mayan miss. How did they get such huge stones to the top of their temples and pyramids? One guess is that they built long inclined planes, and using rollers and man power, pulled the stones up a foot or a yard or more a day. But for all their brilliance, the Mayans never developed the concept of the wheel.

The Mayans believed their gods (principally the gods of death, corn, and rain) must be nourished and propitiated by human sacrifice. The most spectacular sacrifice was, literally, heart-rending, in that the victim's heart was jerked out in a bloody ceremony. To propitiate the rain god in time of drought, they hurled living sacrifices into this sacred well at Chichen Itza. Dozens of skeletons have been dredged from the murky water along with jade and gold jewels.

Following defeat from the Spaniards the Mayans fled westward into the rugged wilds of Chiapas. Now — 400 years later — about one million Mayans speaking some 15 dialects live in Chiapas. To this land where jaguars still devour children came the newly-wedded Beekmans to make peril their choice.

4. *Amado Nervo!*

MABEL KEMPERS WENT with Elaine to the Tuxtla airport and saw her on the cargo plane for Yajalon. The plane was an ancient Canadian relic purchased second-hand by the pilot. Besides Elaine, two Mexican passengers crowded into the cabin, already jammed with bags of sugar, salt, and other foodstuffs. They sat on the bags which came without safety belts.

The single engine grumbled into action, and minutes later, Elaine looked down into the deepest gorge she had ever seen and saw a serpentine thread of brown water gushing toward the Pacific Ocean. Later she learned that four centuries before, terrified Mayan Indians had made suicide leaps into the gorge to avoid capture by slave-hungry Spanish settlers.

Another three minutes and the plane began straining to climb a high mountain. She watched the green forest sliding underneath and speculated on how long it would take a search party to find wreckage. Finally, to her relief, the plane heaved over the mountain and dropped into a long valley. Though it was January, jungle greenery stretched as far as she could see, broken only by bald spots which marked last year's corn fields. As she looked down at the rugged terrain, she shuddered at the thought that John and Kemp had crossed some of the mountains and gorges on foot.

After an hour's flight the plane set down at Yajalon, the Mexican market town that was to be the Beekman's nearest post office for the next seven years. John, sporting a big smile, was waiting at the end of the strip to kiss her.

He escorted her on foot to the four-room adobe house which belonged to another Reformed missionary, Garold Van Engen, then

living over the mountains in the larger market town of Las Casas.
Kemp had already left on a trip to another station.

"I found a village where we can live," John said enthusiastically.
"It's the most beautiful spot in the world. Like Switzerland, except
there's no snow."

Elaine's flushed face betrayed her eagerness. "When do we go?"

"Not until we get permission from the political authorities. We'll
have to wait here for that."

A trace of doubt crossed Elaine's face. "Do the people in the
village really want us?"

"The believers do. They have already built a small church. There
are probably a few unfriendly characters. Kemp has already warned
me that the witch doctor will see us as competition."

Elaine sighed. "Well, if this is where the Lord wants us, He'll
take care of us."

They enjoyed and profited from the few days' delay. News quickly
spread among the Chol believers in Yajalon to market corn and
oranges, that a foreign brother and his wife had come. Soon a steady
stream of barefooted Indians began arriving at their door. Not one
came to Elaine's nose in height, and beside six-foot John, they seemed
like pygmies. He noted the men's narrow hands, unusual he thought
for manual workers. Several had long, narrow eye-slits that under
a canopy of straight black hair gave an Oriental appearance. Their
long acquiline noses with a low nasal index appeared to be a feature
linking them with their Mayan ancestors. John read to them from
the Gospel of Mark which Evelyn Aulie had translated, and practiced his limited Chol vocabulary. Elaine smiled and tried to draw
the women out of their shyness.

Because of the distance from their homes, many Chols had to stay
overnight in Yajalon. The Beekmans invited them to stay in the
house. They slept on the tile floor, disdaining the offer of blanket or
pillow.

With its crooked cobblestone streets and swinging-door saloons,
the town reminded them of scenes in a western novel. Young men
showed off on horseback in front of giggling girls. Sometimes masked
men galloped past as if they were being pursued by the law.

Permission came for John and Elaine to live in Amado Nervo. Since
the mule train carrying their baggage hadn't arrived from Tuxtla, John
decided to make a trip alone into Amado Nervo, to make arrangements
for building a house. He reached the village by six hours of hard riding

on the narrow trail that was boggy with mud. After friendly villagers gave assurance that a hut would be built, John rode back to Yajalon to find the baggage had reached the Van Engen's house safely.

Early one February morning when the peaks to the north and south of Yajalon were still enveloped in mist, the Beekman entourage left for Amado Nervo. Several Chols walked ahead leading mules loaded with baggage. Behind them came another Indian stooped with the weight of Elaine who was seated quite comfortably in a chair strapped to his back. A bark rope looped around the carrier's forehead kept the chair upright as it jolted against the Indian's back. Last came John, sometimes having to trot to keep up with the barefooted Indians.

Further ahead on the trail John tensed as they came near a precipice. He fervently prayed that the Chol carrying Elaine would not stumble.

Elaine sat tight-lipped in the chair, feeling every step the Indian took, even to the heaving of his chest. She tried to look straight back at John panting behind and not down into the gorge. As her breathing increased, she could feel the porter's small body trembling underneath. She steeled to hold perfectly still, fearful that the slightest irregular movement on her part might cause both to topple over the cliff. Not until the trail broke away from the precipice did she breathe freely again.

They reached Amado Nervo in mid-afternoon. The natural beauty of the spot and the excitement of arriving overcame the fatigue of the long journey. Villagers poured down the two sides of the mountain bowl to chatter greetings. Both replied as well as they could in the language, and John wrote down all the new words he could catch.

Elaine noticed that many of the villagers kept their distance. These, she learned later, had voted against their coming. Among them was the witch doctor, Miguel Cruz who stood in the entrance to his dark hut squinting sourly at the crowd around the Beekmans.

Nicholas Arcos, the squat, gap-toothed spokesman for the welcoming committee, pointed to an old hut and indicated that he wanted Elaine and John to go there. This was evidently his house. Why was he taking them there? What about the new hut that was supposed to be ready?

Nicholas had been the first person in Amado Nervo to believe and begin walking the *new* trail following an evangelistic visit from Christian Chols in Tumbala several years before. Since then about 150 Amado Nervo people had professed to follow Christ instead of witchcraft. Under Nicholas' leadership the Chols of Amado Nervo had built the rickety thatch-roofed church on the mountainside.

Elaine strained to understand what Nicholas was saying to John, but with so many adults talking and children and pigs squealing, she could not.

At last John honored her curiosity. "Nicholas says he is sorry our new hut has not been built. He wants us to live in his hut until the new one is ready."

Elaine looked at the string of scraggly children playing around the hut. They apparently belonged to Nicholas. "Where will they live?" she asked.

"He has a pig house," John said. "He said his ten children will sleep well there."

"No, John," Elaine said, "We can't."

"If we don't, we'll offend him," John said. "He feels badly that the new hut didn't get built in time. He thinks this is the least he can do."

Elaine relented and the boxes of belongings were taken off the mule backs and carried through the doorless entrance. She followed them in and looked around. It was larger than some of the other huts, but only about the size of a one-car garage. Walls made of poles set about an inch apart rested on the mud floor. On one side rested the triad of large blackened stones that she guessed was the cook stove. Above the stones a small hole peeped through to the blue sky — the chimney. Beside this, a dormitory room at Moody seemed like the Waldorf-Astoria.

Every new item unpacked drew a chorus of oohs and often giggles. They laughed to see John write down words with a pen. They watched with bated breath when John gave pen and paper to a man. He held it like a hammer until John showed him how to hold it. At first mark the audience howled with delight.

After awhile someone came bringing hot coffee in a tin can and poured it into two cups John had unpacked. Elaine later described it as "black as charcoal, thick as mud, and bitter as medicine, but as welcome as a double malted milk."

When John blew up their air mattress old and young alike watched in pop-eyed wonder as it grew in size. When he sprayed for bugs they covered their faces in mock pain and tittered loudly.

Not until full darkness descended did the villagers begin leaving. Along the sides of the hut Elaine could still hear titters and giggles.

She could make out the frames of dark faces pressed against the pole walls.

An hour after dark, human noises gave way to the lively jungle night. Only when they were absolutely certain that observers had departed did they slip into night clothes and relax on the mattress.

Next morning they awoke to more of the confusion of the evening before, but when John spread shaving cream on his face, the Indians stepped back in respect. Chols have no beard until they are old men, so they reasoned John to be aged.

After breakfast Elaine let the women run their fingers through her soft blonde hair. They had never felt such softness. Their own hair was matted and coarse.

One of the women kept picking at her scalp. Suddenly Elaine realized that she was looking for lice, considered a food delicacy by Chol women who fed them to their children.

The women, Elaine soon noticed, had no style problems. The all-occasion dress was a blue skirt, white blouse outfit accented by a single braid of black hair and bright ribbons trailing down their backs. The blouse was made from a cheap square of cloth with a square cut out for the neck. It was folded over and sewn up the sides under the armpits. Embroidered work, usually squares or diagonals of various colors, was worked in around the neck about six inches deep. The tubular blue skirt made of denim was held up by only a tight knot over the tucked-in blouse. The man's dress was even more simple. A plain blouse-like smock flowed down from the neck and billowed over the arms and below the waist of the wrap-around trousers that were tight at the calf of the leg.

Elaine also soon became aware "that traditions have molded the women; their life is monotonous drudgery; they are always kept in the background . . . trudging several yards behind their husbands on the trail. When they become Christians they are still followers, never learning the songs but mumbling the words after the men at least a phrase behind." She sighed to John, "How I long to see them become active, followers of Christ, not tradition."

The women of Amado Nervo were certainly not unfriendly. "Come to the river and take a bath with us," they invited Elaine. Each had a gourd basin filled with their own brand of "bubble bath," just ordinary ashes. Elaine declined, saying she had to cook, but did accept their offer to wash some clothes.

About a week later, John found Elaine making a Chol outfit. "Who is it for?" he asked.

Elaine giggled and went on working. "Me."

"You're kidding?" John said.

"No, I've decided to wear what they wear. Maybe it will make them think me less a foreigner."

A few days later a rancher came through the village and noticed Elaine in her new outfit. He stared a long time, then his face froze into a frown. After he left, John told Elaine, "He thinks you're demeaning yourself. No self-respecting Mexican woman would dress like an Indian. But don't let it get to you. We're here to win the Chols to Christ, not to convert them to foreign fashions."

One afternoon several men came by armed with reed baskets and machetes. "Come, go fishing with us," they called to John.

John was busy with word lists, but he did not want to seem unfriendly. He slipped on hiking shoes and slid behind the men down the mountainside to the river.

They stopped beside a large puddle that had been cut off from the main stream by low water. Flinging down their nets, the Chols began hacking down small bronze trees they called ak. This done, they cut the trees into short logs which they pounded with other logs.

They threw the bruised logs into the water and soon John saw fish and eels rolling near the surface in a stupor. He watched as the Indians waded into the water and scooped up the stupefied fish in their baskets. That evening he brought home a basket of fish, eels, and crabs which Elaine made into a delightful seafood platter. An extra bonus was a pad full of new words.

Every morning Elaine kept hoping to hear the leaders of the Christian congregation say, "We are ready to build your house." Their promises did not ease Elaine's worry about Nicholas' family living in the pig house. She wrote a letter to their home churches asking that they pray for the new house, which the Indians had promised to build, to be started. John did not want to go ahead on his own for fear of offending the Indians. He did, however, decide to do something about the lack of furniture.

Neither furniture store nor factory was near at hand, so John headed for the jungle showroom a few hundred feet away. The foliage was so thick, he had to crawl underneath to select a tree. After making his selection, he cut away the vines to make a full path. Then he sawed the tree trunk while Chol boys swung from branches to make it fall with their weight. The tree slowly came down stretching vines and bending saplings until it reached the path.

After John trimmed the branches, the boys helped push the log down hill through the undergrowth. When the log stuck, John cleared out room to squat and push harder. At the hut he began skinning bark off with a knife while the boys worked with their teeth. Then he cut the log in lengths and split boards from which he built a kitchen table and chairs.

Outside the hut he built a stone fireplace for boiling water. Near the fireplace he hung their U. S. Army surplus canvas water bag. The Chols named this the "cow" because the six faucets at the bottom gave forth liquid when pressed. An old flat bed spring which he had found in Mexico City fitted nicely over wooden bases. With the air mattress and sheets spread over this, they had a "deluxe" bed — or so it seemed to them.

To solve the embarrassment of dressing before "walls of eyes," he used a sheet and jungle hammocks to rig up a corner dressing room.

All day every day curious Chols came to the Beekman hut. Elaine kept trying to beat the morning rush. But each morning after she emerged from her dressing room, there they would be — a wall of eager-eyed curiosity seekers gazing through openings at the breakfast of cereals, fruit juice, and milk and watching every bite.

Before and after breakfast John conducted reading classes for all ages and built up his familiarity with the language. He kept pencil and pad with him at all times to "grab on paper" new words and idioms which he might hear.

The language detective began to appreciate the richness and variety of the language, so different from English. He learned that jealousy was "a shivering *heart*." Sadness was a "nailed *heart*." Gladness, a "large *heart*." Conviction, a "stabbed *heart*." A troubled conscience, a "talking *heart*." Love, a "pain in the *heart*."

The Chol word for flesh had no metaphysical meaning as "flesh" is used in the English Bible. It meant body, muscle, and meat. The corollary of the Biblical "flesh" was, in Chol, he decided, a "ragged" or "old *heart*."

Actually the hut was more a dispensary than a classroom. Elaine wrote to friends:

> Sickness and pain can always be found in the Chol life of physical obstacles. Because they work hard in their cornfields

under a burning sun, they are often troubled with headaches and vomiting. Bugs and vermin know no master here and open sores develop into running ulcers. Dirt has an easy entrance since they live and sleep on the ground. Round worms, tape worms, and pin worms are common. This is to be expected, as we see the pigs clean up human excreta and then the Indians eat pork half done. Their water is not boiled unless used with coffee. Their fish are roasted without cleaning and everything is eaten but the bones. The same with lizards. Malaria and other fevers, sprains, abscessed teeth, snake bites, and machete wounds are presented to us constantly. We stitch wounds, take temperatures, and give medicines (consulting only the Lord and our medical handbook) until you would think this was the emergency room of Cook County General Hospital in Chicago. Sometimes we fall in bed, too tired to pray.

Communication with their patients was a continual problem for John and Elaine. One woman patient refused to keep the thermometer in her mouth, insisting that the pain was not there but in her stomach. More typical cases were not so laughable.

One morning Elaine examined a three-year-old squalling girl. The child's head was covered with running sores. She cut off the hair which had matted in the sores, applied soap and water, an antiseptic, and concluded the healing ritual by sprinkling sulfa powder on the sores. Later she learned that the traditional treatment for such ulcers was to apply hot ant eggs that had been boiled in water.

John and Elaine soon learned that sickness and native remedies were part and parcel of the tribal belief system.

According to tradition, the devil owned the world and was easily offended. Should, for example, a baby in learning to walk fall upon the ground — the devil's property — he might in anger steal parts of the baby's spirit. Then the baby would become ill.

The devil might cause sickness for the cutting of large trees in clearing a cornfield. Or devil-induced sickness could follow the building of a new hut, because logs and grass, considered the devil's property, were used.

When part of one's spirit had been stolen, the witch doctor was consulted. He communed with the devil to learn what sacrifice was necessary for appeasement: a pig, turkey, or chicken, along with a keg of corn liquor. The sick person procured the designated items and called the witch doctor to his home. The medicine man stuck the animal or fowl and caught the blood in a gourd. Then he mixed a brew from blood, liquor, and herbs which he took into his mouth and spat in a stream on the sick person. He also gave the patient some to drink. Chanting and a crude violin accompanied this ceremony which usually lasted until all participants were in a drunken stupor.

Sickness might be prevented by anticipating the anger of the devil. Parts of a chicken could be buried in the four corners of a field before any corn was planted. Before a new home was finished, the husband could call in the witch doctor to make a sacrifice to the devil. The medicine man would spit the blood of an animal on the walls and into the grass roof and bury parts of the sacrifice under each of the corner posts. With the house dedicated to the devil, a child that falls inside the hut would not become sick. Because a "dedicated" house was considered safe, pagan Chol families frequently buried all their dead under the dirt floor.

John and Elaine learned that many of the Chol beliefs had been merged with the teaching of Spanish priests since the conquest. The Chols thought the sun to be their Holy Father, the great benefactor of mankind. The moon was their Holy Mother, equated with Mary, the mother of Jesus. They thought a moon eclipse was caused by a tiger attacking the Holy Mother. To help her, the old men chanted before burning candles, young men fired guns toward the moon, some beat on drums and turtle backs and shook rattles furiously, while everyone screamed loudly. All this was to scare away the tiger and keep him from eating the Holy Mother.

Neither John nor Elaine were surprised when word filtered to them that the witch doctor, Miguel Cruz, was displeased with their medical successes.

The witch doctor was feared by almost everyone in Amado Nervo excepting a few believers. The villagers believed him to be inhabited since infancy with extra spirits that gave him super-human powers. With his wind spirit he could cause one's corn to be blown down. With his humming bird spirit he could spy on the deeds of others. With his lightning spirit he could strike a house to the ground.

After Miguel made threats, the villagers waited in suspense for something bad to happen to his competition.

John and Elaine ignored his threats and continued to build their knowledge of the language, give medical aid, and teach literacy classes.

One morning John engaged a Christian guide and set out before sunrise to visit other villages. He later recorded this first trip to Elaine in vivid detail:

I had to crouch lest my head scrape the overgrowth along the trail. The long wet grass soon soaked my shoes. All was quiet except the water sloshing in my canteen and the noise of my clumsy stumbling on the trail. We crossed a deep chasm on a swaying rope bridge strung above a raging river and puffed up another mountain. Coming to a village of unbelievers, I suggested we visit the huts. My guide said in a frightened voice, "They like to use the machete and cut many necks." We had prayer and I led the way into the village.

Women and children ran in all directions into their huts. Even the dogs seemed to resent our presence. There were no doors to slam on these huts, so I had ready entrance into every home. I opened the conversations, then let my guide take over and explain the way of salvation. Three men accepted the Lord as Saviour.

We arrived at another village just in time to save a Chol's life. His blood was gushing from a slashed wrist artery. I applied a tourniquet and to the utter amazement of those standing around, the bleeding stopped.

That night I slept on a strip of thin bark laid on the ground. It wasn't long enough and much of me was on the ground. In two days we walked 27 miles. The sun boiled down. My clothes stayed soaked with perspiration. Each step I took felt like I was stepping into a shoe full of water. Two poisonous snakes crossed our path. Monkeys made themselves scarce. We visited four villages, took the Gospel to many families, and returned home tired but rejoicing in the salvation of three Chols.

When John returned, Elaine greeted him and kissed his stubbled face. Her strained face betrayed anxiety.

"What's wrong, Sweetheart?" John asked.

"The witch doctor is telling people he's going to shoot me. He has a gun."

John smiled wryly. "He's only a big wind bag. A small-time quack isn't going to sabotage the Lord's work."

Four days later three tired strangers arrived after a long walk on the trail. When John recognized them, he felt like whooping for joy. They were the three men who had accepted Christ on his two day trip and had come for further instruction.

After the men left with knowledge and John's encouragement to evangelize their own village, a boy appeared.

"My father wants you in our hut," he said. "Bring your medicine."

John and Elaine looked at each other and wondered if this would be walking into a devilish trap.

The boy was the son of the witch doctor.

Above: John Beekman's parents, Thomas and Bella Beekman, as they appeared in 1943, the year John enrolled in Moody Bible Institute. John's father died in 1961.

Right: John at two and one half years.

Below: In 1944 when the country was at war, John was classified 4-F because of his heart condition. Richard Beekman was a pilot in the U.S. Air Force. Jean, their sister, is shown between her brothers.

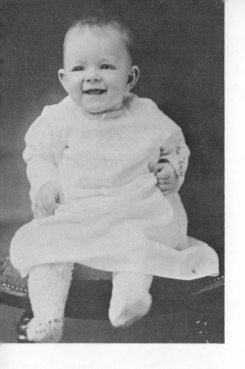

Above: Elaine Beekman at ten months.

Upper right: Elaine and her sailor brother Ben enjoy an excursion in Chicago's Humboldt Park during her early Moody days.

Right: Elaine Beekman's parents, Dan and Helen Hummel, and her brother, Dan Jr., when they came to her Moody graduation in 1945. Both parents are still living.

Above: Elaine took her first horseback ride on a trip to Chicago's Lincoln Park with John.

Lower left: While a student at Moody, Elaine cared for a Jewish baby. Here she arranged to walk with her date and get paid for it.

Lower right: The young pastor and his wife go visiting for the River Grove Bible Church in west suburban Chicago.

Elaine Beekman, the happy and beautiful bride.

Inset: Bride and groom cut the cake.

While president of the Missionary Union at Moody, John planned some interesting programs. At *upper left* he reads a missionary's letter to the Executive Council. At *upper right* he puts realism into a skit on jungle missions.

On the way to the Mexican border John stopped in Texas to check the trailer hitch. He sold car and trailer at the border for $150 and put 43 boxes of belongings on a train for Mexico City. Then he and Elaine boarded a bus and began observing the life of exotic Mexico like two wide-eyed children.

John holds a Mayan idol found in mountainous Chiapas.

On the way into Amada Nervo, Elaine Beekman sat in a chair strapped to the back of a barefooted Indian with a bark rope. The scenery was breathtaking (the canyon and waterfall at left are just below Amado Nervo), but she kept her eyes on John who panted behind while the trail snaked around the edge of such gorges.

Learning a tribal language and classifying strange hard-to-pronounce words is hard, tedious work. John and Elaine (shown here with two native informants) quickly came to appreciate the richness of the Tumbala Chol dialect. They learned that jealousy was a "shivering heart"; sadness, a "nailed heart"; gladness, a "large heart"; conviction, a "stabbed heart"; a troubled conscience, a "talking heart"; and love, a "pain in the heart."

5. *Firstfruits of Love*

MEDICINE KIT IN hand, John and Elaine followed the boy along the path to his father's hut. At the dark entrance John paused and smiled to reassure Elaine. "You wanted to see us, Miguel?" he called.

Miguel appeared. Slight and scrawny with bloodshot eyes, he did not look so formidable. "Come in," he grunted.

John and Elaine exchanged suspicious glances. Then John stooped to enter the hut and led the way.

When they were inside, Miguel pointed to his wife huddled on a pallet beside the cookfire. "Give my wife your medicine," he said.

John knelt on the dirt floor to take the woman's temperature. He noticed her arm was bound with a ragged, bloody bandage. Apparently Miguel had tried to cut the vein in hopes of letting out the evil spirit.

He checked the thermometer in the light of the fire and looked up at Elaine. "I'm almost sure she has malaria. We'll start with atabrine."

John dispensed the pills and told the husband, "I'll return tomorrow and give her more medicine if she is not better."

The man watched stoically as John and Elaine walked away. Their silent but intense prayers were united: "Lord, raise her up. Show Miguel that You are more powerful than Satan." Both knew that more than a life was at stake. Should she get better and Miguel become a believer, many other devil worshipers would be open to the Gospel.

The next day Miguel greeted John with a smile. His wife's temperature had dropped and though still weak, 'she was back grinding corn. He extended a few eggs wrapped individually in dry corn husks for the doctor's fee.

John took the eggs and tried to explain God's way of release from the devil's power. "God sent me with the good medicine because His heart is pained for you and your wife." He held up a bottle of pills. "God has better medicine than these. It will drive out the evil spirits and keep you from getting drunk. God's Son came and died to give you this medicine. He wants you to ask Him for it."

Miguel listened courteously but gave no indication that he was ready to change. "We will pray for you, Miguel," John said, as he stepped out of the hut. "And we will be glad to teach you more."

The following Sunday John and Elaine climbed the hill to church services, announced by an elder's piercing whistle. The men and women sat apart. Children fidgeted under the baleful stares of their mothers.

The Chols sang the few hymns in Chol which had been translated by Evelyn Aulie, and prayed together in a babble. Pad and pencil ready, John strained to catch new words and expressions.

Two of the men from his reading class read from Mark and gave short exhortations. John winced at some of their interpretations, but now was not the time to correct them. *Poor fellows*, he thought, *they're doing the best they can.* A resolution welled up within him to learn the language better and help with translation. If the Aulies at Hidalgo, near Yajalon had to spend as much time with medical work as he and Elaine did, they might not finish the New Testament for 15, even 20 years.

Services over, the believers stood around in groups passing social chit-chat. The elders invited John to confer with them about a discipline problem. A member of the church had taken a young girl for a second wife. He had beaten his first wife when she protested living in the same hut with the younger woman. The elders had tried to get the girl's parents to take her back, but without success.

The elders debated what to do. If they persuaded the man to repent and turn the girl out, she would have nowhere to go. Should the man keep the girl, there would continue to be trouble between himself and his first wife. They asked John for advice. He hesitated for two reasons. First, he honestly did not know the answer. Second, he did not want the elders to look to him for the solution of disciplinary problems. The elders pondered the matter some more and decided to put the offender on probation and instruct him to build an extra hut for his new wife.

A letter from veteran translator George Cowan had helped cement John's feelings that he should major on learning the language and translation work.

Where there are native churches, there is a very strong temptation to be so drawn into the life and ministry with the believers that no time is left for translation work. The desire for immediate spiritual fruit is so strong in all of us that we feel the tremendous urgency of the moment and fail to take a proper long-range view of translation. On many mission fields young believers have gone literally 20 or 30 years without any portion of the Word. The reason: Workers were so taken up with immediate church work, building the walls and the roof, so to speak, that they forgot that one must first lay the foundation in the written Word of God. You will not be neglecting the Chols by devoting your time to language and translation work. Instead you will contribute more in the long run to the future growth of the Chol church than if you gave yourself now to church work.

The Chols presented a different situation from other Mexican Indian tribes where translators were working. Already there were 800 Chol believers. But the work had developed from a Spanish speaking ministry fostered by the Reformed Mission. The Beekmans and their colleagues, the Aulies, were convinced the church could not grow much more unless indigenous work was established in the language. Perhaps less than 10% of the Chol population could even converse in Spanish.

Cool winter gave way to warm spring showers. The Chols of Amado Nervo waited for the heavy rains to stop so they could begin corn planting. But the rains continued, making it impossible to burn off spots for planting.

One morning John and Elaine heard the steady tom-tom-tom of wooden drums. They inquired and were told, "We are trying to soften the sun god's anger so he will shine again."

All that day the drums beat in Amado Nervo, accompanied by drinking, shouting, and dancing. At twilight loud claps of thunder announced the coming of another rain storm. By then some of the men were so drunk their wives had to pull them into shelter.

News arrived that twins had been born to a pagan family in a village over the mountain. One had died. When Elaine asked why, she was told, "It had a bad spirit so they killed it."

Some of the Chol Christians at Amado Nervo had followed this ancient practice before becoming believers. Tradition held that the father could give his spirit to only one child at birth. If a boy and girl were born, the boy was selected to live. When twins of the same sex were born, the largest was usually chosen to survive.

One evening John and Elaine talked and wept far into the night. "If I only knew the language better," John moaned. "If I only had the strength to go to every village with the Gospel. If only there were enough Chol believers trained to evangelize their own people. But they have so little to work with. Only Mark and a few hymns. Christians back home have a banquet with the many different English translations. The Chols have only a few crumbs of God's Word. Oh, if there were a hundred of me to shout from the mountains that Christ can set them free."

Elaine tried to help John relax. "Wilbur and Evelyn are working," she reminded him. "You will learn the language. The translation will get done. Next year there will be a difference. There'll be three of us then."

John relaxed and grinned at thought of the baby who was already making its presence known. "One more will help," he said. "We'd better get some sleep."

He began giving more thought to an airstrip in Amado Nervo for the Missionary Aviation Fellowship plane to land. M.A.F. had recently opened a base near Tuxtla. Carefully, John summarized the need in writing:

> After having traveled the trail between Amado Nervo and Yajalon six times — once by horse, twice by mule, and three times on foot, I've decided the easiest method of travel is by air. . . . I've learned to climb the hills slowly, rest at the top, then run down hill. This way there isn't time for my feet to sink into the mud. It's more like skiing. The disadvantage is that you can plunk into an unusually soft spot and fall kerplunk on your face.
>
> Another challenge is to keep dry. If you don't wear a cape, you're sure to be drenched by rain. If you do wear one, you'll be soaked from perspiration due to the humidity. The only way to escape these difficulties is to fly above them all.

The best spot for the strip appeared to be the length of uphill ground that lay in the bottom of the bowl. The huts stood on the slopes around the three sides. The plane, John figured, could fly in and take off from over the canyon. On one of his trips to Yajalon, he telegraphed the pilot at the M.A.F. base to fly in for a look.

One morning after the rains finally stopped, the yellow bird buzzed low over the village. The men were away in their cornfields.

Howling women and children fled in all directions while John and Elaine waved to the pilot who swooped to within less than 100 feet from the ground. As the pilot circled for another look, John called to the frightened people, "It's only a big bird. It won't hurt you."

E. W. Hatcher, the new M.A.F. pilot, thought a suitable strip could be made, but there would have to be considerable digging and rock moving. Because the men were in the cornfields from sunup to sundown, it seemed practical to put off building the strip until fall. Elaine knew this meant she would have to go out in the porter's chair for the first leg of the long trip to Oklahoma.

They were reluctant to leave, but as John said, "When we were appointed, we agreed to return for another summer's study. Anyway, we can kill two birds with one stone. I can study, and you can have the baby. When we come back in the fall, I'll build a new house."

Before leaving, word came from the Aulies that Gospel Recordings had visited their station and made five records in the Chol language. Extra copies would be sent to the Beekmans.

John told the Amado Nervo church about this, and five young men offered to visit villages and play the Gospel music and messages. But they had no phonographs. Elaine quickly dispatched a letter asking prayer about this from friends at home. She also requested prayer for a typewriter with large type, a fresh supply of medicines, health, the salvation of their neighbors, and that the men would start on the house.

The state elections pushed up their departure two weeks. The Chols were under orders to go and vote in Yajalon. Should they not go, they would be forced to carry rock over the 21-mile-long trail for two days. John felt that after the compulsory trip it might be difficult to hire porters to make a second trip out.

On May 8 Elaine crawled into the chair and was lifted onto the back of an Indian. John plodded behind on foot, followed by a troupe of 20 Chols.

They flew in a rickety cargo plane to Tuxtla. Elaine flew on to Mexico City via Mexicana Airlines, and John followed by bus. They obtained departure papers in the capital and John went on alone to Norman, Oklahoma by bus. Elaine flew up later.

They moved into a dormitory where they were assigned a room. John began teaching a class in morphology[1] and both studied under

[1]Morphology deals with the forms (Greek — *morph*) of words as affected by inflection, derivation, etc.

other instructors. They stayed very busy as they looked forward expectantly to the birth of their first child.

Fair-haired Sharon arrived one hot Monday afternoon in July, very jaundiced and too weak to nurse. Out went the poetic birth announcements, written and illustrated in advance of the joyful occasion by Elaine:

"Sharon Sue Beekman, that's my name,
But like my folks are always sayin'
It's not my name we would uphold,
But Jesus and His love untold. (Phil. 2:9, 10)

"As proud as we are of the weight of me,
Mom and Dad don't want me to stay so wee.
But to grow and grow in body and mind,
And early in life, their Saviour to find. (Matt. 19:14)

"As to the hour of my birth,
My folks had no insight,
Though, now it's all recorded
in black and white.

"So with Christ's coming,
The hour is not shared,
But His Word clearly tells us,
Be prepared! (Luke 12:40)

"Today I began life in this bright shiny world;
But there's more, they say, to be unfurled . . .
A new land, a new hut, and folks with brown skin . . .
Pray for us, please, as we tell them of Him. (II Thess. 3:1)

"P.S. from Mommy and Daddy: Please pray that Sharon might come to know our Saviour early in life."

Elaine brought the baby home to their new living quarters, a small pre-fab house off campus, nine days after birth. The hospital doctor told her, "Because your blood is RH negative and your husband's positive, you may have complications with a second pregnancy. But this rarely happens with the first baby. Sharon looks quite healthy, now."

Both were delighted with Sharon. John couldn't get back to their apartment fast enough from his last afternoon class. He learned to make formula and to change diapers so proficiently that Elaine said over and over, "I never cease to be amazed at how you can adjust to new things."

But on the second Monday morning after her birth Sharon began crying softly and could not be stopped. The temperature stood at 113 degrees outside.

John stayed home from classes and kept trying to reach their pediatrician by phone. He was operating, the nurse said, and could not be called.

By late afternoon they had still not heard from the doctor. Sharon was still crying and was too weak to nurse. Elaine tried giving water from a bottle while John looked over her shoulder. Suddenly the baby gasped and stopped breathing. John tried desperately to revive her with artificial respiration, but without success. When the doctor finally arrived about six p.m. life was obviously beyond recall.

"I'm sorry I could not come sooner," the doctor said. "You can see her heart was enlarged. She almost certainly would have died or been an invalid."

Then the doctor took Sharon from Elaine's arms, and covered her in the bed with a sheet.

An awkward silence hung in the air, with no one knowing what to say. Finally, John pulled Elaine onto his lap and said, "We should pray. Dear Lord, we dedicated her to You before she was born. She is in Your Hands now. You have given and You have taken away. We do not understand this, but we will try to trust Your love."

Services for Sharon were held in a Norman chapel on Wednesday, August 5, with about 100 missionary candidates in attendance. The baby was dressed in an elegant white dress with lace trimming and baby blue ribbon streamers falling from each shoulder. The dress had been purchased in New York by Elaine's Aunt Lena and was intended for the baby's christening.

After prayer, two translator friends sang, "The Rose of Sharon." Then Dr. Eugene Nida, one of the Norman faculty members, spoke.

Looking at John and Elaine who sat within arm's length of the casket, he said, "The death of your baby will probably mean much in your ministry among the Chols. The Chol women lose many babies. You, Elaine, will be able to comfort them with the testimony of this experience."

The grieving parents and friends followed the hearse to the municipal cemetery for the graveside ceremony. They sang together, "Safe in the Arms of Jesus." Dr. Nida gave a prayer of commitment and they watched as the tiny white casket was lowered into the grave.

Elaine wrote home:

Our Sharon has gone to be with the Rose of Sharon. He has transplanted our bud into His eternal garden. We praise Him for the two short weeks we had her with us and rejoice in the knowledge that we shall see her again in Heaven. We're resting in Him that doeth all things well.

A few days later John reflected upon their Gethsemane in a letter to his home congregation.

The principle found throughout Scripture of giving unto the Lord the firstfruits has been a special comfort and joy to us. In Numbers 3:13 we read, ". . . all the firstborn are mine." And in Proverbs 3:9, "Honor the Lord with thy substance and with the firstfruits of all thine increase." Sharon was the firstfruits of our love. At birth we named her after the One to whom she was dedicated. In our birth announcement we asked that she might find Him early in life. In our plans we looked forward to training her and nurturing her that she might become a servant of our Lord. Now, she need not follow the faltering steps of her earthly parents. In His presence she will know nothing but the beauty of His perfection. "Great is the Lord and greatly to be praised!"

John insisted that Elaine stay in Norman for more rest while he returned to Amado Nervo alone. She could answer the more than 400 notes of sympathy they had received. Word had come that the Chol believers were working on a new hut for them and John wanted to oversee its completion. Come fall, he assured Elaine, she could fly to Yajalon and he would meet her there.

Late in August John and another translator left driving a mission owned truck to Mexico City. Packed among other belongings were Sharon's clothes, sent by Elaine to a new missionary mother on the field whose baby had been born the same day as Sharon.

Barely ten months had passed since John and Elaine had made their original departure. Ten months of study, service to the needy Chols, and now they were emerging from the most traumatic experience of their lives.

Ahead lay more sorrows and triumphs.

6. *Shadows*

AFTER BEING DELAYED in Mexico City by dysentery, John finally arrived back in Yajalon. He hired a horse and despite a stomach cramp, rode hard toward Amado Nervo from where he wrote Elaine,

"*. . . Jumping logs, stones, streams, and ducking branches and briers, I completed the 21 miles in four and one half hours in spite of having lost my way. Doubled up like an old man, I greeted the believers who welcomed me home."*

Nicholas proudly directed John to the new house built about 50 yards from the entrance to the mud church.

"*I looked at our new hut. It was much smaller than we had expected; the floor sloped like a ski jump; the holes left for windows were as much circular as square; and the poles placed at the doorway looked like they had a bad case of mumps. But I couldn't help but lift my sun helmet and before the crowd give audible thanks to our heavenly Father."*

John wanted to go to work immediately on the hut, but . . .

"*Calls of medicine had me haul the boxes down and dispense medicines for malaria, infected ears, cuts, etc. An eye disease now rages throughout Chol country. More than 100 Indians have come for medicines for their bloody, swollen eyes. I've tried all our eye medicines and penicillin shots. Nothing has helped."*

Busyness helped stave off pangs of loneliness and longing for Elaine. John worked from six to seven, eating only as he became hungry. Chol women brought tortillas, hard boiled eggs, bananas, oranges, boiled pork, and coffee.

At last he caught up with the medical cases and got down to work on the house. With Chol helpers he dug an outdoor toilet, throwing the dirt inside the house to level off the floor. Made of logs with a grass roof and sides of woven palm tree leaves, the "lounge" was a first in Amado Nervo.

He dug a ditch around the hut and threw this dirt inside. Still the floor sloped. Now doors, windows, and locks had to be made — more innovations in the village. And as before, he had to take time out for the sick.

The most heart-rending case was a baby wrapped in a tattered, dirt-caked damp rag. The skin on its arms and legs hung in loose yellow wrinkles lined by caked dirt. The small eyes deep in bony sockets looked tired and dull. Fever, cough, and vomiting were the only symptoms.

John had already exhausted his stock of penicillin, so he tried sulfa. When the baby vomited this up, the Christian mother burst into tears. "I know how you feel," John said softly. "We had a little one that was very sick. God helped us to trust Him in our sorrow." After John talked some more about Sharon's homegoing, the mother dried her tears. Then they and several believers who had gathered around sang a hymn and prayed.

The baby died a few days later. Three other critically ill babies were brought to John and one of them died. He cried and prayed with each mother and talked about Sharon.

"When I told them about Sharon, their faces brightened," he wrote to Elaine. *"The Lord knew what we needed to give these people sympathetic understanding."*

Elaine arrived in Yajalon on October 3 and ran into John's hungry arms. "A month alone in the jungle with only two letters and Indian food to live on is too much!" he said as she snuggled close.

He gave Elaine his horse and rented a mule for himself. After an hour of whipping the stubborn animal, he sent it back with an Indian.

"The dumb mule didn't want to do more than a pleasure walk," he snorted, "I wanted at least a New York business walk out of it. I grabbed the tail of Elaine's horse and hiked the rest of the way."

Next on the schedule was a thank-you party for the hut builders. Elaine baked four batches of cookies to go with the cellophane-wrapped hard candy and 100 soda pops they had brought in for the occasion. John served the men, Elaine the women. None of the women had ever tasted soda pop before. Some had never heard of it. But after a few experimental sips, Elaine noted, "they guzzled it down like old timers."

John and Elaine smiled and laughed with their Chol friends during the festivities, but their thoughts were about Sharon. Had she lived, they would have been celebrating her third monthly birthday.

They had purposefully planned the party for this day. As Elaine said in a letter to her parents,

> Her name meant "flower-like" and how true it has been. Like a flower she faded and died so quickly, but in her short lifetime we were able to capture some of her sweetness which daily scents our lives. So we gave a party.

Neither attempted to suppress their feelings about Sharon. Elaine wrote to a friend from Moody days enjoying a healthy baby:

> Is Anne creeping now? It sure must be fun to watch them go through all those cute little stages of growing up. I don't suppose a day goes by that I don't think about Sharon Sue and wonder what she'd be like, if she were still with us, for in our dreams we even had her through college. Now when we look at the colored slides taken the day she came home from the hospital, and see again her cute little buttercup curl, her turned up nose and dimple in her chin, our arms and hearts ache to hold her cuddly little body again. But the ache in our hearts is eased as we realize that she knows now only the perfectness of our lovely Saviour and Lord. Already, the Lord has used this experience to give us entrance into the hearts and lives of the Indians. As never before, we have been able to offer understanding words and comfort.

The cool and rainy fall days held more opportunities for service. At the break of morning light, John rolled out of bed to start his men's reading class, already gathered on the board porch in front of the hut. At eight the men left for their work on the coffee ranches and John went inside for breakfast. At 8:30 Elaine became professor for women who had never before held a pencil. The rest of the day was taken up with medical service, including hut calls, and language study. Wycliffe's base headquarters in Mexico City had promised three single girls for literacy work. John hoped they would free him to help the Aulies with translation. He also wanted to start a "school of the prophets" for training young men.

A shipment of supplies, sent by churches and friends in the U.S., arrived at Yajalon and were carried into Amado Nervo by porters.

"Look at the answers to prayer," John told Elaine as each item was unpacked. There were six phonographs, a typewriter with large type, and a large stock of medicines.

That evening Elaine looked over copies of past letters. Then she formed a new one:

LET'S TAKE STOCK OF GOD'S FAITHFULNESS

YOU PRAYED FOR . . . . .

1. Five phonograph players.
   Six have arrived.
2. A typewriter with large type.
   They are no longer being manufactured, yet God found us one for only $30.00.
3. More medicines.
   They're here!
4. The salvation of precious Chols.
   Six became believers while we were in Oklahoma, the result of the faithful witness of Nicholas.
5. A new house for us that will better weather the winds and rain.
   During our absence the Indians built the new hut of grass roof and mud walls. Only windows, doors, and partitions remain to be completed.
6. Our health.
   We've had no serious illness.
7. That Sharon might come to know our Saviour early in life.
   In God's own way, this, too, has come to pass.

Thanks be "unto Him that is able to do exceeding abundantly above all that we ask or think" (Ephesians 3:20).

The phonographs were strapped on the backs of six eager young evangelists of the Amado Nervo church. They set off the following weekend for distant villages. When they returned and gave their reports, John felt inspired to put their daring adventures into writing after the style of the Apostle Paul:

> From below sea level to over 7,000 ft. elevation; through the lashing rains and in the sweltering sun; across acres of cornfields and miles of jaguar-infested forests; through water up to their knees; over treacherous rocks covered with slimy green moss; through chilling rain clouds and shimmering heat waves, they have carried the phonos.
>
> In some villages the fellows have been chased by men with drawn swords; in others threatened with rocks, but none of this deters them from playing the records. Gone for days with only a blanket, they live on whatever is given to them in the huts they visit. When hunger becomes painful, they eat the heart of

certain jungle plants or the roots of certain trees. When no hut is offered for shelter, they roll up in their blankets and sleep in the outdoors.

In all of this the Gospel is being given. Idolatrous Chols are forsaking their idols to trust our living Lord.

Meanwhile back in Amado Nervo, the witch doctor's baby developed a mouth infection and died. He flew into a rage and blamed the believers. All day and night his weird chantings echoed across the bowl. Suddenly Christian mothers by the scores began arriving at the missionaries' house. Each made the same request: "Look at my baby's mouth. Do not let it die."

The witch doctor had pronounced curses upon the Christian babies and predicted they would die in the same way his child died. But not one became ill.

When the baby scare was over, John developed leg ulcers. Sulfa brought no response. Elaine gave him penicillin shots. Eight tries resulted in four takes. One hit the bone. She cried. John laughed.

The heavy rains continued. Even between the showers there was no respite from dampness. Bed clothes gathered the mildew. Pajamas kept under blankets felt like clothes dampened for ironing. Books curled like corrugated paper. Mold grew on everything, even the chairs.

John took time out for a trip to two nearby villages. He held three reading sessions. He returned home with high spirits and a low voice; a high fever and low arches.

The top of their peaked hut was raised to make room for loft quarters. Underneath the grass roof he built a boudoir which afforded a place for Elaine's treasured rose-colored throw rug. This gave them the privilege of ascending a ladder for rest in privacy, away from the wall of eyes that always peered from outside the windows below. This, they desperately needed.

The reading classes continued during the damp rainy season.

"*Believe it or not, when we sit beside these men,*" John wrote, "*we put ourselves in the midst of a circling host of gnats. The bugs are more than a nuisance; they are the cause of fevers and 101 other diseases. Such is the life here where bugs and Indians live together, pigs and Indians eat together, and chickens and Indians sleep together. We can either withdraw from the people or serve them, trusting the Lord for health. We gladly choose the latter.*"

Their choice was not without cost.

For John's 31st birthday on December 2, Elaine baked a chocolate cake. That night she fell in bed with a 102° fever which lasted for six straight days. Her heart pounded with pain, her pulse increased to 110 beats per minute, and her breath came in short gasps. Her muscles twitched and her hands and arms felt numb though hot with fever. There were no chills, the usual indication of malaria.

When the fever broke, her pulse dropped to 45. Weakness and anemia kept her in bed.

While John doctored and prayed, their old nemesis, the witch doctor pronounced Elaine's doom. With fear staring from his eyes, a believer described how Miguel had made a corn cob, doll-like effigy of Elaine and solemnly cursed her in the name of the devil. Upon hearing that, John smiled thinly and declared, "God's power is greater than his. We'll see."

Adoring eyes followed John as he tended to household chores. When feeling returned to her fingers, Elaine penned a poem on musky, damp paper.

"Here I am helpless in bed,
Not even able to lift my head.
But from morn till night John's right on hand;
With utmost of care, I'm fed, pulsed, and panned.
The household runs smoothly — as tho I were there,
More smoothly, I wager, under his watchful care.
Of my appetite I'd nearly despaired,
But it hit a new high on the meals he's prepared.
Does he love me? How could you ask?
That's love in action, no matter how lowly the task."

The days painfully inched toward Christmas. John hummed Christmas carols to brighten the gloom inside the hut where Elaine lay ill. Both longed for snow, a crackling fire, tobogganing and all the memories of past Christmases at home.

John noted that the Chols were preparing for their own celebrations. He marveled at the contrast between the Christian and the pagan ways of celebrating Christ's birth. On the day after, he recorded what he had observed:

It was the day before Christmas among the Chol Indians. The distant figures of four Indian men bent under a load of fresh pine needles soon made their appearance at the church. Men and boys soon busied themselves in stripping the needles from the pine branches while others cut crepe paper with scissors borrowed from us. A blanket of green pine needles was spread on the dirt floor of the church for the barefooted worshipers of the morrow. Streamers were stretched across the room and glued to vines with the sap of a tropical plant. Machete-smoothed bench logs with forked branches for legs were carefully spaced and steadied with flat rocks under the short legs. The mud-walled, thatched roof church was now ready for the services of Christmas Day.

Others were also preparing for Christmas Day. They carried a load for the celebration of the morrow — cheap whisky bargained at great cost from the nearby Mexican ranch. Drums were taken down from the overhead rafters of the huts of the witch doctors.

Before the darkness of the moonless night had been scattered, Christmas Day was ushered in with the monotonous beating of the drums — hollowed logs with the skin of a jaguar stretched over each end. The pagans had begun their drinking and dancing.

Then when the rosy fingers of the dawn began appearing over the mountain, barefooted mothers, fathers, and children clad in ragged cloths gathered at the church entrance. A fond mother would shift her crying baby from hip to back or from back to hip. The little head would hang and nod as the sick infant nestled in the hammock swung from its mother's shoulder. Many little children sat sullenly by, robbed of their normal energies by worms or fever. Others ran about playfully, unmindful of the malnutrition their bared and swollen stomachs betrayed. Some played on feet and legs potted with gnat-filled ulcers.

This was just a typical Indian gathering. Destitute of the necessities of life, these folk would consider our direst poverty wealth. However, mere physical discomforts were forgotten now as their hearts centered on praise to God.

These gathered to pray and to sing some of the hymns we had taught them and to hear one of their own men read and explain the Christmas story in their own language. Often an Indian girl and two Indian men in different parts of the church prayed aloud simultaneously.

In the late afternoon they again gathered to sing and to pray. During this service the women lit fires and heated water in their clay pots to make coffee. As darkness closed around the day, the congregation of about 400 gathered around the fires. Then in a most orderly fashion, groups of 20 were served a cup of coffee and a few crackers.

On a nearby hill drunken men and women lay as if dead, while others screamed like wild beasts and staggered in the

midst of their dancing. The pagan drums were beating un-
steadily now.

Surrounded by this wild paganism, the Christians lingered
around their fires, talking freely of their cornfields and their
joy in the Lord. Then with pine torches lit, family after family
proceeded in true Indian style, single file, toward their distant
huts. The Christ child of Christmas day had become their living Saviour and made the difference as to how they observed
the day.

A few days later, a trail runner brought chilling warning that a
Mexican rancher was coming to shoot the foreign brother and his
wife. He was angry with John for "changing the Indians' religion"
and "encouraging them to act smart toward their employers."

John knew he must get Elaine away for professional medical help.
The shock of Sharon's death, the pressure of tribal life, and the
mysterious fever had been too much. Now with the murder threat
it was essential that they leave as soon as possible. But no one owned
even a mule in Amado Nervo. Horses and mules that might usually
be hired were being worked in the coffee harvest.

At night Elaine teetered on the edge of hysteria. With every small
noise she sat up in bed and shone the flashlight around in fear that
someone was in the hut. One night John sat and read the Bible aloud
from eight until daylight to keep her calm and from screaming.

The next night they heard men fighting a few yards up the trail.
A few minutes later, a Chol came running to tell what happened.
The Mexican rancher had come to kill them, but in his drunken
condition had wobbled off the trail near their house. Neighbors had
jumped him and wrestled him to the ground.

"We helped him forget why he came," the Chol said cannily. "He
is on his way out of the village."

Providentially, a Mexican believer stopped by for a visit the next
day. He turned over to John the mule he had hired from a man in
Yajalon. Early the next morning John and Elaine left on the muddy
trip to the market town. Elaine swayed in a porter's chair, the mule
carried a pack of her belongings, and John stumbled along in front,
fighting a halo of bugs that continually swarmed about his head.

They met the arriving plane from Tuxtla at the Yajalon airstrip.
On board were Iris Mills, a new Wycliffe literacy worker, and two
other single girls, Betty Miller and Arabelle Whittaker. Here were
the long awaited literacy workers for the Chols.

Elaine insisted that John should remain a few days and help the girls get started. The Kempers would care for her in Tuxtla and see that she got medical aid. John could rejoin her after the new workers were settled, and they could enjoy a rest together.

John reluctantly agreed that this would be best since in three months the girls would have to go to the Guatemalan border and have their entry papers renewed.

"Senor, we are ready to leave," the pilot said. John tucked Elaine into a seat behind the pilot and kissed her good-by. "Don't forget," he said, "I'll be waiting here for a telegram on how you feel."

When the plane vanished into the western haze over the mountains, John and the three newcomers went off to a small hotel. They unpacked and immediately began making plans for reading classes. Fortunately, Iris had some knowledge of Chol grammar and knew the rudiments of the language. Betty and Arabelle, John felt, could pick up enough in the villages to help with the reading charts.

Elaine's telegram from Tuxtla came the next day. John understood it to mean that she was doing well and he should stay in the tribe.

John hired enough mules and Indians to carry the literacy girls and their belongings into the village of La Cueva, about 20 miles from Amado Nervo. He went along on the rugged trip and helped them move into a hut the Christian villagers had already built for them. A crowd of eager Chols swarmed around and would not leave until Iris promised that reading classes would start the next day.

He rode back to Amado Nervo, still thinking Elaine to be in no serious danger. Otherwise, he felt, the telegram would have told him to come immediately. Then he heard footsteps and looked up from his desk. It was a runner from Yajalon with a telegram. The message was from Kemp and said John should come as soon as possible. John shuddered. Had the first telegram been garbled? Later he learned that it had.

It was now six p.m. and twilight was giving way to bright moonlight. He sent an Indian out for a horse.

By nine when the man returned with the animal, a small crowd had gathered. "Brother Kwan,[1] will you come back?" one of the men asked, seeking assurance.

John smiled and tried not to betray his concern. "Of course, and my wife will be with me."

But as he mounted, the women began crying softly. "They're

[1] The Chol word for Spanish *Juan.*

afraid you won't return," Nicholas said. "The witch doctor has been saying your wife will die from his curse."

John replied, "Our God can do wonders," and rode down the moonlit trail.

He had expected the moonlight to brighten the path, but just before leaving, dark rain clouds moved in turning the jungle into a mystery land of dark shadows and shapes. He was glad that a Chol believer had offered to lead the way with the Coleman lantern.

Just outside of Amado Nervo the rain began. At one spot the horse sunk so deep into the mud that John had to slide off and whip him out. Further on, a bright-eyed jaguar crossed the trail in front of the guide and flounced into the brush, apparently frightened by the bright light.

Soaked and exhausted, John arrived in Yajalon at seven a.m. The plane, due to take off at eight, was delayed until two p.m. He finally reached Kempers' house at four and found Elaine weak and pale, but in good spirits. Kemp quickly told him the doctor's diagnosis: malaria, anemia, and a bad case of nerves. Recommendation: more intravenous and intermuscular injections and a long rest.

Three weeks of treatment and rest at the Kempers' home in Tuxtla helped Elaine regain strength, but she continued to suffer muscle twitching and depression. The Mexican doctor said there was nothing more he could do. Kemp felt she should go home to Pennsylvania for two or three months of medical care and recuperation. John concurred, so in late February they went to Mexico City to process her diplomatic papers.

The Mexican officials told them this would take a little time. An apartment was available at the Presbyterian Rest Home on the shore of Lake Tequesquitengo. John borrowed a 1930 Marquette from a translator and took Elaine there to wait for the diplomatic green light.

Their living room window faced the small blue lake, fed by underground springs, and set like a jewel in an old volcanic crater. It was a beautiful and restful spot for intimate talks about the future. John wrote their feelings in a letter to his home pastor: *"When we came to the Chols, we expected to have our share of hardships. These things therefore do not move us and as the Lord gives renewed strength we will immediately return to the needy Chols."*

While they waited, John sorted through hundreds of Chol words and phrases which he had not had time to memorize in hectic tribal living.

Finally Elaine's papers were ready. John drove her to the International Airport in the old Marquette and saw her on the flight for Pittsburgh. He considered staying in Mexico City while she was away, to do intensive language study. But a letter written in Chol and addressed by Iris Mills helped change his mind.

kwan bikman
John Beekman:

mik pejkanet ti karta cha'an mik k'ajtibenet erman kwan baki
I talk to you in letter because I   ask you   brother John where
anet.   anetba ti tusla.   kom k'ajtibenet bajche'   a   wilal.
are you. Are you in Tuxtla? I want to ask you   how   you're feeling.
ut'sat   ba'anet   erman.   bajche'   yilal   a pi'vl lak erman?
Good where are you brother?   How   she feels your wife our sister?
kom   k'ajtibenet   baki   oora ma'   cha' titel.   kom
I want to ask you where (is the) hour you again come? I want
i kexol jini karta ti lak   t'an.
its answer this letter in our (Indian) words.

nikolas baskes.

The Christians at Amado Nervo burst into glad tears when John rode in one April afternoon. All wanted to know about Elaine and when he told them she was resting and would soon return, the usually quiet women leaped for joy.

The Reading Campaigners had a thrilling report. They had taught an average of 42 pupils in three classes per day, using syllable charts and primers for raw beginners, and the Gospel of Mark for more advanced readers. Ten men in Amado Nervo alone could now read Mark in Chol. Four had been certified as literacy teachers. They had also treated an average of 25 medical cases daily, and helped a circuit-riding Mexican doctor vaccinate 200 people against the smallpox epidemic that had been sweeping the region.

John accompanied five Amado Nervo lay evangelists on a follow-up trip to villages where they had played records and read the Gospel of Mark. In Carranza, where they had been threatened with machetes and shotguns, he found 20 families of new believers meeting regularly for worship and study of Mark; there were 11 more new Christian families in Paru and Barkararo. All had faced severe threats of persecution. The pagan father of a young Carranza believer had grabbed an ancient shotgun, packed in some powder, and jammed some steel pellets wrapped in cactus fiber down the gun's barrel. Gun loaded and cocked, he jammed the gun into his son's stomach, and snarled, "I'll kill you if you follow this new religion." The boy stood his ground and the old man finally slammed the gun on the mud floor in disgust.

The Paru believers had been confronted by a Mexican rancher with the ultimatum: "Deny this foreign religion or I will see that you have no land for corn planting." "Better to have land in Heaven," John told the Paru Christians, "than land on earth."

John also ran into the multiple wife problem again. Several of the new believers had two wives. "It is better for a man to have one wife," he counseled. "But since you already have two, you must provide for both." He hoped for the time when there would be many strong Indian churches with elders to guide the believers in this and other difficulties.

The circuit took John 200 miles on horseback. Unable to carry food with him, he ate whatever was available. One day he and the evangelists shared tortillas and fried ants. Other days they survived on snails, caterpillars, tree bark, roots, and wild berries. "They all taste good," he wrote to a minister friend, "when one is hungry enough."

Early in June he decided to visit a fiesta in Tila where large numbers of Chols went annually to drink, dance, and make sacrifices for their sins. Five pistol-packing Mexicans overtook him on the trail. "Going to Tila?" the swashbuckling leader asked. John nodded and the man said, "Ride with us."

John trotted his mule along with the Mexicans who joked about the Indian women and drink they planned to enjoy in Tila. At twilight they stopped to rest at a ranch along the trail.

The rancher brought out bottles and offered one to John. "Thanks," he said, "but it's not for me."

Thunder rumbled and lightning splintered the darkening sky. "We've got 20 more miles to go," the leader said. "Let's ride on and beat the rain." He looked at John. "Stay with us."

John prodded his mule and rode on with them, praying for a chance to tell about a new way of life.

Questions flew at John as they rode along. "Why don't you drink? Don't you like Indian women? Are you a Protestant?"

John replied in Spanish, telling how Christ had given him a new dimension of life, and explaining how they could be certain their sins were forgiven.

The darkness thickened and the thunder roared louder. The men pushed their mules faster. John kept pace with them on the never-to-be-forgotten trip.

"We traveled together for opposite purposes," he later wrote Elaine. "They were going for drink and women. I was going for Christ. I couldn't see a bit of the trail, yet the mule trotted along, side-stepping rocks and trees, leaping logs and ditches. Lightning often flashed just a few yards from us as we rode through the clouds on the mountain tops. Once the mule slipped and did a complete turnover. I kicked my feet free from the stirrups and slid around the mule's stomach to freedom, untouched by the kicking hoofs. Upon our safe arrival in Tila, my companions dismounted to find liquor. I found a dry piece of ground and rolled up in my blanket for a few hours' sleep."

Next morning John purchased tortillas and coffee for breakfast. Then he strolled through the village, observing and taking pictures of the processions and drummings. He had begun talking to Indians individually about Christ when one shouted, "Are you a Protestant?"

John replied, "I am one who believes that only Christ can forgive your sins and take you to Heaven.."

"You don't belong here," the man snarled and ran off into the crowd.

A few minutes later a group of 15 rock-carrying Chols rushed in to surround John.

"Get back," the leader shouted to the crowd. "We'll deal with this foreign trouble maker."

7. *The "Nerve Bowl"*

THE INDIANS ADVANCED on John with their rocks. Suddenly a husky Mexican appeared. Grasping John by the arm, he commanded, "Take pictures of my band."

The band leader had seen John photographing the processions and arrived at the right moment. The would-be attackers stood mute as the musician and John pushed through the crowd. They did not dare attack one with so much authority as the band leader.

John took a long time getting each subject in focus. Never had he used a camera so slowly. Not until the would-be attackers had left did he hand the film over to the band leader.

Few would sell him food and none would give shelter. John passed the night again in the outdoors, sheltered from the downpour only by a waterproof rain cape. The next morning he rode into Yajalon, almost too weak to dismount from his horse. He boarded a cargo plane for Tuxtla.

"You have amoebic-dysentery," a Mexican doctor told him. "You can control it but not cure it. You'll just have to learn to live with it as a handicap for living in the jungle."

John recalled reading an anthropological study on Chiapas Indians in which the author described his own case of amoebic-dysentery. He reasoned to himself, *If a pioneer for science is willing to suffer these sicknesses, why should not I gladly suffer for a much greater Cause?*

And after getting the doctor's report, he penned a prayer . . . .
"Lord, give me a heart of gold toward my fellow believers.
> a heart of water toward the lost.
> a heart of honey toward my wife.
> a heart of flame toward my Lord.
> a heart of steel toward myself."

Medication and a few days' rest with the Kempers in Tuxtla brought John's strength back. He had been counting the days until the time for Elaine's scheduled return on June 24th.

That day, a Friday, he was at the Mexico City airport well ahead of the scheduled time for her flight to arrive. They saw each other through the door leading to customs but had to wait an interminably long 20 minutes for her bags to be checked and papers stamped.

When her last bag was okayed, Elaine sprinted for the door and fell into John's arms. The separation had been the longest and hardest of their married life, but John was rewarded by the sight of Elaine's glowing face, fleshed in by relaxation and a regular diet. Her problem had been diagnosed by a Pennsylvania doctor as cerebral malaria. His treatment had put her on the road to health.

The "Kettle" was full, so they spent the weekend in a hotel — a veritable second honeymoon. As John told about the events in Chol country, Elaine exclaimed over and over, "Oh, I'm so anxious to get back."

But John did not concede that this would be best. He recalled George Cowan's letter: *"By devoting your time to language and translation work you will contribute more in the long run to the future growth of the Chol church than if you gave yourself now to church work."*

"Elaine, I think we should stay in Tuxtla for awhile and concentrate on what George suggested," he said. "We can get a couple of Chol fellows to come out and live with us. Before you return, I'd like to have a cement floor in our house and the airstrip built."

They went by bus to Tuxtla where they rented rooms in the Brindis Hotel and sent word to La Cueva for two young evangelists, Mateo and Dominic, to come. John requested the La Cueva church to take care of their families while they were away. He would provide for their lodging and food, but would not pay a salary for translation help. Already he had told Kemp, "I want these fellows to be responsible to the native church, not to the missionary."

Back in Chol country the Beekmans' fellow workers had experienced difficulties. The literacy girls had flown out to have their diplomatic papers renewed at the Guatemalan border. On the trip back they rode in a cargo plane, sitting on their luggage, with squealing pigs as co-passengers.

Pilots sometimes loaded their small planes so heavily with cargo that pigs had to be tossed out to climb over the steep mountains. No pigs were thrown this time, but the load caused the plane to descend faster than anticipated. The plane hit rough ground ahead of the smoothed airstrip and veered to one side. The door sprung open. Iris Mills was hurled out, and suffered a back injury serious enough to necessitate returning to St. Paul, Minnesota, for recuperation.

Wilbur and Evelyn Aulie, blessed with newborn twins, had both come down with malaria and had just left for treatment in Mexico City. This left the Chols with only the temporary literacy workers, Arabelle Whittaker and Betty Miller.

Mateo and Dominic came to Tuxtla and cheerfully began helping John with translation of Old Testament Bible stories. He had decided to begin here for good reasons: Mark had been translated by Evelyn Aulie and contained numerous references to the Old Testament; stories would be easy for the Chols to understand; and he felt he did not have sufficient command of the language for detailed translation.

The Genesis record of creation thrilled Mateo and Dominic. "That's how the world got here!" Mateo shouted. "God did it!"

In explaining the differences between animals and man, John pointed out that animals have no spirit. This, he knew, differed from the Chol witchcraft tradition that held sickness to be caused by the spirits of animals in a human body. The native tradition, for example, said that the spirit of an earth mole in the mouth was supposed to cause tooth decay; to cure the decay, the witch doctor passed a dead mole over the person's mouth to force the mole's spirit to return to its proper home.

John contrasted the Biblical flood story with the flood tradition of the Chols. According to their belief, some wicked men had escaped the flood and tried to outwit God by running up trees. God had caught them and made tails grow out of their backs. This, the Chols believed, marked the origin of monkeys.

When John came to English Bible words not in the Chol vocabulary, he improvised. The baker in the story of Joseph became "one who makes foreign tortillas"; the butler "one who passes tortillas." Chariot became "an instrument of carrying one with four round feet which mules pull." Neither the Chols nor their Mayan ancestors had understood the concept of the wheel and axle.

He finished the Genesis stories and moved into the story of Moses. Repeatedly he had to improvise for concepts unknown to the Chols. Taskmaster, he translated "one who watches workers;" well, "cave water;" hail, "stonelike water;" leprosy, "strange sores."

Besides translation, he and Elaine did other work. They prepared new reading charts which they mailed to Mexico City for printing, and they made a guidebook for literacy teachers. They helped Mateo and Dominic tape evangelistic messages which they sent to Gospel Recordings in California for dubbing onto records.

"The Lord has given us a vision for the work here," John wrote to a favorite uncle. "We are looking forward to the impossible. We are praying for 30 more phonograph machines even though they are on the prohibited list of imports; the starting of a Chol Bible School; the printing of a newspaper in Chol; and the printing of weekly Sunday school material. Of course, the Sunday schools have yet to be organized and teachers trained. Then there are Gospel story books to be made, and more books of the Bible translated. And the ever growing medical ministry with the need of a clinic and nurses."

Mateo and Dominic proved to be cheerful, eager helpers, always anxious to learn more of the strange outside world.

Never having been to civilization before, they were interested in everything — especially the zoo and museum in Tuxtla.

At the monkey island in the zoo, they cackled at the sight of dozens of monkeys frolicking on the denuded tree that was surrounded by a moat. Later in the museum they saw rows and rows of stuffed animals and asked very practical questions: "Why don't they smell? Have they been dead for many days?" John and Elaine laughed with them and patiently tried to explain the ways of civilized people. Such good times helped them forget their own hardships.

On August 8th, John and Elaine celebrated their third wedding anniversary. In three years they had known more suffering and tragedy than most couples experience in a lifetime. Elaine wrote a poem that expressed her feelings:

Your Sweet Smile
Sweetheart, of all your charms,
Your smile is most endearing.
Its steady glow stills all alarms
And shames my bent for fearing.

Seems to me you've beat Mr. Heinz
Producing ten times fifty-seven kinds.
They satisfy the hunger in my heart;
Vie in aptness with cards of Hallmark.
I love to watch your eyes light up,
Twinkling eagerly in anticipation
Of a cherished plan not yet developed;
The hope alone, giving you quivers of elation.
No matter how dreary and cold the storm
That blows in its chilling gale;
The warmth of your smile is as the brightest morn
After a long dark night of sleet and hail.
To think that I can enjoy these smiles so rare
That unfailingly bring courage and delight.
How like our Gracious Lord to let me share
In the fruit of His Spirit from your sweet life.

Manuscript piled up as they continued to work. Thanksgiving passed and Elaine began humming carols and thinking of fall in Pennsylvania. One sweltering day she heard Mateo humming "Silent Night" as he swept the floor. Both she and John knew how well the Chols loved music. In the tribe the believers were already being called "the singers" because they so often sang hymns on the trail, while at work, and by evening fires.

Suddenly Mateo stopped and turned to her. "Sister Elena, what does this song say in my language?"

Elaine looked at the pile of Christmas greetings in which she planned to include personal notes. Quickly she decided. Better the cards go without notes and carols be translated for the Chols. Mateo and Dominic would be leaving for Amado Nervo in a few days. They could carry the words on paper and the tune in their heads.

Elaine mailed the cards without notes and began translating "Silent Night." When she finished, Mateo and Dominic sat enthralled as she sang in Chol about the Saviour's birth. "To think," she told John later, "that I once thought I would have to bury my love for music on the mission field."

Elaine took time to pen another poem for John in honor of his 31st birthday:

Last night I spent a little time,
Working on a little rhyme,
Dropping a phrase or adding a line
To say just right this wish of mine.
I wondered at what ripe old age
A man was fit to be a sage.

Many a man is still a mere child
After 31 years he has piled!
As for your standing in wisdom and knowledge,
Let's look at your marks in that famous college.
"Hard knocks" is the school to which I refer.
Come here, Johnny, and your degree I'll confer.
You'll soon be qualified for the "H.K." ranks
When I've properly administered 31 SPANKS!

John laughed and said he didn't need the spanks to qualify for the degree. He held up his right index finger to display the huge callus he had gained from writing. Elaine insisted and the loving pats were administered.

On the Tuesday before Christmas, Mateo and Dominic packed carbon copies of stories in Chol from the first six books of the Bible. They carefully put Elaine's Christmas carols, neatly typed in Chol, in a folder on top of the Bible stories. John promised the Chol fellows that he would rejoin them in Amado Nervo soon after Christmas.

Four days before Christmas John drove Elaine to Mexico City. After the holiday John intended returning to Amado Nervo to supervise the building of the airstrip. "I can't let you go in over the trail again," he told Elaine. He also hoped to put a concrete floor in their house with cement flown in by M.A.F.

They spent Christmas Day with the Dennis Murphys, a young veterinarian and his wife. Elaine had sat beside Dennis' mother on the plane coming back from Norman the year before and upon arriving had been introduced to the couple. Dennis was working in the Hoof and Mouth Disease Program and was anxious to learn about Indian cultures.

Elaine and Joanne Murphy had one big interest in common. Both were expecting and they planned to make doctor's visits together. Elaine was exhilarated about her four-month checkup just after Christmas. The blood test showed no RH antibodies, although the doctor felt he should keep checking.

A day or two after Christmas, the Beekmans visited Wilbur and Evelyn Aulie who were recuperating from malaria. They talked about the Chols and translation. "I really feel deficient in the language," John confessed.

Wilbur limped across the room to help with a bottle for one of the twins. "That's two of us," he said.

John looked at the short blonde man who limped from a childhood attack of polio. He thought of the rugged Chiapas mountains and thought, "With my bad heart and Wilbur's bum leg, God will have to do it."

Wilbur, a native of Illinois and an ex-accountant, had graduated from Moody the year before John. He sat down and said, "I know you came down to do literacy work, John. But they've got to have something to read first."

John cupped his hands under his chin. "You're right. Well, I'm willing. If the director agrees, I suppose we can work on different books of the New Testament and review each other's work. But you and especially Evelyn will have to be patient with me. I've got a lot to learn."

Wilbur shrugged. "Haven't we all?"

On the last day of 1949, John and Dennis Murphy left for Chiapas. Dennis wanted to spend two weeks in Chol country while Elaine and Joanne watched over one another. Elaine laughed at the idea of being lonesome. Waving a notebook she said, "Between Joanne, typing word lists, and memorizing Chol words, I won't have time to be lonesome."

When John and Dennis reached Amado Nervo they found the Chols already working on the proposed airstrip. Men were piling dirt and rocks on stretchers made of crossed sticks lashed to two poles and in old gasoline cans.

John asked if there had been opposition to the work. "Yes," a church elder admitted. "Some say the airplane will carry away our women and children." Pointing to a crew of men hacking away at a hump of dirt, he added, "The witch doctor says that the ground belongs to the devil and that some of us will die for robbing him."

John looked at the man. "Do you believe that, Tomas?"

The old man grunted. "No. He's only a big wind bag."

About 30 men continued working from sunup to dusk. They refused pay. "Why should you give me money, Brother Kwan?" one said. "If you hadn't given me medicine when I was sick, I would be dead now." Another said, "You told me about the way of Jesus. That's enough pay."

On Sunday the church on the hill overflowed until the children had to be sent outside. John and Dennis estimated that at least 500 had come, many from distant villages. John launched into the story of Joseph in Chol but after 45 minutes his voice weakened. "I will finish the story next Sunday," he said.

The Chols remained seated on the rough backless benches. They pleaded for John to continue and he agreed. The service lasted six hours.

A few days after Dennis left with a guide to return to civilization, E. W. Hatcher arrived. Pointing to his mud-crusted pants and shoes, the new M.A.F. pilot declared, "Walking in to inspect a strip is the worst part of this job."

John smiled. "Now you know how landlubbers feel."

Hatch, who in future years was destined to become a living legend in Chiapas, had been assigned as the first permanent M.A.F. pilot to serve Wycliffe and Reformed Church personnel in the state. A veteran Army Air Force pilot from Oklahoma, Hatch had graduated from Wheaton College in 1948 where he had met his wife, Penny. They had attended evening services at Moody Memorial Church when John and Elaine were in school at the Bible Institute, but had not known the Beekmans.

Hatch sighted up and down the cleared land. "That hump will have to go," he said, "and that rock. Otherwise you might have a bird with clipped wings."

The blond pilot paced off the sloping strip. "Eight hundred feet," he announced when he reached the stone wall at the uphill end of the strip. Behind the wall was the village school.

"Is it long enough?" John asked eagerly.

"Well, it isn't LaGuardia Field," Hatch said, "but it'll have to do. Landing uphill and taking off downhill will compensate for a few feet." He eyed the steep forested slope just beyond the school. "Have to pull up fast if I decide not to land, or the squirrels will have translators for dinner."

Hatch left for the M.A.F. base at Ixtapa. The last dirt and rocks were removed. On February 8th about noon John heard a motor. He ran to the strip to chase the animals away. A moment later he saw the yellow single-engine Piper Clipper dropping through a mountain pass to cross the canyon below the strip.

Wilbur Aulie was in the plane with Hatch. "Tighten your cinch and hang on to your saddle horn," Hatch shouted to him. "We're coming in for the first time."

Hatch cut his speed and dropped lower. Suddenly he jerked back the throttle and said, "Can't make it this time."

To John and the crowd of Indians standing at the side of the strip it seemed as if the plane would hit the wall where a half dozen curious boys had perched. He whispered a desperate split-second prayer and braced himself expecting to hear the crash. When he looked around, the plane had cleared the wall by only a few feet and was banking against the side of the mountain just above the tree tops. The boys had jumped off the wall.

A few moments later the plane slipped over the canyon again; this time at lower altitude. The plane touched ground, bounced a couple of times, and finally stopped about 20 feet from the rock wall.

Hatch threw off his harness and stepped to the ground. "Pasadena can have its Rose Bowl," he said dryly while chewing gum. "We've got the 'Nerve Bowl' down here." Wilbur Aulie climbed shakily to the ground on the other side of the plane and came limping around the nose with the strain still showing on his face. "I was never so scared in my life," he admitted.

By this time the crowd of Chols had grown to about three hundred. They clustered around the plane looking at the pilot as if he were a being from another world. To John's delight, the women did not appear panicky. They had not even screamed when the plane landed, although none of them had ever seen a plane land before.

Hatch took off his cap and scratched his curly blond head. "Well, it might not pass standards back home," he drawled, "but in good dry weather I can make it. Coming in is tricky, though. Got to watch the air currents. I'll have to stay out of the canyon and still touch ground low enough to get her stopped."

The M.A.F. pilot stayed around long enough to take John's first air express order for ten bags of cement and a power plant for generating electricity. Then he turned the Piper around so that it was pointing downhill. "Don't worry if you lose sight of us shortly after takeoff. There's plenty of room in the canyon for us to get out safely."

A few moments later John and the Chols saw the yellow plane ascending over the tree tops of a distant hill.

"The big bird flies high," one of the Chols said.

John nodded. "You bet," he said as he thought that never again would Elaine have to come in over the tortuous trail.

8　The "Miracle Baby"

"HATCH" DELIVERED THE power plant and ten bags of cement. By the time John made the last connection and started the motor, darkness had fallen and a throng of sightseers had gathered. When a light bulb flashed on for the first time in Amado Nervo, he heard an Indian remark, "Let's go to the cornfields. The sun is high."

While the cement floor of the missionary house was drying, John lived in his chicken house. The Chol women kept him supplied with tortillas, beans, and eggs. At mid-day with light blocked off by the visitors at the door of the nine by ten pole hut, John could not see what he was eating. The chatter and laughter made him feel like a monkey in a cage.

He started March with a two-week tour of villages where Chol preachers had already broken ground. The second day out, his horse's belly strap snapped as it turned a curve in a fast trot. John picked himself up from the dirt and limped a half mile before he caught the horse.

Forty new believers greeted John in the village of Agua Azul. They spoke in the Tzeltal Bachajon dialect, interpreted to him by a Chol speaker named Martin. They had been won by the Chol preacher boys and were eager to know more about the Scriptures.

John's first thought was: *Marianna and Florence will be thrilled to hear about this.* Marianna Slocum, the fiancée of dead Bill Bentley, and Florence Gerdel, a Wycliffe nurse were then translating and doing medical work at Corralito, a Tzeltal village several days overland from Amado Nervo by trail. There had been several hundred conversions in the Corralito area, but so far as John knew those in Agua Azul were among the first on the border of Chol territory.

There will be more Tzeltals come to Christ, John thought as he stood among the new believers. *More, because Bill Bentley cared and Marianna and Florence came.*

Bill Bentley's heart had given out before he could return to Chiapas with Marianna as his bride. John's was still beating, although there were times on the rugged trail when he became so tired that he wondered how much longer his heart would hold up.

John looked at his interpreter. Martin's face glowed under the rim of coarse black hair that hung to his eyebrows. When Martin was a pagan his family had experienced a siege of sickness. He consulted a witch doctor who pointed to a hut on the hill and said, "They stole your spirit. You know what to do." Martin did the customary thing: he killed every member of the family on the hill and burned down their hut. Now he was one of the many ex-murderers who were believers and evangelists to the pagans.

After evening and morning services at Agua Azul, John rode on toward La Gloria. The first night out he camped beside a swollen river. The next day he crossed in a dug-out log canoe while the mule swam the river.

That afternoon he rode into the scraggle of huts called La Gloria. The Christians came running to greet him, babbling the latest news. The pagan idol had been destroyed. All but two families in the village had become believers. A new thatch meeting-house had been built.

John spoke that evening amidst flickering torch lights while hordes of insects hummed around his face. Afterward, he slept fitfully on a bark pallet in a believer's hut surrounded by the discordant noise of babies crying. By morning his body was tingling with the itch caused by night-riding bugs, always present in an Indian hut.

The men usually went to their cornfields at sunup, but this day was an exception. They wanted "Brother Kwan" to teach. At half hour intervals he suggested it might be time to quit. No, they begged, go on. And he did until noon.

At Carranza John met the multiple wife problem again. Several new converts had two or three wives. They gathered around him after services, asking for advice.

He took each man aside for private counsel. Generally, he advised: "Do as the Amado Nervo elders suggested. Don't turn any of your wives out. (He recalled that one believer had done this with the result that the excluded wife, desperate for food and shelter, slept in the cornfields offering her body for pittances of food.) Build another hut for your extra wives and children. Provide them with corn, beans and firewood. Live with only one wife in your present hut."

On the last lap of the two-week trip he arrived at a racing river less than one day's ride from Amado Nervo. Bleary-eyed from trying to sleep in huts with crying babies and blotched from bug and tick bites, his body ached for clean pajamas and the air mattress. But try as he would, he could not budge the stubborn mule. Finally he walked upstream and crossed on a bridge of vines strung between two trees.

John arrived as late afternoon shadows were creeping over the village. As if by magic the sick cases appeared at his door. He treated a snake bitten baby and then turned to grieving parents with a dead baby. The grave had been dug and would Brother Kwan give a prayer and some of God's Word.

While shadows lengthened, he followed the burial party to the hillside grave near the family's hut. Red-eyed and hoarse he read, "I am the resurrection and the life. He that believeth in me shall never die." After he prayed, the father tenderly placed the thin body wrapped in a white shroud in the recessed ledge cut alongside the bottom of the grave. Other men jabbed pointed sticks into the ground to seal off the niche from falling dirt and then the grave was filled.

Back at the hut more Chols were waiting. He treated the sick until midnight then fell across the air mattress in exhaustion.

He rose before six the next morning to eat breakfast. Shortly after sunrise Hatch landed to take him to Tuxtla, the first leg of the trip to Mexico City and reunion with Elaine.

As John left for the capital, Arabelle Whittaker and Iris Mills were travelling back to Chol country to the village of Allende where they planned to continue literacy work during John's absence. Wilbur and Evelyn Aulie were building a house near the Chol village of Esperanza and anticipating a stepped-up translation schedule. Plans were for John and Elaine to stay in the capital until after their baby was born, then return to join the other members of the team in an all-out effort to complete the Chol New Testament.

Elaine welcomed John into an apartment rented for their stay. There was simply not enough room in the overcrowded Kettle.

He conferred with Wycliffe's Mexico director, George Cowan,[1] about specific translation projects. "Wilbur and Evelyn plan to finish the Gospels and Acts," the dark haired native of Canada said. "Perhaps you should work on the Epistles."

"I'd like to do some more Old Testament stories between Joshua and Malachi first," John said. "The Chols need to hear about Daniel and Jonah and the Messianic prophecies. Then I could begin with James. The application of this book should help settle a lot of problems in the Chol church."

After Director Cowan agreed to this program, John radioed to Chiapas for young Mateo to come to the capital and help with translation of the additional Bible stories.

Meanwhile, he and Elaine were becoming more anxious about their expected baby. RH antibodies had shown up in her blood tests. However, the doctor assured them that birth of a second RH baby was unlikely, even with Elaine's RH negative blood and John's positive.

Mateo arrived and John tried to concentrate on the Bible stories while Elaine worked on two hymns, "I Must Tell Jesus" and "God Will Take Care of You."

On Thursday evening, May 11, the pains began. John immediately called her obstetrician, Dr. Ernesto Chavez, who said, "Come directly to the hospital."

About 9:30 they reached the British-American Hospital on Marino Escobedo Avenue near the famous Paseo de Reforma. The pains were coming faster as John rushed Elaine into an elevator.

John was hardly settled in the waiting room when Dr. Chavez rushed in. "You have a girl, six pounds and 13 ounces." Noticing John's worried face, he quickly assured, "Everything's fine."

But the next day's developments cast doubts about Judy Beth's health. The pediatrician, Dr. Julia Baker, reported her hemoglobin had dropped, apparently the result of negative antibodies destroying her positive blood. A Mexican donor was recruited for a transfusion. Then Judy was put in a small, heated bed.

The hemoglobin rose, but only temporarily. The same donor came again to share his blood. Finally, ten days after birth, Dr. Baker permitted the parents to take Judy home with the understanding they would bring her in for check-ups three times a week.

[1]George Cowan is now President of Wycliffe Translators and area director for Europe.

More transfusions into the veins of Judy's thin hands did not raise the hemoglobin count for more than a few days at a time. Dr. Baker ordered a bone marrow test, a blood culture, a blood chemistry test, and a series of kidney X-rays. But the tests furnished no solution to the deepening mystery.

Dr. Baker assigned another doctor to temporarily care for Judy while she flew to London for a scheduled medical conference on blood disorders. There she presented the results of the various tests done on Judy. Some of the world's greatest blood specialists conferred and decided that it was a rare RH negative incompatibility. They telegraphed their opinion to the Beekmans and requested a sample of Elaine's blood serum be sent to Boston for study. John personally took the sample to the airport. However, no worthwhile help came from this effort.

Meanwhile, another remedy was being proposed by the Beekmans' colleagues at the Kettle. "Do we believe God can make John and Elaine's baby live?" Harold Key asked a group of translators.

They felt God could do something.

"Okay," Harold said, "Let's go to their apartment and pray."

Ethel Wallis, who had first presented the need of the Chols to John and Elaine and who had been present at Sharon's funeral, went with the group to the apartment.

"When I first saw little blond Judy lying in her bassinet," Ethel recalls, "I thought, 'Why, she looks just like Sharon. If God doesn't do something, she'll go the same way.'"

Harold Key spoke to John and Elaine. "Before we pray, we would like assurance that you are willing to accept whatever God wills about Judy. We cannot command God. We can only ask him to help."

John looked at Elaine who nodded gravely. "We are willing," he replied in a whisper. "God knows best."

The group knelt around the bassinet and prayed earnestly for Judy's recovery within God's will.

"Our faith was exercised and we really prayed," Ethel Wallis says. "Soon after that a steady but slow improvement was noted in Judy's condition. The hemoglobin count stayed above the danger point. Judy became known among us as the 'miracle baby'."[2]

[2]RH disease is a condition in which antibodies in the blood of an Rh-negative woman destroy the blood cells of her unborn Rh-positive child. It can only

John and Mateo finished the remaining Old Testament stories for binding. He suggested to Elaine that she wait with Judy until January to come to Amado Nervo. He would return and "batch it" for three months while teaching the Chol preachers and working on translations.

The two men went by bus to Yajalon and waited for the weather to clear so Hatch could fly them in. The heavy rains had produced thigh-deep mud making it impossible to go by trail.

Finally on October 5 the rain clouds cleared away from the green mountains. Hatch picked them up at the Yajalon airstrip for the nine-minute flight. As they flew across the canyon John strained to see the people whom he expected to be running toward the strip.

"Keep your fingers crossed and pray," Hatch exclaimed jokingly as he eased the plane earthward. "You can never tell about this mud."

The wheels touched ground, bounced a few feet, then skidded forward to a stop. Hatch pumped the brakes as much as he dared, coming to a stop with plenty of ground to spare.

John leaped out to greet his old neighbors. To his surprise, only a few came rushing toward him and they were smiling through sunken cheeks and eyes.

One man cried, "Brother Kwan, why didn't you come sooner? My children are dead."

The terrible truth hit John. An epidemic of malaria had swept the village in his absence.

---

occur in pregnancies in which an Rh-negative woman is married to a man whose blood is Rh-positive. One out of eight couples are faced with the possibility of having a Rh-diseased baby.

When the father carries two genes for the positive blood factor, the baby inevitably inherits his Rh-positive blood type. Then during delivery of the firstborn, some of the baby's Rh-positive cells may enter the mother's body. When this happens, the mother's body responds by producing antibodies to destroy the foreign cells as if they were invading bacteria or viruses. In subsequent pregnancies such antibodies may travel from the mother into the baby where they attack and destroy its blood cells.

About the time of Judy Beekman's birth, doctors in other countries were beginning to save a percentage of Rh diseased babies by replacing with transfusions the entire blood supply. Recently, Science News (Nov. 25, 1967) reported a new vaccine will soon be available that will prevent Rh-negative women from ever producing antibodies to Rh-positive blood. If there are no antibodies, there will, of course, be no destruction of the unborn infant's blood —thus, no disease.

9. The Power of the Enemy

A CRIPPLED MAN clung to John's right arm. "Brother Kwan, come to my hut, please." Another man pulled at John's sleeve. "My children are coughing blood. Please help them, Brother Kwan."

Not knowing what to say, John looked at the small crowd of hollow-eyed men. Some he recognized as mere shadows of their former selves. Some could hardly speak for coughing.

"How many have died?" John asked.

A church elder counted on his fingers. "Over twice times ten graves we have dug. And many more are close to the grave." The old man then fell into a fit of coughing while John stood silently. "My wife," he gasped, "is one who is close to the grave. She lies now in the hut. Oh, Brother Kwan, we had no hope until you came."

Hatch had already started unloading supplies and medicine. John quickly put men to work carrying boxes to his house. When he began stacking boxes inside the house, a deadly snake ran from under a board and within inches of his hand. He smashed the snake's head with a board and finished the work.

Grabbing a jar of paludrine tablets and his medicine kit, he hurried outside. He noticed rain clouds closing in and quickly donned his black rain cape. Then he began making rounds.

The epidemic was as bad as he could imagine. Whole families lay on bark mats, rising only to cough and spit blood to the cockroaches that skittered across the bare earth floors. The huts reeked with the odor of death and disease.

Most pitiful were the children, many of whom had fallen into convulsions. One boy about eight had been in a coma for a full week. The constant spasms, the twitching face, the rolling eyes, and the jerking of the arms and legs tore at John's heart. He gave injec-

111

tions for malaria and liver extract shots to build up the boy's blood while the Christian parents sat by murmuring prayers.

Two premature babies arrived. One died a few hours after birth. The mother of the other, due to her illness, could not produce any milk. John prepared a formula which could be fed to the baby through an eye dropper but on the fourth day the baby died.

Heavy rains came every day turning the trails between the huts into rivers of mud. In three weeks John dispensed 4,000 paludrine tablets and gave over 100 injections. "Imagine your husband," he wrote to Elaine, "flitting around like a fairy or angel — whichever you prefer — draped in a rain cape, wading through ankle deep mud on the trails, or leaping from one rock to another in a hurry, sometimes both feet slipping together and his rear receiving the hard end of a rock. Some days he does not get back to our house till the sun is setting, after eating what is offered in the homes of the sick. Upon reaching home, he finds the porch filled with women and men wanting medicine or a visit from the man with the needle, and inside the downstairs floor criss-crossed with sleeping Chols who have walked through the mud for help. What a heart-ripping sight it all is. But I'm glad to be here."

Hardest for John were those who stubbornly clung to witchcraft. Some of the unbelievers who could stand stared sullenly at John while he ministered to their Christian neighbors. Inside the unbelievers' huts children moaned and convulsed while parents applied weird concoctions. Sometimes when the witch doctor's remedies had been exhausted and the plight of the patient especially desperate, the parents called John as a last resort.

For one case the witch doctor cooked up a batch of onion juice and blew it on a boy's body. Then he killed a chicken and painted the boy with blood while chanting. When the boy continued having convulsions, the witch doctor next prescribed turkey blood, then pig blood. When the boy worsened, the parents called John who sloshed up the hill with medicine kit in hand.

The boy painted with onion juice and chicken, turkey, and pig's blood looked a weird sight. He lay squirming, screaming, clenching his fists, and crunching his teeth while the family, fearful of punishment by evil spirits, looked on. John injected penicillin and gave paludrine tablets. "It was a sight I'll never forget," he wrote Elaine, "an excellent opportunity to tell of the power of the blood of Christ."

Not for six weeks did Amado Nervo return to normal. Thirty-seven deaths occurred in families that trusted in witchcraft, but not one of John's patients died.

Despite the epidemic, the church building stayed packed on Sunday with Chols attending from eight different villages. Many came on Saturday afternoon to be ready for the Sunday services which started at eight a.m. and lasted into the afternoon.

One Sunday John talked for an hour, followed by some spontaneous hymns and prayers. An elder then stood and said hopefully, "Maybe Brother Kwan can give us another short message."

John continued teaching literacy and doctrine classes. He finished the Epistle of James and checked it with four Chol language helpers for sense. When they failed to understand some difficult verses, he decided to check with others.

An unsought opportunity came one morning when six Sanchez brothers, all professed believers, came to the house. "We've been feuding over land," the eldest explained, "and have even shot and thrown rocks at one another. The church elders asked us to come to you for help before some of us are killed."

"Will you listen to God's writings?" John asked as he took the fresh manuscript in hand. They nodded and meekly sat down.

John read the epistle through without comment, then he began a second reading with applications. One by one, the brothers broke down and began to confess in prayer their sin, and to ask the forgiveness of one another.

A few days later the brothers invited John to a love feast. The date was November 23, by chance the American Thanksgiving Day. He wrote home gleefully, "I had my turkey after all."

John went back to Mexico City in December. He and Elaine packed baby food, play pen, crib, high chair, food and bedding — 36 boxes in all — and took them to the bus station. Through all the packing Judy, face glowing with health, fanned the air with her hands, breaking out with coos and gurgles that Elaine interpreted as, "Who's this strange man in our house?"

They arrived in Tuxtla ahead of their belongings, just before New Year's, 1951. John and Mabel Kempers were already packing to leave for vacation in Guatemala and graciously invited the travelers to live in their home while waiting the freight.

On Monday, January 8, Hatch flew them into Amado Nervo. Elaine walked on the new concrete floor and inspected a new screen door, a cabinet for pots and pans, and the wooden bed John had built to replace the sagging springs. "It isn't the Taj Mahal," John cracked, "but it's the best I could do for my queen."

The women flocked to see Elaine and stood wide-eyed while Elaine explained the purpose of each baby thing. They had never seen a baby rattle or a pacifier before.

After tending to the medical cases that had piled up, John did more modernizing. He adapted the old Army surplus canvas bag to supply running water to an inside sink that sported a drain. A small refrigerator flown in by M.A.F. completed the most modern kitchen Amado Nervo had ever seen.

But the most appreciated comfort was X10PPA, a short wave receiver and transmitter licensed by the Mexican government and installed by Red Brown, M.A.F.'s newly arrived radio technician for Chiapas. This provided communication with the M.A.F. base at Ixtapa, the newly established Wycliffe Jungle Survival Training Camp near the Guatemalan border, and Wycliffe's Mexico City headquarters. Emergency messages could be sent and received and Hatch could be spared unnecessary trips by being notified when Amado Nervo was socked in by bad weather.

The one big disappointment was that thieves had broken into the hut while John and Elaine had been away. According to village gossip, the thieves were professing Christians.

The next Sunday John talked to the Amado Nervo church about restitution and confession. Everyone knew who had stolen from the hut, even John, himself. After the service he waited for the culprits to come.

Not until after dark did the thieves come down the trail loaded with jars, saws, cannisters, rat traps, and other booty. One carried money to pay for some sugar he had stolen.

"I have already forgiven you," John said. "But you must tell God what you have done."

Tears flowed freely as the men prayed for divine forgiveness. They also promised to make public confession before the church.

But the following Sunday only two rose to tell what they had stolen, what they had returned, and how they had asked both John's forgiveness and God's. The third fellow sat tight on his bench.

That night he slipped to John's hut. "I couldn't confess before the church today," he blurted. When John asked why, he said, "Because I remembered taking a mousetrap which I didn't tell you about. I broke it and threw it away. But I will pay you for it and confess Wednesday." He kept the promise.

John put James aside and worked on First, Second, and Third John between interruptions. Twice each week he held morning classes for about 50 teenage preacher boys who evangelized outlying villages on the weekends.[1] On a typical Tuesday morning, John arose to see the boys already waiting beside a fire near the front porch with water for coffee simmering on the fire.

Class got under way as soon as John could dress. He climbed down the ladder and greeted them cheerily, leaving Elaine and Judy still in bed upstairs. Then after coffee with the boys outside he said, "The sun isn't going to wait any longer on us. You will soon have to go to your cornfields." About half of the boys moved inside the Beekman living room. The rest sat on the porch. Only those who felt they could hold their spit could come inside. John had a practical reason for this: Many of the boys were mild tubercular cases.

"Brothers, choose your message for next Sunday," John said.

By consensus the boys settled upon a paragraph of Scripture. After one stood and read it aloud, John asked each fellow to tell what he thought it meant. Not until all had finished did he begin asking leading questions.

After the boys settled on a reasonable interpretation, John asked them to think of illustrations from tribal life. A favorite showed the distinction between true and false believers: "The outside of the corn looks perfect. But when we pull back the husks, we find crooked rows of little kernels. In other ears we find that rain or worms have gotten inside the husk and the kernels have rotted. We open other ears of corn and find even rows of large kernels. It is what's inside that counts."

The preacher boys had trouble understanding many Biblical

[1] At first the absence of older believing men among the volunteer lay preachers puzzled John. Only one older man came to the classes and went on weekend trips. Later he came to connect this practice with a Spanish imposed cultural practice. The Spanish colonizers in Chiapas required the Indian men to donate a few days *servicio* — donated labor — to the village each year. Only the old men were exempt. The Chol believers borrowed the word *servicio*, with its primary meaning to them of donated labor to work in the congregation. It came to mean both attendance at the church building and witnessing or evangelizing outside the church. One of the preacher boys made this parallel to John: "We do *servicio* in the village because we are compelled by threatening words. We do *servicio* for Christ because the Holy Spirit compels us by filling our hearts with love." John now feels that the older men, being exempt from town service, may also feel exempt from the more active parts of church work.

symbols. Sheep, goats, and even plowing were unknown to the Chols who planted their cornfields with the primitive dibble stick. Yoke was a difficult word to translate. One explained John's first rendition as meaning "the necktie that the Mexicans wear which we don't." John then proposed "bark" which was immediately understood. "Take my yoke upon you" (Matthew 11:29) became: "Hang my bark upon your forehead." The Chols were accustomed to supporting and balancing heavy back loads with a cloth or bark band secured around the forehead. Frequently the load was switched to another back, using the same bark bond.

When John felt the fellows had mastered the content of the Scripture passage and had two or three good illustrations from Chol culture, he asked for a volunteer to give a talk on the material.

When he finished, John asked, "Brothers, how can he improve?"

"He should look straight at the people," one replied. "Even when he reads the Scripture he can look up some."

Another added, "He should speak so people on the back row can hear."

And another said, "He should not scratch his ear while talking. People will think he has a bug there."

The preacher quietly received the criticism. Then at John's request, he gave a short re-run, keeping in mind the suggestions made.

By the end of the Friday class the boys had their messages and illustrations prepared and were ready to work out their itineraries.

John did not say, "Francisco and Jose, you go to this village." Instead, he asked each to "name the village where you think God's Spirit is leading you." When more than two mentioned the same village, he said, "Brothers, Jesus' disciples went two by two. Perhaps one of you would want to go with Jose to La Gloria." Then, the circuits agreed upon, John equipped the young evangels with precious copies of Bible stories in Chol, phonographs and records, medicine kits, including a medical handbook prepared by Elaine, and literacy charts to place in each village.

The following Tuesday they gave reports of their troubles and successes. Always, some told of death threats from fanatical opponents of the Gospel. More than one bore the marks of beatings and machete cuts when he stood to report. After hearing their reports, John declared to Elaine, "It's the Book of Acts all over again."

One Friday, 20-year-old Francisco, a thin, wiry youth with a shock of thick black hair to match his black eyes, volunteered for San Pedro.[2] Domingo, two years younger, volunteered to be his partner.

"Brothers, bitter enemies of the Gospel are there," John warned.

The boys refused to be turned. "We will tell them about Jesus," Francisco said, his eyes flashing. "If we die, we go to be with Jesus that much sooner."

Friday the boys left with phonograph machine and Gospel records both in Chol and Spanish. Saturday noon they arrived by foot in San Pedro.

Soon a large crowd of Indians gathered to hear the "talking tortillas." A Mexican rancher arrived to survey the situation. "Let's get them," he snarled to a friend. "They'll cause these Indians to follow the foreign devils and quit buying liquor from us."

Gun in hand, the rancher slipped through some undergrowth behind the boys and sprang at them. "Tie them up," he ordered two of his employees.

The Mexicans tied Francisco and Domingo and dragged them away to the home of the rancher. Like Paul and Silas in the Philippian jail, they kept courage through the night by singing and praying.

The next morning was Sunday. The rancher took the fellows in a canoe downriver to the Mexican village of Salto. He marched them to the village plaza where he handed a written accusation to the municipal president. The accusation charged them with attempting to burn a sacred Indian idol in San Pedro and disturbing the peace.

A large crowd quickly gathered around. "Did you try to destroy the idol?" the president asked.

"No," Francisco said. "We came to tell our poor Chol brothers in San Pedro about the true and living God. I used to dress in rags," the thin boy continued. "I didn't know how to read or write. What money I had was wasted on drink. That's how the Chols of San Pedro still live. I want to give them that which helped me. Now I have a good home and clothes. I can read and write. The Word of God has made me different. My friend and I came here not to burn

2The explorer, John Stevens, visited San Pedro in 1841 and wrote: "If a bad name could kill a place, San Pedro was damned. Everyone we met on the trail cautioned us against the Indians there. Fortunately, however, when we went through, most of the men were away for a fiesta in Tumbala. A few Indians were lying about in a state of utter nudity and, when we looked into the huts, the women ran away, probably alarmed at seeing men with pantaloons."

the idol, but to tell our brothers the Gospel which can change them, too. If you want to hear the message we are spreading, let us play the phonograph machine for you."

The official nodded, ignoring the rancher's scowl. The boys played several Gospel messages in Spanish.

"Let's see your books," the mayor asked.

Domingo handed them over, but asked permission to read from one. The official agreed and he read the Ten Commandments in Chol.

The official looked hard at the shifty-eyed rancher. "These fellows have broken no law." He ripped the accusation in two and said to the boys, "Take your machine and books and go."

The boys left the plaza in triumph and visited the town jail where they played the records and preached for the prisoners, guards, and prostitutes who hung around the jail waiting for new prisoners with money.

Tuesday they arrived back in Amado Nervo, singing as they came up the trail to the Beekmans' house. After they told him of their deliverance, John said to Elaine, "The Gospel is touching the ranchers where it hurts most — in their pocket books. They don't want to let the Indians out from under their thumbs."

John fell into silent contemplation. He thought that the Chols and their Mayan kinsmen from other tribes in Chiapas were not unlike the Israelites enslaved in Egypt. The Indians, like the descendants of Abraham, had been under the control of foreigners for about 400 years. But unlike the Israelites, the Chiapas Indians were not slaves in a foreign land; but serfs on land that had been taken from their ancestors by the Spanish colonists.

He and Elaine had found the great majority of Chols pitifully poor, illiterate, and shackled to the economy dominated by the coffee ranchers. Federal law prohibited one person from owning more than 250 acres of land, but a clever man could increase his holdings by spreading titles among members of his family.

Thousands of acres were classified as government lands (seized from big land owners after the Revolution) and supposed to be available to the Indians in 25 acre plots upon application. But because the Indians were illiterate and afraid of the ranchers, the best land remained untaken and the Indians planted corn only on land the ranchers did not want. The ranchers also kept the rumor mills busy with stories to discourage the Indians from applying for land. One story described the land offer as a federal trick to conscript Indians for military services.

A typical rancher was called "master" by his Indian serfs. He permitted them to farm a small plot of his land to produce food for their families. For this "privilege" they were obliged to work in the rancher's coffee fields whenever he requested it. Sickness was never an excuse. The "master" paid wages in tokens, worth less than 50¢ for a day's work, and redeemable only for high priced merchandise in his commissary.

Many Indians stayed in perpetual debt because they sought to drown their miseries in drink purchased from the ranch store. After a spree an Indian who owed 100 pesos might discover his bill to be 700 pesos, with the explanation that he had ordered drinks for others.

An Indian father might not even call his children his own. In payment for debt, a rancher could demand a child to be his life-time servant or concubine.

A minority of ranchers treated the Indians more kindly, but even they did not try to overturn the system that kept the Indians in submission. They boasted of "taking care of our poor Indians," by doling out emergency food and medicine in a patronizing attitude that seemed to John a parallel to the attitude which some U.S. pre-Civil War slave owners had taken toward Negroes.[3]

"The believers are going to do something about this land business," John told Elaine. "They've been talking to me about it."

Elaine looked at John, fear written in her eyes. "The ranchers

[3] An in-depth study of ethnic relations between the Indians and Spanish speakers (which also includes a minority of Indians) has been done by Professors Benjamin N. Colby and Pierre L. van der Berghe of Harvard University. Using the term "ladino" (meaning "cunning" or "crafty" person) in reference to persons of Spanish language and culture, they documented numerous distinctions between the ruling and subject classes. Indians do manual, agricultural, and servile work. Indians get the less desirable locations in the market place. Indians must buy all their durable and manufactured products from *ladino* merchants. *Ladino* merchants often put aside diseased and spoiled meat for Indians. A check of male prisoners in the market town showed 49 of 53 inmates were Indians. Until recently, Indians were not allowed to ride horseback in one area. They were expected to fold their arms and bow submissively when speaking to a *ladino*, whom they must address as "Don," "Senor," or "Patron."

Ladinos treat Indians condescendingly, but often with a touch of affection. They think of them as primitive, uncultured, ignorant, irresponsible, unreliable, and childish. *Ladinos* call Indians "children" regardless of age. When an Indian wants a hair cut, he must sit on a chair instead of the regular chair reserved for *ladino* customers. He is given a rough five-minute haircut for which he pays about one-third the price charged a *ladino*. Always, Indians are expected to act the role of subordinates and in many cases avoid close associations and familiarities, except that the Indian is welcome to perform domestic duties in the *ladino's* home.

might organize and who knows what might happen, then. They've got political friends in the Mexican towns."

"Sure, but we know that the federal government wants the land distributed and the Indians lifted out of poverty. If enough Indians applied and the ranchers knew we were sympathetic, they might back off. There's good land available now. If the Indians had it, they could grow their own coffee and sell it. They could band together in cooperatives and break the backs of the exploiters."

"John, you're really dreaming," Elaine said.

"Maybe not. Look what God has done in Amado Nervo since we came. The first man to own a mule was a believer. The first family to wear shoes was a Christian family. Look how they hold their heads up. They're becoming proud of their ancestry and their language. That's how it should be. And life will be better when they get back their lands and become their own bosses."

John stood up and paced the concrete floor. "Elaine, Christ drives out fear. I'm going to encourage and stand behind those Christians who want land. Let them lead the way. When they get land, others will want some, too. By the power of the Gospel, Chol country will one day be transformed."

Elaine looked at Judy playing in the doorway with a Chol boy. "John, we're all alone out here," she said with anxiety edging her voice. "If the Indians start getting land, the ranchers will believe we put them up to it. They might hire people to kill us. Remember that Mexican who almost got to our hut. It's not that I'm worried about you or me, but Judy. They might try to do something to her."

John stopped abruptly at the mention of Judy's name. "If they did . . . ." He stamped his foot. "No. God will take care of us. We'll continue to serve and let the Holy Spirit do His work. We've seen more than once that God is more powerful than the devil."

10. *The Arm of the Lord*

WITH THE RADIO installed and working off the power plant, John felt free to leave Elaine and Judy for a three-week circuit through other villages. The converts of the preacher boys needed encouragement and more teaching. He felt more at home in the language and wanted to do some preaching himself. And he wanted to visit La Gloria where Arabelle Whittaker and Viola Warkentin, a new literacy missionary, were working.

The May heat sapped his strength on the first day out. Food seemed scarce in every village. One day for breakfast he had a banana with coffee; for lunch, two hard boiled eggs and chili; for supper, two thin tortillas and another banana. His hosts ate less.

He reached La Gloria early in the second week and found the two literacy girls teaching almost the entire village. He asked the believers about a village of escaped murderers which he had heard existed several miles up the river. "Brother Kwan," an old man said, "there is such a village called La Lucha. But they might kill you if you go."

John ignored the warning and hired a canoe. Several miles up the jungle river he left the canoe and continued by trail. He recognized that there was no food shortage here. Tropical fruits of all descriptions lay in his path.

He entered the village and stopped at a hut. Suddenly a man leaped out and ran into the jungle. He learned later the man was the witch doctor.

As news of his arrival spread, men stood in doorways with machetes in hand — a silent warning that a visit could mean trouble. Nevertheless, John stopped at each hut and explained the way of salvation in Chol.

121

However, one sullen man began scraping his face with the blade when John addressed him. This, John knew, meant, "Go or else." Yet he stood his ground and continued talking about Christ. The man scraped his face until the blood came but he never swung at John.

In another village John saw fear on the faces of the believers. Inquiry produced the reason. The rancher for whom they worked had spread a story that the foreigner — John — was gathering people to send off to a foreign war. "It's true that Someone is coming to take you away," John told the restless crowd. "That Someone is Jesus. He is coming back to take all believers to Heaven."

The circuit confirmed John's feeling that an ingathering was taking place among the Chols. He estimated the Chol church had swollen to over 3,000 with 1,500 new converts coming during the past three years. Not one of more than 20 churches had a foreigner or a Mexican national pastor. All were being served by the trail hiking preacher boys.

"God is doing a great work among the Chols," he announced triumphantly to Elaine. "How I'd love to spend more time in village work. But I've got to get on with my share of translation."

That night after Judy was asleep, John and Elaine looked from their second floor window across the natural bowl around which the huts of Amado Nervo were clustered. Darkness had fallen and the first stars were glowing in the clear sky. A fragrant symphony of sound wafted through the trees. The believers were enjoying their nightly custom of family hymn singing just before retiring. Some of the hymns Elaine had translated. Words went unspoken as they listened to the vibrant voices singing of new-found peace and happiness. Both were remembering the trials and struggles of past days. At last Elaine said, "I mourn the day I ever said my musical training wouldn't count in tribal work. It's worth it all just to hear them sing. This must be the sweetest music this side of Heaven."

Amado Nervo rose with the first rays of dawn. John usually rose first even on days when he did not hold class for the preacher boys. Often he found guests that had arrived during the night sleeping on the porch. By the time he had tended to their needs — usually medical — Elaine was up and starting breakfast with blonde Judy tugging at her skirts.

Judy was their constant delight. Now almost two, she was speaking a polyglot mixture of Chol and English. Elaine had to keep her quarantined in the kitchen while she gave shots and handed

out medicine. Judy amused herself by giving injections to her doll
with a pencil. Then after the sick were cared for and breakfast
done, Judy could go outside and play with neighbor children on a
swing John had hung from a tree limb. At any reasonable distance
away she was easy to spot, her blond head bobbing among the dark-
skinned Chol children like an isolated spring dandelion on a hillside.

As he saw them leaving Friday and Saturday, John envied the
preacher boys to the extent that he wanted to do their work. The
temptation to major on direct witnessing was great and while dreading
the absence from Elaine and Judy, he looked forward to the periodic
trips. Although he had not studied extensively in the history of missions, he knew instinctively that the Chol church must attend to its
own propagation, support, and government. Unlike God's power, they
must lead the way in escaping from oppression.

One evening after a long session at the translation table with
young Mateo, John slumped in a chair while Elaine finished dinner.
"I don't like to sit so long in one place," he yawned. "But it's necessary. A verse, a chapter, a book at a time will get the job done.
The Word in Chol, preached and applied by Chols will bring salvation to people in these mountains. The by-products will be education, health, land, and good crops."

Elaine turned from stirring a pot of beans. "How much progress
did you make today?"

John grinned. "Finished Second John. It was easier than James.
All I lack is Third John to be ready for Gene Nida in Tuxtla."

The oppressive heat lay heavy in Amado Nervo when John finished this small epistle. With the temperature in the 90's, he began
shaking with chills. He could not hold a cup of water without
spilling it. His hands and feet shriveled and he felt numb and frozen.

After a few hours the chills switched to fever. He joked to Elaine,
"I think I'm in the furnace room of a steel mill."

Paludrine tablets did not halt the cycle of chills and fever. Right
on schedule the M.A.F. plane landed to fly John into Tuxtla for
checking James and First, Second, and Third John with Dr. Eugene
Nida of the American Bible Society. With Dr. Nida's okay, the
Society would print a quantity in pamphlet form for distribution to
the Chol congregations.

"I'm going," John said stubbornly, and clutching the precious
manuscripts he climbed into the plane.

Nida scolded him for coming with a fever and insisted he go to bed. Wilbur and Evelyn Aulie were already in the hotel with some manuscripts of other New Testament portions. For the conference, the whole party moved into the room where John was in bed.

John and the Aulies explained to Nida that they had been exchanging manuscripts through the courtesy of M.A.F.'s plane service. "We don't always communicate well with one another," John noted, "but we try to understand one another's opinions."

The Aulies, who by this time had four children, hoped with John that the entire New Testament might be ready for checking by the end of the year.

The ideal, all agreed, would be for the translators to work outside the tribe with language helpers, uninterrupted by medical work and other necessary ministries when living in a village. John laughed from his bed and said, "That's dreaming."

The conference ended and Grady Parrott,[1] another M.A.F. pilot, flew the translators back into their villages. John felt better and told Elaine, "The tonic I needed was Nida's okay and promise that the Society will publish the epistles."

John leaped into Romans and worked persistently between interruptions for treating snake bites, malaria, ulcers, machete cuts, and pulling teeth. Written instructions from Elaine's dentist uncle, Dr. Harold Keeney, was his guide for the latter. Through trial and error, he learned to put novocaine in the right nerve.

One dental patient came from La Lucha, the village of escaped murderers, which John had visited on his last circuit. The man reported 20 believers standing firm in the faith but enduring much persecution and ridicule.

When a literal translation made little sense, John turned to the tricks of the translator's trade. He adjusted figures of speech, rearranged sentences, and used phrases or clauses to approximate complex words not in the Chol vocabulary. For example, Romans 6:2 translated literally meant, "We who have fully surrendered ourselves to sin, how can we become more active in sin?" He changed this to: "We who are like dead people, how can we respond to sin."

Some of the believers did turn back to the old ways. The most frequent cause was drink. On one occasion John found all the men in one village drunk. Those who had once professed to follow Christ greeted him with slobbering hugs, mumbling, "Read to us from the Holy Father's Book, Brother Kwan."

[1]Mr. Parrott is now president of M.A.F.

Usually persecution became the seed of stronger faith and more believers. When he read Romans 8 to the preacher boys, ending with, "nothing shall stop God's love for us through Christ Jesus, our Lord," the fellows grinned with confidence as if to say, "We knew it all along."

Reports kept pouring in of new victories throughout Chol country. A new believer in the village of Kahkwalatal invited the preacher boys to witness in his village. Four fellows went and began hut to hut visitation. Suddenly a shotgun boomed and pellets splashed around them. From around a boulder came several men waving weapons and shouting, "Liars! Thieves! Leave or we will kill you." The young evangelists ran into the jungle with the guns booming behind them.

To add insult to the incident, the attackers went to the nearest Mexican town and made charges against the believer who had invited the preacher boys to the village. The magistrate called him into court and fined him 50 pesos. His neighbors drove him and his family from their home and stole his corn. After believers in another village gave him food and a place to live, he said, "God is taking care of me."

Unbelievers in still another village cut down trees so that they fell across the path leading to the nearest church. The next Sunday they followed the families of believers to the part of the trail which had been blocked. Here they began shooting into the air. The families scrambled over the logs and through the brush with the wailing children. They arrived at the church scratched and cut from briars. Instead of complaining, they asked for prayer that they might remain faithful.

Personal tragedy frequently struck within the families of believers. There was hardly a family in Amado Nervo that had not lost at least one child. Many had buried two, three and even four from tetanus infections, intestinal diseases, and other tropical maladies.

Nicholas Vasques lost a child on the first Good Friday John and Elaine were in Amado Nervo. Three years later his five-year-old daughter, born with six fingers on one hand and six toes on one foot, became critically ill. Elaine gave both malaria and penicillin shots in a desperate effort to halt the fever and infection that raged in the child's body. But on Good Friday morning Nicholas came bearing sad news.

That afternoon John, Elaine, and a line of believers climbed a hill to the freshly dug grave. They sang hymns and prayed, then watched Nicholas place the child in the grave. As the mourners turned to leave, Nicholas said to John, "It is strange that my children died on the day the Lord died, but I know that just as He rose from the grave, they, too, will rise."

The believers at Amado Nervo killed a bull and celebrated Easter, 1952, with a fiesta that began Saturday morning and did not end until Sunday evening. The Chols had celebrated fiestas for centuries and John saw no reason to discourage the practice, only to refine it. He felt strongly that the Chol church should develop in its own culture without impositions from foreigners. Indeed the praying, testifying, talking, feasting, and mild horse play was a witness by contrast to the wild pagan fiestas.

The traditional Chol fiesta had developed from an ancient feast held at corn planting time. The first Spanish priests had tried to modify the pagan rituals to include the resurrection. The result was a strange syncretism of pagan and Christian practices.

On Monday of "Holy Week," the pagans draped a black cloth over a man-sized wooden image. They removed the cloth on Easter, but not to symbolize the resurrection.

John learned that the entire ritual was almost completely pagan. They covered the "god" (crucifix) so he would think it dark and cloudy and remember to send sunshine to dry out the recently felled trees and underbrush for burning. They removed the cloth to show the "god" the blazing sun, so he would remember to send rain on the newly planted corn in the burned-over fields. They made animal sacrifices in the corners of the fields to beg good will from the devil who owned the earth.

Liquor was always preferred over food during "Holy Week" and other festival days. As the week progressed, the adults became more and more inebriated until by Sunday almost the entire adult population lay in a drunken stupor. It was a pitiful sight to see little children climbing over the drunken forms of their parents and crying for food. At the same time the clear-headed believers in the church on the hill were praising God for deliverance from darkness.

At first the believers included prayers for their crops during the festival. A Mexican pastor who made annual preaching visits among the Chols had tried unsuccessfully to get the evangelical congregations to abolish the fiestas. John encouraged them to continue and center the celebrations around Christ's sacrificial death and resurrection.

Christmas and Easter became the major feasts of the Chol church, but two others of importance were the harvest and the "consolation" fiestas.

The harvest fiesta included the tithing of the corn harvest to a central storehouse maintained by the congregation. This offering was utilized for three purposes: Food for widows and families unable to work their fields because of illness; a reserve for distribution or sale in years of poor crops; and a source of financial revenue for the church treasury.

A "consolation" fiesta was given for a family that had recently lost a member through death. Believers brought gifts of food and money to the church for the elders to present to the bereaved Christians.

As John told Kemp, when the Kempers family arrived for a series of summer Bible schools among the Chols, "I see no reason to destroy those elements of Indian culture that can be brought into the life of the congregation."

Dr. and Mrs. Kempers came in June, bringing their daughter Margie and a seminary student and his wife. Margie and little Judy became instant playmates.

The first week's Bible study was held at Tumbala, the second week in Amado Nervo where about 400 attended daily. "I'm heartened by the enthusiasm and interest of the Chols," Kemp declared. "John, the Lord has used you in a remarkable way. Frankly, when you arrived I had become quite discouraged with the Chol field."

John smiled at the older man, recognized as one of the evangelical leaders of southern Mexico. Kemp, a graduate of Princeton Seminary, had helped develop many Spanish speaking congregations throughout Chiapas.[2]

"I'm willing that the Chol congregations be related to Spanish-speaking churches," John said, "but I think it's good to keep in mind

[2]John Kempers and other Reformed Church of America missionaries in Chiapas work within the structure of the National Presbyterian Church of Mexico. Chiapas was alloted to the Presbyterians in the so-called "Cincinnati comity plan" of 1917. This ecumenical agreement has been blamed by many leaders for thwarting evangelical growth in proceeding under the assumption that one mission board would do all that could possibly be done in a heavily populated state. Non-cooperating missions have freely ignored the plan. The Assemblies of God and Seventh Day Adventists were not a party of the "Cincinnati Plan." They both have strong communities in Chiapas.

Donald McGavran in his analysis, *Church Growth in Mexico* (Eerdmans, 1963, p. 45), notes that had comity been strictly observed in Mexico, the Congregational Church, with only about 300 members in nine small, static churches, would today be the only Protestant force in 800-mile long Sinaloa state.

the differences between the Chol and Spanish cultures."

"Yes, there are differences," Kemp noted. "Language is the most important one. I've really come to appreciate the work you Wycliffe people do in putting the Scriptures into the native dialect."

"We only consider ourselves servants of the whole Church," John said. "Wycliffe, as you know, is not an ecclesiastical body. We are officially in Mexico as 'scientific investigators.' This enables us to have the support of the ministry of education and government leaders in other agencies. But each of us as individual translators are committed to indigenous church principles and the translation of the Word."

The congregation had already gathered for the morning session and Nicholas Arcos was leading a hymn. "Before we go in," Kemp said, "there's something I've been thinking about along the lines of our discussion. How would it be if our Mexican church in Chiapas recognized you and Elaine as 'cooperating missionaries'?"

John smiled broadly. "I think we'd like that very much. Of course, we'd continue as we are within the Wycliffe organization."

"Naturally," Kemp said. "Maybe we had better go inside now. We'll have time to talk more later on about how to maintain the ties and good fellowship between Chols and Mexican believers."

The week of Bible Study at Amado Nervo climaxed with a giant Saturday cookout in honor of the preacher boys. At three a.m. men lit the morning fires and began butchering two bulls purchased from a rancher for the event. Women came bringing firewood and clay pots.

Later in the morning the missionaries introduced dodge ball and the potato race to the Indians. They caught on quickly and could not find enough time to play all they wanted.

After the games, the preacher boys stood before the congregation and answered doctrinal questions. Then John rose and charged them to be faithful and loyal servants of Christ. Later he told Kemp his feelings: "Chills rolled up and down my back to think that just a few years ago these young fellows could neither read nor write. Here they were being recognized as the teachers and leaders of more than 3,000 Chol believers."

Top left: Man clears cornfield for spring planting. Chols follow slash-and-burn agriculture. *Lower left:* Boy slashes trail through thick jungle. *Top right:* Balsa logs are used for church buildings. *Center right:* Poles, vines, and grass are all the materials Chol carpenters need. *Lower right:* No house is complete without a steam bath. Water is poured on red hot stones to provide the steam.

"Maize" (corn), says a Mexican economist, "is the most important single item in Mexico's diet, cuisine, mythology, and politics."
The Mayan ancestors of the Chols noted that the sun, wind,
rain, and fire all played a part in growing corn, so these elements
became personified as gods to be appeased and obeyed. Many
Chols still worship the ancestral gods.

Shown above are three stages in preparing corn for food: *upper
left,* children shelling corn; *center left,* woman preparing to wash
corn at drying-up waterhole; *upper right,* girl grinding cooked
corn into paste for balls which men use for food on long trips.
Lower right is a crude sugar cane grinder.

Upper left: Children came to the Beekmans' house every day
— asking questions, bringing a gift of tortillas or an egg, wanting
ice from the refrigerator. *Lower left:* Judy Beekman plays on
swing with neighbor girl. Amado Nervo evangelical church is
in background. *Upper right:* Girl catching snails. *Lower right:*
Boy returning with machete and jungle bird for supper.

Upper left: The missionary house after the roof was raised to provide space for working and sleeping. The first floor was reserved for cooking, eating, and receiving visitors. *Center left:* The missionary translator is dentist, doctor, and pharmacist in his village. *Lower left:* A neighbor they could not heal. *Upper right:* John assures the little girl that the pills are good medicine. *Lower right:* This woman, a believer, displays proof that her baby has recovered.

Upper left: The Beekmans and their colleagues rode horseback and walked in country like this before Missionary Aviation Fellowship came to the rescue (see next page). *Upper right:* Iris Mills, now Mrs. Alen Wares, helped in literacy programs among the Chols. She, Elaine, and other women missionaries were carried like this around the edge of dizzy precipices. *Lower left:* John sometimes rode through mud up to the horse's stomach and swam rivers too deep to wade. *Lower right:* Judy Beekman had piggy-back rides that lasted a whole day.

The opposition of the witch doctor didn't keep Chol men from clearing an airstrip. *Upper left:* They load dirt .and rock onto a stretcher made of cross sticks lashed with vines to two poles. *Center left:* M.A.F. plane takes off. *Lower left:* Chol boys built wooden model planes after seeing their first airplane on ground. *Upper right:* John and E. W. "Hatch" Hatcher, M.A.F. pilot, study map of rugged Chol country. *Lower right:* John cranks power supply while Elaine radios news to M.A.F. base in Ixtapa.

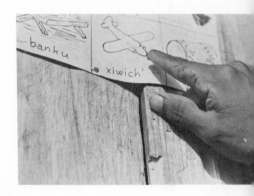

John trained over 100 Chol lay preachers who gave weekends to village evangelism. This was a major reason for the rapid growth of the Chol church. *Upper left:* A class at Tumbala. *Center left:* A young preacher, about 16, ready to hit the trail. He carries food supply and phonograph on his back, *Lower left:* Three preacher boys stop at water hole to eat corn balls. *Upper right:* Family listens to the "talking tortilla" give a gospel message. *Lower right:* Literacy followed evangelism.

Upper left: Group of presidents of Chol congregation. John felt the Chol church must attend to its own propagation support, and government. *Lower left:* Boys' Sunday school classes taught by native believer. *Upper right:* Arabelle Whittaker helped with literacy and also translation. *Lower right:* (Westminister Films photo) Elaine leads a women's literacy class at Amado Nervo. Note that she wears the native dress.

Upper left: John entered this village of ex-murderers called La Lucha at risk of life. But in time the strong church that is pictured here sprang up. *Lower left:* (Westminister Films Photo) John addressing the Amado Nervo Church. The streamers are from a recent fiesta. *Upper right:* Believers enjoy a tug of war at a church fiesta. The hut frame at right of the rope's center is the beginning of a structure to represent the Jewish tabernacle in the Old Testament. John intended the giant visual aid to teach that animal sacrifices were superseded and fulfilled by the sacrifice of Christ. *Lower right:* Fiesta meal. The men always ate first.

This Amado Nervo mother suffers from crippling arthritis and has been unable to walk for over ten years. After she was crippled, her husband beat her and brought a young girl in to be his second wife.

The Chol prisoners, three of whom served seven years for a trumped-up charge of arson. This picture was taken when John brought their families to Yajalon and the men were not allowed outside the bars.

Wycliffe translators, Chol native informants, and Dr. William Wonderly, representative of the American Bible Society, at the translation table in Mitla. John Beekman and Dr. Wonderly sit at left between two Chols. Elaine sits in the center foreground with back to camera. To her right is another Chol informant, then Evelyn and Wilbur Aulie and Arabelle Whittaker.

Missionary Aviation Fellowship plane lands at Carranza with load of Chol New Testaments for a dedication ceremony. These Chols are about to see for the first time the complete New Testament in their own language.

One of three dedication ceremonies for the Chol New Testament. Here in the crowded Tumbala Church, Cristobal Arcos, a Chol evangelist, pays tribute to the translators and publishers. Several years before Wilbur Aulie took this man to Puebla, Mexico, for hernia surgery, making him the first Chol to be operated on in a hospital.

Part of the crowd that could not get in the Tumbala church for the dedication ceremony.

11. *Counterattack*

THE WOODS AROUND Amado Nervo sparkled with the gay colors of early summer. Wild orchids, dahlias, white and yellow Mexican poppies, and poinsetta grew profusely within easy gathering distance of John and Elaine's front door. Coffee trees shaded the well-named hair flowers. Composed of long, hair-like strands of deep red stamens, they were also called *cabello de angel* or angel's hair. A wild cotton tree, bearing large yellow, poppy-like flowers, stood close by, its branches fluttering in the breeze. Elaine frequently said, "How can drunkenness, disease, and witchcraft flourish in this lovely Eden?"

"Never underestimate the power of the Enemy," John replied one June morning after breakfast. Then sighting down the trail, he said, "Speaking of the Enemy, here comes one of his agents."

Elaine looked. It was Miguel, the witch doctor, who had once put a death curse on her.

The beetle-browed witch doctor staggered onto the porch and greeted them cordially.

"You haven't been to see us in a long time," John said. "Come in and hear the new records."

Miguel entered and in a shaking hand took the coffee Elaine offered. John put a gospel record on the phonograph. After a few moments Miguel seemed to sober up.

"We've often prayed for you," John said quietly. "We want you to find the same joy your neighbors have."

The old man's face crinkled. He leaned forward and mumbled, "My evils are many." Suddenly the dam burst and his woes poured out like a brook after a rainstorm.

Forgetting his translation goal for the day, John listened until the sorrowful medicine man ran down. Then he knelt beside him and prayed, "Lord, help Miguel know that You love him and that You can forgive him of all the evil he has done."

Miguel came to the house three or four more times, then one Sunday morning he appeared in the church service for the first time. He seemed unusually interested in the sermons and even tried to sing in a croaking voice. Prayers were intensified for him. Not only were John and Elaine concerned about him as a person, but they knew he could mightily influence the unbelievers of Amado Nervo.

One day he asked John and two men from the church to come and teach his family some hymns. They agreed on a date. But when they approached his house, they heard loud incoherent singing and talking coming from inside. Miguel wobbled to the doorway and greeted them gaily. John peered over the old man's shoulder to see the drinkers. One he recognized as a member of the Amado Nervo church. Miguel's influence was at work. John turned around and said wearily to his companions, "Let's go. We'll return another time."

More discouragement awaited John back at the house. A young girl named Maria stood crying on the porch. "Brother Kwan," she sobbed, "My brother, Francisco, cannot hear. He is much worse."

John knew the sad case. Francisco, only 16, one of the preacher boys, whose mother had recently died, was serious and mature beyond his years. The boy had contracted tuberculosis on one of the weekend trips. John hurried to the hut to see the boy whom he had taught to read and write, and whom he hoped might one day become a leading pastor among the Chols.

Francisco lay on a pallet beside the smoldering cook fire that pushed wisps of smoke into the long blackened ceiling and through the small escape hole. Thin and racked with coughs, the boy managed a weak smile when John entered.

"How do you feel?" John wrote on a slip of paper.

He began coughing again. John moved an old tin nearer the pallet and waited patiently.

"I'm going to die," the youth said between labored breaths.

John did not try to contradict him. He had seen other Chols die from T.B. and knew the marks of approaching death — thin, wasted body, bloody cough, and yellow pallor.

"I'm going to be with Jesus and my mother," the boy said.

There was little John could do beyond asking Francisco's father and sister, neither of whom could read or write, to make him comfortable and let him sit in the door of the hut when strength permitted.

When John arose from prayer, another Chol stood in the doorway. "Brother Kwan," the boy begged, "come fast. My father has cut himself with a machete. The blood, it races like a river." John hurried to tend to this medical case.

Francisco seemed to get better and was able to sit in the door of the hut where his coughing could be heard all over the village. Dressed in coarse white muslin shirt and trousers, poring over the epistles recently translated by Wycliffe's Chol workers, published by the Bible Society, and sent in by M.A.F., he became a familiar sight.

One rainy day in July, Maria ran down the path to the missionaries' home. This time her eyes were wrung dry from crying. "Francisco no longer speaks or moves," she told Elaine. "He has gone to see Jesus and our mother."

Elaine held the slim girl close and tried to give comfort. She could feel Maria's body shaking with grief. "One day you will see Francisco and your mother again," she assured her. "No one will get sick or die there."

The next morning John and Elaine walked to the grave. They found it encircled by the preacher boys of Amado Nervo who had come as a group for the funeral. Three told about the courage of Francisco in facing persecutions while on evangelizing trips. "I saw a man stick the blade of his machete under Francisco's chin," one said, "Francisco didn't flinch. He just kept on telling the man about Jesus."

Miguel appeared at church again and claimed to be a believer. Five pagan families followed him into the church and became believers. Later he told John, "I cannot give up drinking completely; I have obligations to unbelievers who want my services."

"Brother, the Lord said we cannot serve two masters," John declared. "You must leave the old life completely."

"Not yet," Miguel replied. "This way I will bring the unbelievers to church."

John found it hard to understand the man for whom they had prayed so long. He no longer opposed them, but he was not willing to stand with them. A few weeks later Miguel indulged in another ceremonial drinking spree and fell into a stupor from which he never regained consciousness. His end was a pathetic sermon to the unbelievers of Amado Nervo.

The rains continued heavy through October. The air strip became so eroded and muddy that it was impossible for M.A.F. to land, and so John and Elaine went without mail for about a month. Through their short-wave radio they learned that President Eisenhower had been elected to his first term in the November 5th vote. But U. S. elections were secondary in their minds as they prepared for the first Bible translation conference scheduled for January in Amado Nervo.

The entire New Testament had been finished in first draft by the Chol team, but John needed to do much checking and rechecking of portions done by the Aulies, who were on furlough, and by Arabelle Whittaker before Dr. Nida arrived.

Following a memorable Christmas fiesta and New Year's service at Amado Nervo, the visitors flew in on two M.A.F. planes.

The Beekmans, Arabelle, and Vi Warkentin caught up on Wycliffe family news and rejoiced together at the rapid growth of the Chol church. The Nidas filled them in on news from the States and their impressions of the election campaign. Then they spread out manuscripts on the Beekmans' screened-in porch, usually used for the Indians' reception room, and sat down to five days of hard work. Through it all, Elaine was the smiling hostess, ready with coffee and other refreshments, and keeping Judy and friendly Chols out from under foot.

Their purpose was essentially to put the message of the New Testament into Chol. John had come to feel that this involved much more than a literal word for word and phrase by phrase translation of the purest New Testament text. He wanted the Biblical message put into native Chol idioms.

The original form of the Scriptures," John noted later, "is full of idiomatic expressions. The authors under inspiration of the Spirit wrote in a form which was common to their day. They used expressions in accordance with the whole linguistic structure of the language."

In this and future conferences, the Chol translators came across many places where it was necessary to translate idiomatically. For example, the Chol meaning of "heaviness of heart" (Romans 9:2) was quite different from the English meaning. If a Chol husband is mean and beats his wife into submission, the wife may decide to make his heart heavy. She removes a piece of her fingernail and cuts it into small pieces. After the husband eats this in a tortilla, his evil and meanness is supposed to change to tenderness. "To say that Paul had 'heaviness of heart,'" John told his colleagues, "would make a Chol think that Paul had a wife who had gone through this ceremony." Instead of "heaviness of heart," the translators used the Chol idiom, "a heart that is nailed," to express Paul's sorrow for his Jewish brethren.

It quickly became obvious that the entire New Testament could not soon be made ready for printing and binding. Dr. Nida approved Galatians through Jude and asked the translators to do more work on the remaining books. They did not grumble. John said, "The Chol New Testament will be the single most important factor in the growth and development of the Chol church in future years. We want it to convey accurately God's inspired message to them."

After the visitors left, John and Elaine talked about the accomplishments of the conference. "We did more together in five days than we can do apart in five weeks," John said. "What could we do in five weeks away from the tribe."

The germ of an idea was beginning to form in John's mind. What was needed, he felt, was a central translator's workshop, where translators could bring their language helpers and share insights and concentrate on the main job apart from the distractions of tribal life.

Life in Amado Nervo resumed its hectic pace after the Nidas and the others left. Some days there were so many medical cases, tooth pullings, classes, and chores related to jungle living that John didn't get a single verse translated. Between housework and caring for Judy, Elaine was his girl of all trades: receptionist, office girl, nurse, and dental assistant. She also translated the hymns, "Living for Jesus," "Holy, Holy, Holy," and "Work for the Night Is Coming." They were to be included in the new hymnal marked for a printing of 4,000. Their stock of old hymnals had long been sold out. On hymnals and other items of value, their policy was to sell at half cost, low enough for the Chols to afford and high enough for them to maintain their dignity.

John clapped when Elaine sang for him, "Work for the Night Is Coming." "They've never felt very important down here. But they'll be right in the front ranks of Heaven. And, by the way," he added, "I haven't heard you complain lately about your musical training at Moody being of no value on the mission field."

A whooping cough epidemic in December brought death stalking

through the huts of Juarez, a village two hours' trail hike from Amado
Nervo. The local witch doctor chanted and sprinkled blood day and
night but to no avail. More than 40 children and adults died — all
from pagan families. Not one of the believers who accepted medical
aid from John and Elaine died.

This contrast caused considerable talk within the ranks of the
pagans. Believers told John about overhearing such conversations as:

"Maybe we should believe, too. Nothing happens to their children."

"No. They are cursing us with black magic."

"If that is true," said the first, "their God is more powerful than
ours."

Diphtheria and chicken pox added to the misery of Chol country
and caused more deaths.

One day a couple arrived from Allende with their sick one-year-
old boy. The preacher boys were studying in the living room so John
took them into the kitchen. The child's blistered, peeling feet spoke
of days of high fever. The rolling eyes suggested approaching death.
A throat examination revealed a diphtherial membrane. John gave
Elaine an aside there-is-no-hope look. To make the parents feel
better she gave an injection. Then John directed the parents in
prayer. By the time he said Amen, the baby had stopped breathing.

A few days later John made a trip to Allende, arriving by M.A.F.
plane at the nearest air strip on a river island. The believers from
Allende came down to meet him. As some crossed back to the mainland over a log which served as a bridge, a girl fell into the river and
was whisked downstream by the strong current toward a fifty-foot
waterfall. One of the men and John leaped to the rescue. They
reached shore with the girl within five yards of the waterfall. To
John's surprise, she did not need artificial respiration. Her blue skirt
had billowed over her head, forming an air pocket, keeping her
from inhaling water. John, however, could feel his tired heart
pounding with great effort.

A friendly rancher gave the rescuers a change of clothes, and
they walked up the hill to the village. John taught and counseled
for a week, and helped the elders resolve spiritual problems and
personal quarrels that had arisen in the congregation.

Back in Amado Nervo word came of a new kind of trouble.
Eight Christian families living in the village of Chich Lum had been
approached by pagan men from another village seeking wives for
their sons. When the Christians had refused to give up their daugh-

ters (who averaged about twelve years of age), the leader of the
pagans shouted angrily, "We'll be back."

The Christians then gathered their few belongings and fled into
the jungle. At midnight the thwarted fathers returned armed with
machetes and clubs to find only empty huts.

John understood why they had refused to give up their daugh-
ters. The pagan husband frequently beat his wife unmercifully with
the flat end of a machete, and forced her to carry heavy loads from
distant cornfields over the rugged trail. The husband's weekend
drunken sprees kept her and the children cowering in a corner of
the hut. In contrast, a Christian husband treated his wife with
respect, singing hymns with her, leading the family in prayer, and
teaching her and the children to read from a primer.

The affair had a happy ending when the refugees were invited
to build new huts in a Christian village. In good time, the daugh-
ters found Christian husbands.

Christmas, 1952, came and again the Amado Nervo church overflowed with festive worshipers. For the special services the men
built an outdoor model of the Hebrew tabernacle using a blanket
for the veil, a gourd for the laver, and a pillar of rocks for the altar.
They constructed the rest with sticks and bark and much imagina-
tion. While the people clustered around to watch a demonstration,
John explained the Hebrew and Mayan sacrificial systems and how
both had been completed by Christ's atoning death.

He dedicated three new preacher boys to be roving weekend
evangelists. The other boys from Amado Nervo reported on their
adventures to the congregation. By piecing together what they said,
John estimated that the believers' ranks had swelled by more than
a thousand during the past year. But their reports also showed that
the opposition had not abated.

The power structure of Mexican land owners was still determined
to keep the Indians in economic captivity. Barely a month later at
the end of a wild four-day fiesta in Tumbala, the ranchers found an
opportunity to strike back.

The fiesta was marked by drunkenness and carousing against the
believers. At the close of the fourth day, candles were left burning
before the patron saint in the Catholic church. Apparently some
drunks knocked the candles onto the floor carpeted with dry pine
needles. The fire spread rapidly through streamers and other decora-
tions that hung from the rafters. The roof beams burned, collapsing

the limestone walls which crumbled into powder. The saint collapsed in the inferno.

Early the next morning men from Tumbala rode into the Chol
cornfields with summons for twelve evangelicals to appear at the
municipal building. The men summoned did not know until they
entered Tumbala that the church had burned.

Six of the twelve were tied and thrown into the dirty jail. The
other six were released with warnings.

During the next four days, the six prisoners were kept on a starvation diet while pagan mobs milled outside, screaming for the death
penalty. An influential man demanded that they be hung by the
toes. Several powerful ranchers and *ladino* businessmen who sold
liquor were seen inciting the mobs. One of the businessmen was
overheard saying, "We must kill them and stop the evangelical movement or our businesses will fail."

Once the prisoners were brought out to face the mob and were
soaked with gasoline. An accuser struck a match and held the flame
perilously close to their clothing. "Confess and tell the truth," he
demanded, "or I'll burn you alive." Other men behind him shot into
the air.

The prisoners refused to speak and were thrown back into the
dirty jail that stank with uncollected human excrement. A rancher
pushed his face against the bars and yelled, "You're going to die in
this hole. Where is your God now?"

News of what had happened quickly reached Amado Nervo.
"Because we are foreigners, our hands are tied," John told Elaine
sadly. "We know and right-thinking Catholics know that this is not
a religious conflict. But if we step in, the ranchers will tell the
state authorities in Tuxtla that we are protecting arsonists and fighting against the Catholic church."

The Beekmans and fellow Wycliffe Translators in Mexico had
worked to establish friendships with reform-minded Catholics. They
had stressed repeatedly to Catholic clergy and government officials
that they primarily were Bible translators. But translation produced
native churches in areas where Catholic and pagan rituals had
merged in the unholy wedlock that had degraded the Indians instead
of uplifting them. A few courageous priests did admit that the Indians were more pagan than Catholic and called for reformation.

A Tumbala rancher showed the prisoners a paper containing words
in Spanish. "Sign this and you may go free," he promised. The Chols

signed and unable to understand Spanish did not realize they had been tricked into signing a confession.

On Monday, February 9, the six Chols were tied and carried out of the Tumbala jail to face the howling mob shrieking, "Death to the Protestants!"

Then began a march to Yajalon led by soldiers and accompanied by 400 men carrying clubs, machetes, and pistols. Later it seemed miraculous to John and Elaine that the prisoners were not murdered on the trail by the mob.

Two months later the Chols were still in jail and no date had been set for their trial.

John wrote home,

"Persecution is in the air. I, along with my Indian companion, was nearly clubbed last week in a village of unsaved Chols. We have been accused of instructing the Indians to burn down the Tumbala church along with a lot of other false statements. Keep praying. Our Lord is the One in whom we are always victorious and abounding in joy."

12. *City of the Dead*

JOHN WAS STRIDING down the hill, medicine kit in hand, when he heard Elaine call, "Hatch is on the radio."

He hurried back to talk to the pilot. "Just thought you and anybody else listening on the network would want to hear the latest news," Hatch said. "Joseph Stalin died yesterday in Moscow."

John interrupted, "Thanks, Hatch. You're better than the *New York Times*. When are you coming to see us?"

"Whenever you need me. Just push the button."

"We're due for furlough this summer. I'll give you a call in plenty of time."

"Righto," Hatch said. "Over and out."

John thought about Stalin's death while he made the medical call. The Chols knew nothing of this fallen dictator on the other side of the world. Indeed, he believed that a nuclear war could destroy both the United States and Russia and life among the Chols would not skip a step. The Cold War might as well be on another planet so far as they were concerned.

Neither he nor Elaine felt anxious to go on furlough. "With the six fellows in jail and persecution intensifying," John said, "we need to be here just to show the believers there is someone on their side. But I suppose some checkups and rest will do us all good. And if you should be pregnant as we hope — "

Elaine broke in. "Better make that as we are almost sure."

John grinned shyly. "I wouldn't know. You're the mother. But maybe I'd better call off that little swing around the bush Domingo and I were planning to take next week."

"No, don't," Elaine said. "I'll watch myself. And the women will look after Judy when I need to rest. Look at her now, playing with

150

little Jose. There are probably six pairs of friendly eyes watching every move she makes."

"Okay, Sweetheart, if you think you'll be all right, we'll go ahead."

The following Monday, John and the preacher boy, Domingo, took off for the lowlands on the teaching and witnessing trip.

The sun boiled down and the hot winds blew clouds of dust in their faces as they rode through the jungle. They stopped to feast on wild cherries and drink water from vines while monkeys howled from the trees overhead. Later in the day they swam in a swift river to gain brief respite from the heat.

That evening John preached to about 300 and later slept on a bark mat in a believer's hut. The next day they hurried on to La Lucha, the village of escaped murderers where he had once been greeted with threats. Almost 200 believers greeted them in a new metal-roofed church building.

After services, some of the men asked John if he would like to see some old ruins. He followed them ten miles into the tangle of jungle to an old pyramid covered with vines and thick undergrowth. From the size of trees growing up along the side, John knew it was very ancient.

As the Indians cavorted on the high mound, time seemed to stand still in the rain forest. John had never taken time to dig among the Mayan ruins that were scattered throughout Chol country, but he knew a bit about Mayan history. He could easily picture the ancestors of the Indians on the mound stealing through the jungle in pursuit of wild game.

He guessed the unexplored pyramid to be at least 1,000 years old. The great monuments of Palenque, only a day's trail hike away, had been built, according to scholars, about A.D. 800. Some historians estimated that as many as 15 million Mayans might have lived in Palenque and other great cities at that time. About A.D. 1000, the Mayans had vacated their great temple cities because of war, disease, earthquake, social decadence, or some other mysterious reason. Palenque had remained lost until 1773 when discovered by Indians who told a Spanish priest.

John imagined that it would be fascinating to dig around the old pyramid. But that, he felt, was the task of the archaeologist and the historian. He and Elaine had been called to bring spiritual light to one tribe of the present-day Maya, represented by the small, dark-skinned and expressive dark-eyed men who had taken him to a monument of their tragic history.

Early the next morning John and Domingo rode hard on the day's journey to Potoja, a village John had never visited before. The first Indian to spot them whistled up the rest of the men in the village. Within minutes about forty cursing Indians, all waving clubs and machetes, had surrounded them.

Knowing he could not be heard above the din, John merely stood smiling with Domingo at his shoulder. The inner circle of the crowd moved closer, brandishing machetes almost under their noses. Only then did John raise his hand and shout, "We will leave and go sleep on the hill."

The curses stopped and the Indians stepped aside to give John and Domingo a path. A few yards up a nearby hill they unfolded their blankets on a soft underpadding of leaves. They had ridden all day and were very tired. Sleep came quickly. Next morning, after prayer for the unfriendly village, they rode on through the jungle.

At the next village John met a runner from Amado Nervo. "Sister Elena is very sick," he said.

That was enough for John. Handing the reins of his horse to Domingo, he said, "Take care of him. I'll take the short way back."

The short way back — over trails and across chasms which horses could not travel — was 27 miles. He arrived to find Elaine weak but resting comfortably after a miscarriage. Quickly he pumped the radio to life and called Hatch to fly in a nurse.

After treatment by the nurse, and a few days' rest under John's watchful eye, Elaine felt able to travel. Hatch flew them to Tuxtla where they caught a north-bound bus.

Sixty miles south of Mexico City, they stopped at Puebla for medical checks at the hospital founded and directed by the veteran Baptist leader, Dr. Fealand Meadows. Both John and Elaine were coughing blood. The examinations showed a pharynx infection, but clear lungs. John and little Judy also had parasites.

News of the Chol prisoners awaited them in Mexico City. Word had come via radio from Chol country that two of the six Chol prisoners had been released on bail. The other four had been transferred to the large prison in Tuxtla.

The Kettle being full, as usual, John rented a hotel room. He then went immediately to the immigration office to arrange for diplomatic clearance for a short furlough home. Director John McIntosh encouraged them to take the time off and assured that efforts would be made to get the prisoners released.

At the immigration office, a clerk riffled through files for 15 minutes, then shrugged. "Mr. Beekman, I cannot find your entry papers. Without them you cannot leave the country. Please be patient. We will keep looking."

John and Elaine had entered under a special working arrangement between Wycliffe and the Mexican government.[1] Their residence was further complicated by Judy's birth in Mexico City, giving her dual citizenship with the U. S. and Mexico.

He thanked the clerk and went back to the hotel. After a few days, they found cheaper quarters and began work on a Spanish-Chol dictionary. No one could predict when the papers might be found. Several other translators had also had similar problems.

Sad letters began arriving — three to five a day — from Chol believers who had learned to read and write.

"How long, brother and sister, will it be when you come with us again?"

"Please, brother, tell about me (ask for prayer) in church, because I want to do the Lord's work."

"We are sad because it is not seen how those in jail will end. I am sad also because I have no house. My home burned down. I don't know why."

And glad letters.

"I am telling the truth to a new brother daily in his house."

"We use the new book of hymns. Thank to God. May God help you in the making of more new books."

"Great is the power of the Lord. God moves on the heart of the new brother."

Summer dragged into August and still no immigration papers. They finished the Spanish-Chol dictionary and drove through the mountains to Acapulco for a short vacation. Elaine gasped at the beauty of the world-famous spa with its luxury hotels studding the beaches around a bay of cool blue water.

They registered at a small motel and, since it was the summer off-season, got rock-bottom rates. They swam (three-year-old Judy

[1]No U. S. citizen is allowed to enter Mexico as a "missionary." Those denominational missionaries now serving there are officially classified as "rentistas" — aliens who can prove a guaranteed income from savings or an out-of-the-country source. The Southern Baptist Foreign Mission Board, for example, must deposit the salaries of its missionaries one year in advance in Mexican banks.

wanted to live on the beach), loafed, and read — mainly a biography of Hudson Taylor. Stretched on the white sands and sheltered by a striped beach umbrella, they talked about the faith of the famous missionary who had founded the China Inland Mission. "Listen to this," John said, " 'God chose me because I was weak enough. God does not do His great works by large committees. He trains somebody to be quiet enough, and little enough, and then He uses him!' Isn't that great?

"Here's something else I like. 'I am always on the run, but I am more happy in the Lord, than ever I have been . . . . Things may not be, in many respects, as I would wish them; but if God permits them so to be, or so orders them, I may well be content!'"

After they returned refreshed to Mexico City, John called again at the immigration office. The clerk was smiling and apologetic. "Your papers were here all the time. Please forgive us."

They went by train from Mexico City to Elaine's home in Clearfield, Pennsylvania where John left Elaine and Judy, while he started a round of travel and deputation work. Her first Sunday in church, Elaine broke into sobs when the organist began the prelude. The sound of the music she had loved since childhood overwhelmed her. She hadn't realized how much she had missed it.

John's accounts of Chol victories gripped his audiences. Many churches offered regular financial support. To each John said, "God has already provided for us, but I have a list of colleagues who are short of their quotas."

Furlough plans called for them to remain in the States until the next summer. But Missionary Aviation Fellowship asked them to return for a few days to appear in a film, "Of Wings and Missions," intended to show M.A.F.'s work in Chiapas.

M.A.F. flew them down early in February. John immediately checked on the plight of the four men charged with the Tumbala church burning.

John accompanied families and friends to see the four prisoners in the Yajalon jail. He smelled the stench half a block away. Then, as he peered into the semi-darkness of the one-room, stone-walled, dirt floor jail, he felt transported back to the Dark Ages. The men had no toilet facilities, no wash basin, and only piles of rags for beds.

The prisoners were not permitted to come out and be with their families. John blinked back the tears as he watched one reach through the bars to stroke the face of his little boy. After this and other greetings, John led in a worship service of singing, prayer, and Bible study while the guards looked on sullenly.

On February 5, the first anniversary of the Tumbala church burning, an earthquake shook Yajalon, demolishing several buildings. Falling stones caused serious injury to a ringleader of the Chols' accusers. Because of the date, talk spread that God's judgment had fallen.

When M.A.F.'s film was completed, John and Elaine flew back to finish their furlough. A hectic schedule of missionary meetings kept them exhausted. One Sunday evening after a long missionary program, Elaine sighed, "I'll be glad to get home to the Chols for some rest."

Hudson Taylor had written his furlough feelings after visiting an English church: "Unable to bear the sight of a congregation of Christian people rejoicing in their own security, while millions were perishing for lack of knowledge, I wandered out . . . alone, in great spiritual agony." John and Elaine sensed how he felt when they compared the well-dressed, contented people whom they met to the Chols.

They enjoyed most the times spent with their families. There was an unforgettable week at Camp of the Woods in upstate New York with John's folks. When they parted to return to Mexico, Judy frowned at John's mother and said, "Grandma, why are you making a funny face?"

Good news and bad awaited when Hatch dropped them down into Amado Nervo. The two men out on bail and one of the jailed prisoners had been freed from indictment. The remaining three had been sentenced to seven years in the Tuxtla prison.

John called on the families of the unfortunate men. They were sad but not disheartened. "Oh, Brother Kwan, how can we give up?" one wife said. "The church is feeding us from the storehouse. Everybody is so good. We will just have to keep on praying."

"It's wonderful how the Chols are helping one another," John reported to Elaine. "They're not depending on us, but on one another and God."

Six weeks after the Beekmans' return from furlough, a stock of medicines arrived in Yajalon. They had collected the medicines during furlough but had to leave them at the border until approval for importation came from higher authorities in Mexico City.

The shipment included thousands of vitamins. Elaine explained to the women that "they are like food and make us strong." One woman picked up a pill and asked, "If I plant some, will they grow like beans?"

A translation conference with the Chol workers and Dr. Nida was scheduled for November in the neighboring state of Oaxaca. John worked furiously to get ready. The preacher boys wanted special classes. Medical emergencies kept arising. He could not save one baby who had been fed hot pig's blood by a witch doctor. Part of the grass roof had rotted away and needed replacing. Rats had made nests in other parts of the roof. Whenever it rained, moving the furniture was like playing musical chairs with the leaks.

But the roof was repaired and the medical work done — including pulling fourteen teeth the day before leaving.

They arrived in Mitla, Oaxaca, in time to celebrate Thanksgiving with Arabelle Whittaker and the Aulies, now grown to a family of seven. Houses were rented easily and cheaply and the translation table was spread when Dr. Nida arrived. Besides Nida, the Aulies, Arabelle, and John, three Chol informants were at the table. After a week Nida left the Chol committee to continue with the revision of the manuscripts. The task of the committee was to check through the entire Chol translation, revising inaccuracies and obscure meanings.

For example, Luke 4:25, ". . . when the heaven was shut up three years and six months." John suddenly realized that this was a Chol idiom meaning that it was ready to rain. They changed it to read in Chol, ". . . the sky was clear for three years and six months."

Mitla, an ancient ceremonial capital of the Zapotecs with about 3,000 population, seemed to John and Elaine an intriguing, but tragic place. In the Zapotec language it was Yoo-paaa, meaning "Place of the Dead." Here were buried ancient Indian priests in stone tombs discovered deep inside buildings that had perhaps been built when Nebuchadnezzar was destroying Jerusalem and carrying off the Jews to their first slavery. The Zapotec civilization was generally held to be older than the Aztec but more recent than Mayan civilization.

Already several translation teams had started work on various Zapotec dialects[2] in the state of Oaxaca. But in Mitla, where many Zapotecs spoke Spanish, there was not a single evangelical church.

[2] Work is now progressing in eight Zapotec dialects; two more are scheduled to be entered.

On New Year's Eve the Chol workers went to observe the Zapotecs literally make prayers with their hands for the New Year. John and Elaine had seen Indians pray *to* images, but had never watched people pray *with* images.

In the light of hillside fires they watched the Indians make miniature replicas and symbols of whatever they wanted in the New Year, praying as they worked. They built small stone houses enclosed by walls, inside which they placed smaller stones representing oxen, sheep, and goats. Rows of cactus strips set into the ground represented cornfields. A pile of small pebbles symbolized money. A wee hammock, a baby.

Zapotecs in their colorful costumes chanting and chipping at stones in the light of flickering fires under a pale moon cast a spell upon John and Elaine. The ceremony, they knew, was probably older than the New Testament. "Think of all the generations of American Indians," John said somberly, "that have lived and died, never hearing about Christ. Why, when Columbus sailed to this hemisphere, this was already an ancient civilization."

On the second Sunday of 1955, the translators held a service in Spanish at John's house. Zapotec neighbors crowded in to listen. A quick warning came from the house's owner: "No more services or get out." Not wanting to interrupt work on revision of the Chol Testament, they began going to a nearby village where there was an evangelical witness for Sunday services.

April came and the temperatures climbed into the nineties. The revision continued. John, Arabelle, and the Aulies reached I Corinthians in making corrections. Behind them came Viola Warkentin doing the final typing, and behind her, three proof-readers.

Elaine and two translators serving among the Zapotecs did the proof-reading. One read the original from which the final typing was done. Another followed the typewritten manuscript, and another the Spanish text to check for omissions and spelling of proper names. The completed text was to be bi-lingual with the Chol version in larger print and occupying most of each page and the Spanish version at the bottom.[3]

John began having heart pains. He said nothing, thinking they

[3]Wycliffe translations are usually bi-lingual to help the tribespeople become better acquainted with the national language, and to aid national language speakers in Christian work among the tribespeople.

would go away. Lately he had been tiring easily, but thought he might be out of shape from a lack of trail hiking.

In May the translation committee decided to take a two-month break so the workers could return to their tribal posts. They had been working hard for six months and felt that a change of pace might help before returning to Mitla in August for the final wrap-up.

Parched fields and hearts greeted John and Elaine when they arrived back in Amado Nervo. The corn had withered in the fields from lack of rain and famine threatened. More discouraging, however, were the land squabbles and backslidings among believers. John shook off the feeling that he should have his heart checked and plunged in to help the needy people.

John walked through a mountain-side cornfield where thin stalks drooped under a rainless sky. The first crop of the year had failed, a disaster on two counts: The Chols had been robbed of both food and seed for the second planting.

He radioed to Wycliffe headquarters in Mexico City and stated the problem. A staff member asked the Federal Department of Indian Affairs to help. In a few days, 1,000 pounds of seed corn reached Tuxtla where it was picked up by M.A.F. and flown into Amado Nervo and other Chol villages having landing strips. When John saw the corn, he said, "Thank God that the Indians have some friends on the outside."

Now the Indians had seed corn but no rain. Old timers could not remember when the area had suffered from such a long drought.

John traveled through the villages, encouraging the believers to pray. Near one village he met an angry crowd of pagans at a scum-covered water hole. "The rain god is angry because so many people have become Christians," a spokesman said.

John looked at the sky, flecked only with scattered white clouds. "Rain will come," he said. "Wait and see."

The crowd began grumbling. "We have waited — one, two, three, four, five months. No rain. Why should we believe you now?"

A few hours later the sky darkened and the wind began rising. Suddenly white streaks of lightning splintered the sky and thunder boomed. Then the blessed rain descended, soaking the parched earth and driving the amazed Indians into their huts.

After the heavy shower ended, the awed villagers gathered around John and listened respectfully to the message of Christ.

More showers followed and then the men swarmed into the

cleared fields to make the second planting. John gave attention to the land quarrels.

Chol heads of households staked their claims on unused land by simply declaring, "This is my field." Unfortunately, this type of possession made it easy for the strong to take the best fields, leaving the weak no appeal. When a man died, the greedy usually moved in and took over his lands, leaving the widow and children to starve in poverty. The elders of the congregations were supposed to protect the widows and decide land disputes between believers.

John had never tried to tell the Chol believers what to do about such problems. "If I should and they followed my advice," he had said in the beginning, "they would come to depend on me too much. They must learn to settle their own problems in the light of the way they understand the scriptures."

Accordingly, he and Elaine started four weekly Bible classes: two morning classes for the women which she taught, and two for the men which he taught. Both taught from James and the teachings of Jesus about the requirements of discipleship. One by one, leading members of the church began to admit their failings and within a month he and Elaine sensed revival was spreading.

John challenged the elders to take the initiative in correcting misdeeds and solving land disputes. A particularly glaring case was Juan Cruz, a new believer.

Early in the spring, Juan had finished clearing his land for planting when his nephew, a professed believer, moved in and began planting.

Juan meekly began clearing another plot, only to have the nephew move in again by force. Juan did not realize his right to present the case to the church elders. Instead, he skipped Sunday services and drowned his grief in liquor at a ranch store.

Wobbling home on the trail, he fell into a drunken stupor. A notorious murderer came upon him and pounded him with sharp stones. Hours later, wounded and bleeding, he staggered into his hut.

His flesh wounds healed but walking brought pain. He finally came to John, who had no medicine for dislocated vertebra. However, John and other believers nursed him back to spiritual health, and the elders saw that he got part of his land back.

John and Elaine began packing to return to Mitla and help with what they felt must be the final checking of the Chol New Testament.

However, before Hatch flew in for them, they learned of one more tragedy that had occurred during their last absence.

Sebastian Lopez had been the first ·believer in the village of Carranza. He had won many of his neighbors who came to regard him as their spiritual leader. He had been convicted of defacing an idol — which had actually been an accident — and assessed a heavy fine which he paid with borrowed money. He hoped to pay the money back from future corn crops, but while working in his corn-fields — two days' trail hike from home — he was snake bitten. Anti-venom secured by his friends from a nearby ranch did not help. They started carrying him home, but on the way he begged, "Please let me rest here and bring my family and friends to see me before I die."

His family and church friends reached his side. They sang a hymn together and then Sebastian prayed for his flock. After encouraging them to read the Scriptures and pray every day, he turned to a young lay preacher and said, "Please see that my children do not have to bear my load of debts. Sell my corn crop to pay them."

The young preacher who stood before John was in tears. "Brother Kwan," he sobbed, "with the drought there was not enough corn to pay any of the debts. Now they are upon his children."

John conferred with Elaine. An offering from Vacation Bible School children in the Sixth Reformed Church of Paterson, New Jersey had just reached them. It was enough to pay the 500 pesos which Sebastian had borrowed to help pay his fine.

Suddenly news came that one of the four prisoners had been released from the Tuxtla prison, and that a man of high influence had promised to intercede for the others. "Our Lord is still a God of miracles!" John exclaimed to Elaine.

The Mitla conference lasted only two weeks. Dr. Nida pronounced the Chol New Testament acceptable for publication. The translators were elated and enjoyed a service of praise and prayer together. But the strain showed on John's face. "You've been working too hard," Dr. Nida joshed him.

What Dr. Nida and the others did not know was that John's heart pains had grown worse. Lately at night Elaine had felt the bed shaking as his tired heart labored to pump blood. She insisted that he consult a heart specialist as soon as possible.

13. *The Great Aorta Mystery*

DR. DEMETRIO SODI-PALLARES, a world-famous cardiologist,[1] gave John an electrocardiogram, X-rays, the works in Mexico City. Then he confronted the couple with his findings.

"How you have walked the trails in Chiapas and lived this long is a mystery to me." He pointed to a diagram of the heart, "Here at the top of the left ventricle is the aortic valve — the takeoff point for the great artery which carries blood for general body circulation. It is a flutter valve; that is, it opens with the force of the blood coming down from the left ventricle, then closes to prevent blood from leaking back into the ventricle. It opens and closes with every heart beat.

"Now coming to what I believe, Mr. Beekman, is your primary problem. Your aortic valve is simply not functioning. You suffer from aortic insufficiency — that is, some of the blood after leaving your left ventricle, regurgitates — flows backward — into your heart.

"This primary problem has caused some other problems. Your heart has had to work harder and has enlarged to compensate for the deficiency. Your blood pressure has risen abnormally. In short, your heart is in congestive failure."

John gave Elaine a why-hasn't-someone-told-me-this-before look, and said, "That's why my heart has been beating like a trip-hammer lately."

"Yes," Dr. Sodi-Pallares said. "You were probably born with this deficiency or had rheumatic fever in your childhood.

"This can't go on much longer," he continued. "In two years or less you'll reach the point where medication cannot give relief."

Dr. Sodi-Pallares paused as if in deep thought. "I've read," he

[1]Dr. Sodi-Pallares is renowned for his findings in the relationship between sodium and potassium in heart cells.

finally said, "that Dr. Charles Hufnagel at Georgetown University Hospital in Washington has developed a plastic valve for aortic problems. He might be able to help you, if you are willing to take the risk."

John and Elaine exchanged glances. "When can I go?" John asked.

"You're not ready now," the doctor said. "First, I want you in bed for two weeks for a daily intravenous injection of digitalis and a salt-free diet."

John followed the doctor's orders. The rest and medication took away the pain and he felt able to drive. On September 20, they left Mexico City for Washington, D.C.

Elaine wrote in her prayer letter:

> We've had eight happy years of service among the Chols, and have been privileged to see the Chol New Testament finished at the end of August. We thought that the way led north to our Wycliffe biennial conference in Arkansas and then back to Mexico for many more years of teaching that translated Word among the Chols. *But the Captain of this tour has chosen a route with a DETOUR for us.*

The 1950 Plymouth station wagon made the 3,000 mile trip in eight days. John went immediately into Georgetown Hospital.

After the diagnostic procedures had been completed, Dr. Hufnagel talked to John and Elaine together. "Dr. Sodi-Pallares had the right idea. The basic trouble lies with your aortic valve. But in addition, you have stenosis. At some point it is about the size of a matchstick when it should be as large as your thumb."

"Is that why I've always had cold feet?" John asked.

"Yes."

"What about the operation?"

"There's considerable risk involved," Dr. Hufnagel replied. "Of the four who have had it, only two have survived. That record gives you a 50-50 chance."

"And if I don't have the operation?"

"It won't be long till you'll be an invalid. Should the operation be successful, you could enjoy maybe five more years of restricted activity."

"I understand," John said without blinking. "When can the surgery be done?"

Dr. Hufnagel showed surprise. "Mr. Beekman, I don't want you to make a quick decision. Take a few days to think about it."

"No," John said resolutely. "I'm ready now."

The doctor called Elaine aside. "Apparently your husband doesn't understand the seriousness of this operation."

"I believe he does," Elaine replied. "We've talked about it and feel God has led us up here. This seems to be the one door open to us."

Dr. Hufnagel scheduled the surgery for October 11, 1955, just two weeks following John's arrival at Georgetown. As the date approached, John told Elaine, "I have no assurance the Lord will pull me through. But I have perfect peace that whatever the outcome, it will be the Lord's will."

Elaine had already asked their home churches in Pennsylvania and New Jersey to pray. Other churches were praying, including the River Grove Bible Church in suburban Chicago and the Chol congregations back in Chiapas.

On the evening of the ninth, John called Elaine. "Good news," he said jovially.

"You don't need the operation?"

"Not that. I'm going in tomorrow morning instead of Wednesday. They've decided to put me ahead of another fellow."

Elaine hadn't expected to sleep the night before the operation. She tried reading Scripture, beginning with Psalm 91.

Silently she repeated in her mind the confidence of the psalmist, *He that dwelleth in the secret place of the most high shall abide under the shadow of the Almighty. I will say of the Lord, He is my refuge and my fortress: my God; in him will I trust.*

Other times of testing passed before her mind. John's visit to Dr. Johnson at Moody for advice on his future work. The apartment fire which had destroyed all her earthly belongings. The difficulties in crossing the border the first time. The curse of the witch doctor in Amado Nervo. Sharon's death. Malaria and her physical breakdown. The saving of Judy's life. The miscarriage. The recent trip to Washington.

And now John, who had said in the marriage ceremony, "Elaine, you are my best earthly friend. I promise to love and protect you, to be considerate of your happiness, and in all things to seek your welfare."

God had permitted Sharon to die. She had leaned on John for strength to trust and to bear the sorrow. But what if John's life should end on the operating table?

She closed her eyes and saw him — standing tall and handsome and oh, so serious at the wedding. She saw him again returning to Amado Nervo thin and sporting a three-day growth of beard after an exhausting circuit through the villages. There was a gleam in his eyes when he returned from a trip that had always excited her. She could hear him saying, "Elaine, there are five new families of believers in Carranza." She saw him bending over a Chol baby, wracked with disease and wrinkled with dirt, his steady, gentle hands giving an injection of life-saving penicillin.

She wanted to cry, "God, you can't take him from me and Judy. There is so much for him to do. He is only 36." Then she remembered his words, "I have perfect peace that whatever the outcome is, it will be the Lord's will."

"I will say of the Lord," she murmured, "He is my refuge and my fortress: my God; in him will I trust." Then she added, "Even if it is Your will for him to die."

And she fell asleep.

At eight o'clock the next morning the doors of the hospital surgery suite swung open to admit John, already under anesthesia.

Preliminaries completed and the incision made, Dr. Hufnagel moved his skillful fingers down the defective aorta to a distance away from the heart and below the branches that went to the arms and head. He could not risk working closer to the heart. He clamped the aorta shut here and at another point about two inches further down from the heart. From this instant he moved rapidly, knowing that he had to get the blood moving again within five minutes to prevent damage to the legs.

The surgeon severed the matchstick-sized section of the aorta between the clamps; at his signal, the nurse presented the replacement valve — a rounded chamber containing a ball, and two ends projecting from opposite sides of the central chamber.

He inserted the two ends into the upper and lower segments of the divided aorta and clamped firmly upon them. This stopped the regurgitation of blood back into the heart from all but the arterial branches going to the arms and head.

With the artificial valve in place a dangerous flutter began causing John's heart to beat irregularly fast. Dr. Hufnagel grimly watched the wavy writing on the electrocardiograph that indicated the heart was working against itself. The doctor assisting Dr. Hufnagel reported, "Blood pressure rising and falling irregularly." The surgeon knew that unless the fluttering stopped soon the patient was doomed.

The seconds ticked away as the surgical team worked desperately to save a life. Suddenly the cardiograph writing leveled out to indicate a steady rhythmic beat. Dr. Hufnagel smiled and said, "We can get ready to sew him up." The operation had taken four and one-half hours.

Late that evening John was wheeled back into his room where Elaine and Pastor Van Ostenburg from Midland Park were waiting. Dr. Hufnagel came in and looked at John who was thrashing about restlessly. He patted Elaine's arm and said sympathetically, "We can't do anything now but sit tight and wait."

The doctor left and Elaine and the pastor sat beside John, praying and listening to the rhythmic tick-tock coming from under the oxygen tent. The sound, they knew, came from the ball rising and falling within the artificial valve in rhythm with John's heart beat and the movement of life-sustaining blood in his body. "What a wonderfully reassuring sound," Elaine said. "As long as he's ticking, we know he's alive."

John steadily improved. On the eighth day after the operation Elaine found him propped up in bed and reading his mail. "Here's one from Amado Nervo," he said cheerily. "They are praying for me and want to know when we'll be back."

Dr. Hufnagel stopped by for a bed check. "You're doing great," he told John.

"When can I leave the hospital?" John asked.

"Not for a couple of weeks," the doctor replied. "Then I want you under the observation of a heart specialist for several more weeks."

"By the way, Doctor," John asked, "what happened to the fellow whose place I took? Has he had surgery?"

"Yes. He had aortic insufficiency, too. But he didn't pull through. He was only 21 and strong physically. From that standpoint, he should have lived and you should have died. The only reason I can think of is that he didn't want to live as much as you did."

John left the hospital on November 1 and joined Elaine in a friend's house. Elaine hardly slept the first night. She kept waking up to listen for the tell-tale tick-tock that assured her John was alive. The next day they flew by Allegheny Airlines to Phillipsburg, Pennsylvania, where Elaine's family met them and took them on to Clearfield where John recuperated.

When John became well enough to walk around, Judy, now five, badgered him to play hide-and-seek. After John would hide, she would stop, listen, and say, "I hear you ticking, Daddy. You can't hide from me." The ticking sound could be heard clearly across a large sized room.

In December they went to John's parents in Midland Park. John had become an uncle again. Sister Jean's Mark had been born two days before John left the Georgetown Hospital.

Everyone in the church wanted to listen to and learn about his ticking heart. The elders of the church were more curious than the youngsters. Jake Vandermeer, Elmer Van Dyke, and many of his old acquaintances were there, but Coffee Pot Jake had passed on to his reward. "How I'd like to have a cup of coffee with him," John wished, "but that will have to wait until I get to heaven."

John and Elaine exclaimed about the missionary budget of the church that had tripled in recent years. Several of the church members replied, "You're the ones who made us realize just how important missionary work is."

The older members who remembered John as a tow-headed, mischievous boy seemed to take special pride in their missionary. One was heard to remark about a certain troublesome boy in the church, "We must be patient with him. Who knows but that he might grow up to be another John Beekman?"

On New Year's Day, a Sunday, Jean and Pete presented little Mark for christening. Pastor Van Ostenburg requested John to give a brief charge to the parents.

The church grew deathly quiet as John walked toward the front. Suddenly as he began climbing the steps to the raised platform, the ticking seemed to stop. Shock swept through the congregation. Some expected to see him collapse because they thought his heart had stopped. John reached the pulpit and stood still for a few seconds to catch his breath. Then the ticking became audible again and the congregation sighed with relief.

One week later, five young evangelical missionaries met their baptism of death in the rain forests of Ecuador. John and Elaine were with his parents when the shocking news came of the Auca massacre. His mother gasped, "John, how terrible!" John's heart did not skip a tick as he said, "God knows what He's doing. I think it would be a great privilege to die for Christ."

A "thanks" letter went to churches and friends who had contributed almost $3,000 to pay the hospital and doctor bills. "I feel like shouting Psalm 103:1, 4," John wrote. *"Bless the Lord, O my soul: and all that is within me, bless his holy name. Who redeemeth thy life from destruction; who crowneth thee with loving kindness and tender mercies."*

On February 22, John pointed the Plymouth southwest for the long trip back. The first day out, Elaine read a devotional reading from Psalm 32:8, *"I will instruct thee and teach thee in the way which thou shall go: I will guide thee with mine eye."*

When they stopped at the border early in March, John was unable to help unload crates and suitcases for inspection. The sound of the ticking heart and an explanation from John to the curious border inspectors prompted the chief official to hand him a newspaper and say, "Sit down and relax. We'll do all the work."

A thin tire gave no trouble until they were three blocks from the Kettle when John felt it deflating. He slowed, opened the door, and leaned around to see his fears confirmed. Suddenly Judy chirped, "Don't worry, Daddy. It won't go clear flat until we get there, 'cause I prayed to Jesus."

They reached The Kettle with air to spare, and as they were getting out, a husky Mexican stepped up and offered to fix the tire.

John's heart immediately became the talk of The Kettle. The translators held a prayer and praise service to celebrate his safe return.

Hugh Steven, a tall blond Canadian, and his wife Norma were new Wycliffe members. They were not at The Kettle when John arrived and saw him first at a formal dinner when they sat near him. When Norma became aware of the ticking sound, she punched Hugh. "Listen, that man has an alarm clock in his pocket."

A few evenings later John spoke to the Wycliffe group. When he took a deep breath the ticking could not be heard. A veteran translator, who had experienced his share of rugged living, was sitting near the back. When he thought the ticking had stopped, he fainted and had to be carried out. "When I close my mouth, inhale, or swallow," John explained, "you can't hear the ticking. But that doesn't mean I'm about to die."

John presented himself to Dr. Sodi-Pallares for an examination. The Mexican doctor was delighted with the results and noted there was less tension in the heart beat. John immediately asked, "Can I stand a trip to Chiapas? I'm anxious to get back."

The doctor shrugged and laughed. "You, Mr. Beekman, are impossible, but I don't see why not if you fly all the way. No trail hiking, though."

"I want to look over the site where the Chol Bible school and our new home will be located," John told John McIntosh, who had succeeded George Cowan as director of the Mexican branch. "And the Chols will be glad to know about my heart."

The director okayed the trip. John rented a small apartment for Elaine and Judy. Elaine drove him to the Mexico City airport and saw him off on the Mexicana flight for Tuxtla. Hatch picked him up there and flew him into Amado Nervo.

The first Chols to reach the landing strip saw him and leaped for delight, shouting, "Brother Kwan is alive! He is back!"

Within minutes the excited Chols had surrounded him, all babbling about the ticking sound and wanting to know about the operation.

Suddenly the thin high whistle that marked the announcement of church services split the air. "It isn't time for services," John said.

"Yes, it is," Nicholas Arcos declared. "Come and gather with us to praise God for what He has done. We also have some questions to ask you about some hard sayings in God's Word."

John climbed the hill to the church with measured steps, the crowd of welcomers streaming behind him. Once inside, they sang and prayed with such fervor that John would not have been surprised to see the grass roof rise into the air. At times he could hear a dozen Chols praying and thanking God simultaneously for the success of the operation.

When the long service finally ended, John asked to be excused to make up a bed in his house. "Not yet, Brother Kwan," Domingo exclaimed. "We want to see where the doctor put the tick-tock in your body."

So John sat on a large rock and bared his back to show the red semicircle that marked the incision around his rib cage. First the women filed by to take shy glances. Then came the men, the first ones just looking, then one touched the mark and ran his finger to the end. Those behind followed suit, making the examination, as John recalled later, "a ticklish experience."

14. *Onward Christian Soldiers*

JOHN SKY-HOPPED out of Amado Nervo and joined Al DeVoogd, a new Reformed Church missionary assigned to the Chols, at a landing strip beside the Tulija River. They inspected a site for the Beekmans' new home and the proposed Chol Bible school and clinic. Realizing that he could no longer walk or ride the rugged trails in village evangelism, John wanted to make his life count for the maximum during his predicted short life expectancy. He reasoned that he could contribute the most by teaching the Chol New Testament to preacher boys who would come from all over Chol country and adapting the translation to a new Chol dialect that had just been surveyed. The school and clinic he envisioned would be owned and directed by the Reformed Church mission. He and Elaine would serve, as Kemp had already proposed, as cooperating missionaries.

Amado Nervo was a delightful spot, but neither centrally located nor easily accessible because of the deep gorge in front and the steep mountain behind. The "Nerve Bowl" strip was tricky for landings even in good weather. It was, as Hatch said, "like driving into a garage at 60 miles per hour."

John wanted the new site to be near a better strip on which small cargo planes could land if necessary. He desired level ground so the foundations of buildings would not be washed out by heavy rains, and the ground needed to be fertile enough for demonstration crops to grow.

While he had been away, the great land rush had started. The first man to defy the ranchers' threats and organize a colony of homesteaders had been a believer. After his party had gotten land, other Chols began trekking to the land office.

John and Al agreed that having land of their own would not boost the Chol economy enough. They needed know-how and seed and equipment to plant new crops. "No one knows how many centuries these Indians have depended upon corn," John told Al. "Poor nutrition is a major cause of poor health. They must develop sources for a broader diet. What better way to start an agricultural revolution than to train the lay preachers in both the Seed of the Word and the seed of the soil?"

The new site was only 500 yards upstream from the landing strip. Twenty-four acres of fertile and mostly level land banked on the river and extended back into a timbered area. They named it Berea, in honor of the Asia Minor church which the Apostle Paul had commended for searching the Scriptures daily.[1]

"This is lower than Amado Nervo and much warmer," Al said. "Do you think you can take the heat?"

John smiled. "Yes. It will be easier for me here than on the side of the mountain in Amado Nervo."

The two men walked around a bit. John stood near the river and looked back toward the beginning of a forested slope. He visioned the future buildings: a dormitory, a dining house, a class room building, a clinic, missionary houses, and yes, a shed for sheltering agricultural implements — perhaps even a tractor. He saw young Chols crouched behind desks, studying the Chol New Testament, preparing sermons to preach the next weekend in outlying villages. He saw a bedlam of chickens, turkeys, pigs, calves and other animals — a means of building a stable diet for the Chols. He saw young Chols assisting in the clinic, learning how to minister to the sick in the villages where no doctor ever visited.

"When the Word of God takes root in a people," he told Al, "improved health and living conditions follow. We've seen evidence of this in Amado Nervo. The first man there to wear shoes was a believer. So was the first man to own a mule. And land — the first man to defy the ranchers and apply for land from the government was a believer. Believers leading the way, that's how it should be."

John itched to see the new house started, but first timber had to be cut, lumber sawed, and aluminum and other materials brought in. Building could not be expected to commence until after the rainy season. He had to be patient and wait.

After the deaths of the five missionaries in Ecuador the year before, John had asked himself, *They were healthy, strong, and in*

1Acts 17:10, 11.

*the prime of life. Why did God let them die and leave someone like
me with a frail body?* Then and there he had resolved: *"I must use
my remaining time wisely. Step by careful step I must finish the
tasks yet to be done."*

John returned again to Mexico City. He and Elaine worked ten
to twelve hours each day in May correcting printing mistakes in the
Chol New Testament. Then, after the type was set, they read proofs
until their eyes were sore. No chance for error could be granted.
The change of a single letter in a word could change the meaning of
an entire sentence. They gave the marked-up galley proofs to the
printer who, to their disappointment, did nothing further for several
months.

Chilling news came of severe persecution in the Tzeltal village
where Chol preacher boys had evangelized at risk of their lives. The
Tzeltal believers had first been told by the pagans, "Kwan Beekman
and the foreigners are going to kill you and put you up as canned
meat." When this and other lies had not affected their faith, the
unbelievers attacked the Christians, chasing them from their homes
and killing one.

John and Elaine read and marveled at a dispatch from Bernabel
Lopez, one of the Chol evangelists among the Tzeltals.

*"They beat their drums, and then shot at us. The bullets landed
beside Pasqual's house. He is a real believer and has a phonograph
machine and records. He says he is never going to leave the Word
. . . . Once our path was blocked and a man said he was going to
shoot us in the navels. He put ten pellets into the barrel of his gun,
and fresh powder, but nothing happened when·he pulled the trigger.
He said if I came back he would use shells. It will be seen whether
these will fire for him. God is powerful. He takes care of us as we
preach His Word."*

John's ticking heart speeded up from excitement when he heard
that hundreds of Bachajon Tzeltals had turned from paganism to
Christ on the borders of Chol country where Marianna Slocum and
Florence Gerdel would later go to translate this dialect of the
Tzeltals. "Praise God," he exclaimed to a colleague. "He is really
honoring His Word and the courage of His people."

He thought of Bill Bentley who had dreamed of serving the
Tzeltals before his fatal heart attack. "Bill must be rejoicing with
the angels over the Tzeltals," he said to Elaine. "And he must be
very proud of Marianna."

A hopeful break appeared in the struggle to get the Chol believers released from the Tuxtla prison. A high United Nations official and a cross-section of important Mexicans endorsed a petition asking the governor of Chiapas, who was scheduled soon to visit Mexico City, to pardon the Chols. A friendly state representative from Chiapas volunteered to present the petition to the governor upon his arrival.

The governor arrived, met with political cronies, and departed. Nothing was said about the petition. Too late, the petitioners learned that the representative had deceived them and held back the petition to spare the governor political embarrassment.

Those working for the release of the prisoners were bitterly disappointed. "We are not giving up," a Mexican spokesman vowed. "We will try to get a conference with the president."

In September John McIntosh called John into his office. "John, you made a major contribution to the Chol New Testament. Your colleagues speak very highly of you."

John broke in. "I hope it will be printed soon."

"I hope so, too," Mr. McIntosh said. "Unfortunately, the commercial printer used by the Bible Society has a lot of work stacked up. We'll have to be patient. But that isn't what I wanted to talk to you about."

The Director continued. "Roy and Margaret Harrison have finished the first draft of their Zoque New Testament. You know about their good work in Chiapas."

John nodded. The Harrisons had been working tirelessly for many years on this dialect.

"Like all others, it needs checking before the Bible Society will approve the cost of publication. Usually Gene Nida or someone from the Bible Society wants to check the copy and approve it. Perhaps the process might be speeded up if one of us who had been over the road before could help the translators. To come to the point, John, I'd like for you to volunteer your talents."

John folded his arms and leaned back in his chair. Only the steady tick-tock of his heart valve could be heard in the quiet office. "Well, John," he finally said, "you're the Director, but you know how anxious we are to get back to the Chols and work with the Bible school."

"I know that," the Director said understandingly, "but a few weeks with the Zoque translators here at headquarters might mean a great deal."

"Okay," John said. "I'll work with them and make any suggestions that come to mind."

"We're not here for the purpose of producing a masterpiece of translation," John told the Harrisons, "but only to make God's Word intelligible to the native readers and faithful to the original text. We'll work toward that."

They checked lexicons, grammars, dictionaries, the Greek text, and various English translations, to arrive at the meaning of difficult passages. Then they worked to put the passage into a form understandable to the native speaker who sat with them. They gave special attention to such key theological words as sin, love, grace, salvation, etc.

As had been true in checking the Chol Testament, they found numerous corrections necessary.

For example, ". . . in the shadow of death" (Luke 1:78) translated literally in Zoque meant that death cast a shadow under which the deceased could rest and keep out the heat of hell. They decided to use the simple statement, "death is near."

The Zoque translators had rendered "mystery" in I Corinthians 2:7 as "hidden." Investigation showed that "hidden" in Zoque referred to a dog hiding a bone from other dogs, or a person hiding a stolen object to keep his guilt from becoming known. The clause implied selfishness, stealthiness, and guilt, none of which they wanted to apply to God. They used a word which meant "not revealed in first times."

All the corrections were listed, catalogued, and reduced to a number of general principles which the Zoque translators and workers in other languages could use. John jotted down several meanings to share with Elaine and use in devotional messages.

Joy in Zoque was "heart sit down" and John noted, "True joy is yours if your heart keeps sitting down in the midst of the problems and activities of the day."

Disobedience was "a shrunken heart." Pride for the short Zoque people was "walking on tiptoe."

While John was working on the Zoque translation, Arabelle Whittaker and Viola Warkentin wrote from Chol country where they were conducting literacy schools in preparation for the publication of the New Testament, "Remember, John, the man in La Lucha who threatened to kill you when you explained the way of salvation? Well, he is now a believer and a regular attender in church services."

The heart valve ticked merrily along. Indeed, he had never felt better when he finished checking the Zoque manuscript. He yearned to get back to Chiapas.

John McIntosh eased his restlessness by assigning another checking job. This time it was the Popoluca language spoken in the torrid coastal state of Vera Cruz.

Finally in December he became free to go to Chiapas. A carpenter, hired in the capital, and Ron Manus, a Christian university student, accompanied him. They left on Christmas Day, 1956. Elaine remained behind with Judy to insure the safety of the new baby due in February. Both she and John were concerned about a report that showed the RH negative antibodies increasing in her blood again.

Thirty-eight volunteer Chol laborers greeted them at the home site. The Chols had already carried hundreds of rocks and all the gravel needed for the foundation. By Saturday they had the foundation walls up. Within a month they had completed the superstructure of the house. Ron became permanently interested in Bible translation, and later took linguistic training. He now serves with his wife, Phyllis, under Wycliffe in Peru.

Hatch dropped by and flew John to Amado Nervo. His old neighbors gave him a hearty welcome and ushered him into his house which they had cleaned in advance. The women insisted on preparing all the meals and washing the dishes. No one would let him do anything except speak in the church and answer questions on the Scriptures.

Before returning to Mexico City, John visited the Chol believers in the Tuxtla prison. The friendly guards permitted him to hold a service for all the prisoners. Afterward, the head guard said, "The General wants to see you."

John's heart picked up speed, betraying his anxiety, as he entered a well-furnished cell. The General closed the door and directed him to a chair. "Now," he said, "would you tell me how to become a believer?"

The General, John learned, had been reading a Gideon Bible in Spanish. John turned to Acts 16 and read the account of the Philippian jailer's conversion. Then he prayed and invited the General to receive Christ. "I am not quite ready," the distinguished man replied. "I want to think more about what you have said."

Later John learned that the General was a political prisoner, not a prison official. He subsequently became an evangelical and actively witnessed for Christ.

Thomas Wesley Beekman, seven and one-half pounds, was born February 8. The anticipated change of blood became unnecessary when tests showed that the baby's blood was RH negative — the same type as Elaine's. Judy had hoped for a little sister. "A boy is okay, I guess," she chirped, "so long as he isn't mean to me."

The remainder of 1957 moved swiftly along for the four Beekmans. John continued to divide his time between Chiapas and Mexico City.

With his reputation established as a translation consultant, he was given checking assignments in four more languages. The basic problem he found with each translation was a failure to follow the lexical structure of the native language.

One translator had rendered Mark 3:26, "If Satan has risen (gets out of bed in the morning) at himself and is divided (as an orange is cut in half) he is not able to endure but is coming to an end."

It was not easy for some translators to depart from literal translation. They, like John, had been schooled to believe in the verbal (word-for-word) plenary (full, complete) inspiration of the Scriptures. John patiently pointed out that "when we go to translate into another language we find that theologians have already made a valid distinction between the linguistic form and the meaning of Scripture. They say, and we agree, that both the linguistic *form* and *meaning* of Scripture are inspired in the original. The Holy Spirit used the linguistic forms of the Hebrew and Greek languages as He found them. To communicate Scripture in another language we must use the linguistic form as we find it. Only in this way can we be faithful to the meaning of Scripture."

He suggested, "There is no standard system by which the same set of meanings is assigned to words by the different peoples of the world. Each has its own inventory of words with meanings and usages which are both similar and distinct from all others.

"Imagine a foreigner hearing one of us say that, 'I dressed a chicken,' or 'a gun went off,' or 'I stepped on the gas.' These are figures of speech peculiar to North Americans who speak English. There are many figures in the New Testament that readily show the necessity of adjusting the linguistic form in the translation process: John 8:52, 'taste death,' Acts 17:20, 'bring strange things to our ears,' and Romans 3:14, 'whose mouth is full of cursing and bitterness.'

"Think of the linguistic structure of a language as a 'conveyor' or 'vehicle' carrying meaning," he told the translators. "Let a highway be one language and a waterway another. To carry a passenger (the message) by highway one will need a car; to carry the same passenger by water to the same place, one will need a boat. To carry or convey the same message in two different languages one will use two different linguistic structures. Now, just as one wouldn't attempt to transfer parts of the car to the boat when changing vehicles, so one wouldn't try to transfer the linguistic structure of the original when translating into the receptor language. The language into which one puts his translation is merely the vehicle to get the message through to the people. If the meaning does not get through, it is because the translator doesn't know how to manage the vehicle. He is not well enough acquainted with its structure. Perhaps he is trying to run a boat as though it were a car."

Once the translators knew that they were not betraying the evangelical view of inspiration, they began, as John said, "to translate in the form which the receptor people spoke." Before understanding and accepting this view, one worker almost despaired of producing a translation that would communicate the gospel message. John patiently explained each problem, set down principles for him to follow, and advised that he re-work it carefully with a language helper from his tribe. His revision was remarkable and needed no more than two changes on an average per chapter.

As an indication of how highly they regarded the "man with the tick-tock heart," John's colleagues in Mexico — over 150 in 1957 — elected him their representative to Wycliffe's world-wide biennial conference. He was also named to the Executive Committee of the Mexican branch.

Not until the first month of the new year did the family move to the Bible school site at Berea. Elaine had already started teaching Judy, now eight, with the Calvert system. Their new "tin" house with aluminum walls and roof was not quite finished so they moved into the two-room clinic building, and Hatch flew in their household goods from Amado Nervo.

John's pride and joy was a new outboard motor and fiberglass boat which he planned to use in visiting twenty-two villages along the banks of the river. "It'll beat trail hiking," he told Elaine, and added, "which my heart won't allow anyhow."

Almost immediately Indians began arriving for medicine, though the nearest village was two trail hours away.

To the twenty men and boys who arrived on Sunday morning, John said, "Stay and hear the story of Jesus." All stayed.

Now that the Chol New Testament had gone to the printer, and the Bible school was being readied for the first students, John and the Reformed Church missionaries began giving further attention to the organization of the Chol churches.

Both John and Kemp hoped the Chol congregations could continue to operate within the fellowship and control of the Chiapas presbytery, but the big question was: How much control should the Spanish-speaking pastors and elders exert over the Indians?

"The Apostle Paul," John noted to Kemp, "let his churches learn through their mistakes rather than keep the control so tight as to prevent mistakes. We are tempted toward the latter, which usually results in a struggling church rather than the development of a responsible Christianity."

Both men agreed that there were two distinct cultures in Chiapas — Indian and Spanish. "I think this will continue," John declared. "The Spaniards came here 450 years ago and imposed their political and religious bureaucracy upon the Indians, but the Indians have stayed within the pre-Conquest pattern. Most of the population is still Indian.

"I know," John continued, "that some say the Indians will change their ways and merge into the *ladino* culture within a decade. I doubt this. Some Indians will continue to move into the national culture. Modern medicine will reduce the death rate and it seems likely that the distinctive Indian societies will grow faster than they lose adherents. There are 40,000 Chols in Chiapas now, more than when I came ten years ago."

Kemp nodded in agreement. "I think you understand the situation better than most of us. You've lived with the Indians and speak their language. My work has been mainly with the Spanish-speaking people."

John smiled in admiration of the older missionary. "You've done a great work, Kemp. You've built some strong bridges between Indians and Spanish speakers here in Chiapas. Now with the Chol and Tzeltal churches growing rapidly, you can make the bridges stronger, and still the churches will develop within their own cultures without too much outside interference."

The two men talked on, sharing views, and agreeing on basic principles they felt essential to growth and fellowship among the *ladino* and Indian cultures.

They decided it would be unwise to have rulings handed down to Indians from a Mexican-dominated presbytery or Spanish speaking pastor who would neither understand nor appreciate the Indian way of thinking and doing things. They recognized that the love of Christ had not completely broken through the prejudice which the evangelical *ladinos* held toward the Indians.

They concluded that the Indians should have their own governing body consisting of representatives from their own churches. Disciplinary matters and other needs could be settled by the Indians themselves in their own language. The top Indian leaders from all the Chol congregations would meet periodically to discuss mutual problems in Coordination Institutes. This, John and Kemp believed, would keep the churches indigenous. Both the ordained Chol and *ladino* pastors would be members of the Chiapas presbytery, thus providing opportunities to better understand their cultural differences. This, John felt, would permit the Chols full citizenship within the church body.

As the spring of '57 came on and the house was finished, John and Elaine looked forward to the actual opening of the Bible school scheduled for that fall. They were both surprised and disappointed when the Wycliffe Board requested John to become the interim director of Wycliffe's translation force in Guatemala.

When John protested that he did not want to leave the Chols, Cameron Townsend said, "Guatemala City and Chiapas are close enough for you to handle both jobs. Anyway, you'll only be needed in Guatemala until we can appoint a permanent director."

Elaine was aghast at the idea of two jobs. "Think of your heart. You'll be working harder instead of less, as you're supposed to."

"The question, Sweetheart," he reminded her gently, "is not whether my heart will stand it or not, but whether God wants me to. Wasn't it Hudson Taylor who said, 'God's work done in God's way will never lack His supply'?"

"You, you," Elaine replied in mock anger. "You always have a good answer."

A few evenings later, they held hands and walked beside the smooth flowing river. Elaine tugged at John's hand and they stopped beneath a spreading oak. "When we were married," she said softly,

"I promised to love, comfort and assist you in the Lord's work. I love the Chol work and have looked forward to living in this new house. But if you're also needed in Guatemala, then I'll love, comfort, and assist you there."

John bent and kissed her. "No one could ask for a better assistant," he said. "No one."

Pictures taken by the author on his trip into Amado Nervo, ten years after the Beekmans left. *Upper left:* Wycliffe Translator Viola Warkentin (see next page), steps out of the plane to greet a crowd of Chol women. All wanted news about Brother Kwan and Sister Elena. "How's his heart?" was on every tongue. *Lower left:* Amado Nervo boys examine the plane. *Upper right:* An unbeliever from over the mountain was passing by and wanted news about John's heart. *Lower right:* The Amado Nervo lay pastor behind his "pulpit."

The Beekmans have departed, but missionary work continues among the Chols. Wycliffe Translators Viola Warkentin and Ruby Scott (also affiliated with Conservative Baptists) are adapting the Tumbala Chol New Testament into the Chol Tila dialect. They also teach school in the flatland village of Chivalito. *Upper left:* School boys cut grass before class. They bring their own machetes. *Lower left:* Class in session. *Upper right:* Ruby helps boy with homework. *Lower right:* Boy looks at picture book in viewing gallery of missionary home.

John Beekman's dream come true is the Chol Bible School at Berea where Henry and Charmagne Stegenga now serve as representatives of the Reformed Church of America. Students from the Berea School serve some 9,000 Chol evangelicals. *Upper left:* The administration building. *Lower left:* Working a math problem. Young Chol men are trained to be community leaders as well as pastors. *Upper right:* Student prepares for next day's lessons. Beside his left arm (on viewer's right) is the Chol New Testament. *Lower right:* Pole bed in the bunkhouse.

Reformed Church missionaries are introducing new food sources to bring nutritional variety to Chol diet. *Upper left:* Henry Stegenga points to a demonstration rice crop. Close by are plots of watermelons, honeydews, and cantalopes — all new to Chol country. *Upper right:* Stegenga holds a goat, flown to Berea. *Lower left:* The "tin house" which John Beekman had built and where the Stegengas now live. *Lower right:* The Stegengas prepare to board an M.A.F. plane for a trip to the dentist and mission meeting in the market town of Las Casas.

15. *New Frontiers*

A FEW DAYS LATER, after John told the Board he would go to Guatemala, he felt a tightening in his chest accompanied by severe pains. Gasping for breath, he collapsed into a chair. Elaine paled.

"I'll be all right," John stammered, trying to assure her. "Just, just let me rest a few minutes." After an anxious (for Elaine) hour, John felt like walking and went back to his desk work. Nevertheless, she insisted he consult Dr. Sodi-Pallares when they returned to Mexico City to make final preparations for the trip to Guatemala.

"There's apparently no damage," the doctor reported. "The artificial valve has not completely solved the problem. There's still a good bit of blood regurgitating back into the ventricle. Better pace yourself."

On May 21, 1958, John, Elaine and the children flew to Guatemala City. John had already arranged to have the car driven down from Tuxtla. The tiny country that snuggled up to Mexico on the north and El Salvador and Honduras on the south was then tense from fear of a revolution. Terrorist attacks and exploding bombs had become a part of daily life in the capital.

They moved into a quaint little Spanish-style house in which each room opened to a large outdoor patio. It was provisional headquarters for Wycliffe members (eight couples and six single girls) who served tribes in Guatemala.

The many facets of directing a Branch challenged John. As head of the Guatemalan translation family, he was administrator, coordinator, and technical and spiritual advisor. Also, he had to keep the wires up to key government people whose support was vital in advancing the translation effort.

John and Elaine spent much of June becoming acquainted with

their colleagues and getting oriented into the work. They also worked to improve their Spanish because of expected contacts with government officials. After Cameron Townsend's initial success with the highland Cakchiquels, Wycliffe had lagged in the Central American countries in favor of more populous Mexico. Then in 1951, twenty years after Townsend left the Cakchiquels, Harry and Lucille McArthur began translation work among the Aguacateco Indians. When the Beekmans arrived, teams were busy in nine tribes and hopes were set on entering eight more.

One of John's first conferences was with David Fox, translator to the Quiche Indians, a Mayan tribe. Dave brought the Gospel of Luke for checking. Talks with Dave and other translators convinced John that Guatemalan tribes believed and practiced the Christopagan religiosity that was so obvious among the Chols. Like the Chols, these Mayan tribes had absorbed Catholic concepts and Biblical names into their wells of pagan tradition.

For example, he discovered these ideas among the Ixil Indians where Ray and Helen Elliott had been working since 1952:

• God is a crochety old man who can't control his world any more, so he sent his strong young son to keep order and prevent skullduggery.

• Jesus Christ is the Son, but the Son is also "Our Father." This son used some very effective tricks to keep things under control. One day Jesus was captured by some Jews who tied him up in a corner and sat down to celebrate with a pot of chicken stew. Jesus blessed the chicken, and it jumped in the pot splashing chile into the eyes of the Jews. While they were wiping their eyes, Jesus escaped.

• The Apostles are the twelve men who hung Jesus on the cross.

• Of the two thieves who were hung on crosses beside Jesus, one was a liar and thus very bad. He could not be forgiven. The other was not a liar, but had merely killed another man. Jesus could pardon him.

• The custom of burning incense began when God's sister had trouble in childbirth. Because smoke from burning incense relieved her, its power has been recognized since that time.

Always the pioneer, John moved to start work in new languages. After a new tribe was discovered (usually by translators working in a neighboring tribe), the first step was to secure permission from government authorities for a language survey to see if a translation was needed.

After hearing about the Jicaques of Honduras, John flew to the capital, Tegucigalpa, for talks with officials. They gave permission for a survey and translators Clarence Church and Dave Oltrogge visited the area.

They found the Jicaques living several large families to a long-house and quite unfriendly to outsiders. Nevertheless, several men who claimed to speak "some" Spanish submitted to tape recorded interviews. The procedure was for the surveyors to speak in Spanish with the Indians replying in their own language. The object was to see how well they understood Spanish.

A typical interview began with a story: "A man's house burned down, destroying all of his seed corn. He started to town with money to buy some more seed. When he got to the store, he discovered he had lost the money on the trail. Feeling very sad, he went to a friend and asked, 'Will you share some of the seed you have stored?' The friend said, 'Yes, I will.' So even though the man's house had burned and he had lost his money, he still had a corn crop that year."

Having told the story, the interviewer then asked the tribesmen: "Please tell that story back to me in your language."

The tape-recorded response of the Indians to this and other questions were painstakingly checked by informants who could translate the answers back into Spanish. A report was prepared that showed the Jicaques almost totally lacked comprehension of Spanish. With this evidence before them, government officials readily invited Wycliffe to send in translators.

Back in Guatemala City John and Elaine were eagerly reading a report from an evangelical lawyer in Chiapas. Two of the Chol prisoners had been paroled from the Tuxtla prison and the other was expected to be released shortly.

Both felt very thankful. "It's been a long fight," John said, "but think of the victories. At least twenty prisoners have come to the Lord through the witness of the men. The injustice has given opportunities for us to tell the Gospel message to officials and intellectuals in Tuxtla and even in Mexico City."

Other news from Tuxtla was not so encouraging. After returning from furlough in June, Wilbur Aulie had come down with both malaria and typhoid and was being treated in the Tuxtla hospital.

John impatiently slapped his hands together. "Oh, if I could only be two men and one of me be in Chol country now. No, if

I could be two thousand and one of me go to every needy tribe in the world."

Elaine sensed his restlessness. "We'll be going back in December; try to be patient. Now, how about some tea for the one man who is in Guatemala?"

Pursuant with plans for a four-month absence from Guatemala — divided between Chol country and a translators' workshop scheduled for Mitla — John trained Clarence Church to serve as acting director. This done, the Beekman entourage drove north on the newly opened branch of the Pan-American highway. Two very dusty days later they pulled into Tuxtla.

Christmas in Berea was a gala affair. The Al DeVoogds and about twenty Chol visitors joined the Beekmans for a Christmas Eve carol sing in Chol, Spanish, and English. For Christmas dinner, they enjoyed a "love feast" of chicken tacos, beans, rice, coffee, Koolaid, ice cream and cookies. As Elaine poured the coffee, she said, "Isn't it thrilling to know that 5,000 Chol believers are having 'love feasts' in their churches today?" John said, "Amen," and added, "Don't be so thrilled that you spill that hot coffee on us."

Early in January the Coordination Institute for Chol elders convened in Berea. John joyfully greeted each of the forty men who came and patiently answered the recurring question: "How's your heart, Brother Kwan?"

Many of the elders were newly-elected by their congregations. John recognized several as former drunkards, thieves, and wife beaters before being transformed by the Gospel.

The elders brought minutes of past consistory[1] meetings. As John paged through them, he swelled in pride at the wisdom shown in their disciplines. The records confirmed the conclusion he and John Kempers had reached that the Chols could best govern themselves.

A typical action involved a Chol boy named Pedro who had stolen. The elders heard his confession and decided he should be placed on six months' probation. They informed him that during the probation he must sit in the rear of the church, and refrain from participating in public worship — singing, praying, and giving offerings. Pedro submitted to the punishment. Six months later, he walked a half-day over the trail to a church which had elders and

[1]Consistory is the lowest court in the Reformed and Presbyterian Church tradition. Its members include elders elected by local congregations and pastors.

reported completion of the punishment. The secretary of the consistory wrote, "Pedro has fulfilled the requirements of the probationary period, therefore, we have forgiven him, as it is recorded in II Corinthians 2:10 and other places in God's Word. Now he may again be looked on as a brother in our Lord Jesus in the fullest sense."

During the "Coordination Institute" at Berea, the elders asked questions of one another and attempted to reach common agreements on what elders should do and what disciplines should be imposed for specific law breakers. One group explained how they visited the sick in systematic fashion. Another group explained how they gave free will offerings to bereaved members. A third group told about receiving corn tithes to provide for needy families.

Some of their conclusions were applicable to the whole Chol church: A brother who had more than one wife at the time of his conversion should be asked to support both wives, but cohabit with only one; a man with one wife should be warned not to take another; elders should go in groups of two or more to visit the sick (to avoid immoral implications); any elder who could not teach his children the ways of the Lord should be removed from office.

After three days of deliberations, the Coordination Institute concluded and the Chol elders left by trail for their villages. John took off with Hatch for Lacandon country where he had a date to check the Gospel of Mark with translator Phil Baer. Elaine and the children stayed on at Berea.

As the yellow Cessna edged over a green mountain, Hatch pointed to a bluff. "Fellow crashed over there last week. His old bus couldn't get over the top."

"Too bad," John said over the roar of the engine.

"Yes, it is. These bush pilots are so reckless. They take chances I wouldn't take in a million years. Fly old crates in all kinds of weather. Load them to the gills with passengers and cargo, then start dumping stuff when the plane balks at flying over a steep mountain. All I know to do is trust the Lord and take all possible precautions."

"That's what Elaine says I should do. But Hatch, having a bad heart isn't like flying with a bad engine. You can trade the engine in for a new one. With a bad heart you've just got to keep going on the old one."

A few minutes later Hatch dipped down to the narrow strip

sliced between two banks of trees. Phil Baer and his attractive blue-eyed wife, Mary, were waiting with a thermos of hot coffee.

Phil, a rangy, dark-haired Jewish-Christian, and Mary had been living among the Lacandons, a Mayan tribe, since 1940. They had learned the language and completed the gospel of Mark for those whom anthropologists called the most primitive tribe of Mexico.

John got his first glimpse of a Lacondon religious ceremony later that day. He was touched deeply while watching the Indians pray earnestly before their clay god pots.

About a dozen of the god pots rested on palm leaves underneath a thatched-roofed shelter that came without walls. The Indian making the sacrifice spread pitch on top of the gods and set it afire. The pitch slowly melted and ran down the sides of the bowl-like faces until the sacred objects were enveloped in yellow flames. Then the worshiper began weaving back and forth behind the flames, waving sacred palm leaves in the smoke and chanting in a weird, high-pitched monotone.

"It gets to you, doesn't it?" Phil said quietly.

"Yes," John agreed, "when you think that they've been worshiping this way for no telling how many centuries."

The two men began walking toward the Baers' house. "Well, Professor," Phil drawled, "I'm anxious to see if you can live up to your reputation."

John laughed. "I don't know what my reputation is, but I'm ready."

After a week's hard work with Phil, John left via M.A.F. for The City of the Dead in Oaxaca. Elaine remained in Berea.

Ten translators — each with a native language informant, two translation consultants in training, and John (the director) began work in February. In his first lecture John said, "This is a dream come true. We have before us two months of uninterrupted work and fellowship — no sick calls, no teeth to pull, no witch doctors to endure, no corn grinders to fix, no shotguns to repair. Think what William Carey would have given for this privilege."

The four-fold program which John introduced at Mitla set the pattern for future workshops: seminars on translation principles and methods; consultations with individual translators about their particular problems; actual translation under the supervision of a consultant; training of new translation consultants.

John carefully pointed out the problems and challenges of translation. "The Greek text of the New Testament is full of metaphors, similes, synecdoches, litotes, ellipses, and other items that pose problems for translators. First century Greek speakers understood these, just as we understand expressions like 'get on the ball,' 'pain in the neck,' and 'slow as molasses.' Every tribal language has idioms and expressions which only the native speakers uniquely understand.

"Let's look at ellipses in the New Testament. These are omissions which were implicitly understood by the Greek reader. About half were filled in by the King James translators and appear in italics. There are hundreds of examples. Look at just one verse, Romans 8:18, 'For I reckon that the sufferings of this present time *are* not worthy *to be compared* with the glory which shall be revealed in us.' 'Are' and 'to be compared' are only *implied* in the Greek text and had to be supplied by the English translators. We translators for Mexico's Indian languages must also fill in these ellipses if our translations are to be meaningful to the people whom we serve."

John paused and waited for questions while his heart ticked in perfect rhythm. Sometimes he asked specific translators to give examples in their languages. Often he gave illustrations from Chol and other languages on which he had worked.

The workshop moved on and the translators waded deeper into the maze of translation problems. They noted that abstract nouns of European languages (beauty, love, redemption, etc.) often had to be put in a verbal form for Indian languages. "God is love" sometimes came out "God is One who loves," or even, "God loves people." English grammatical patterns had to be adapted to new forms: "He told her" to "he spoke, she heard"; "He saw him yesterday at sundown" to "when set the sun saw he him yesterday."

John and a consultant-in-training worked long hours with each translator. The trainee watched as John checked to see that figures of speech, style, and grammar did not slavishly follow English, Spanish, or Greek patterns. He also learned to watch the Indian helper as he read passages in the tribal tongue. Hesitation or stumbling by the Indian, John pointed out, might indicate an awkward or an obscure translation.

Two weeks before the scheduled end of the Workshop the participants took a break for a short Easter vacation. John flew to Berea on the afternoon of March 25 to give Elaine a happy birthday kiss and share cake with the family.

After Easter, the Beekman family went to Mitla together for the conclusion of the workshop. Tommy unexpectedly came down with typhoid and cried all night long for two nights in a row. Just when antibiotics were beginning to calm him, his crib began creaking, and the heavy beams over their heads began shaking. The family awoke and carried the children outside. However, the earth tremors lasted only a few seconds. "I'll drag the mattress into the patio and we'll sleep outside," John said. "There might be more."

The Workshop closed on April 14, and the translators scattered to their tribes. The Beekmans drove to Mexico City to get U. S. passports for their children. Diplomatic relations had just been severed between Mexico and Guatemala, and Mexican passports would not get them across the border.[2]

Before they left the Mexican capital, the new Mexican Branch director, Dr. Ben Elson, announced plans for a second Translator's Workshop the following spring. In asking John to again direct the Workshop, he said, "We had planned to wait two years, but the reports from the last one were so good that there are people who want to attend sooner."

They got back to Guatemala City in time for the Inter-American Indian Congress. Wycliffe's general director, Cameron Townsend, flew in from Peru for the meeting of social scientists, political leaders, missionaries and others concerned for improving the lot of Indians in the Americas.

This was John's first opportunity to get well acquainted with the gentle and diplomatic missionary statesman and pioneer of modern Bible translation.

"How's the work going, John?" Townsend asked.

"Doors are opening," John said. "We've signed a contract to work in Honduras and are trying now to get into Costa Rica. We could place ten new translators tomorrow if we had them. But we need a new headquarters building."

"You do, huh. Well, let's go see the President."

To John's amazement, Townsend secured a quick audience with President Ydigoras, who was then trying to keep his shaky government from falling. After exchanging courtesies, Townsend got right to the point. "Mr. President, over forty years ago I came to your country to study the Cakchiquel language and translate the New Testament. Since then many Cakchiquels have developed into out-

[2]Children of U. S. citizens born in Mexico have dual citizenship until the age of 21 when they must choose between the two countries.

standing citizens. Perhaps you've heard of Dr. Elena Trejo who practices medicine here in the capital. She was one of my students. The present head of your Department of Indian Affairs is an old Cakchiquel friend. There are many others."

President Ydigoras, a short, stocky man with rakish black hair that kept falling over his forehead, smiled. "You don't have to convince me. The work you people are doing should have the support of good-hearted people from all religions."

"I'm glad you feel that way, Mr. President," the missionary diplomat said. "Now we need a little land here in the capital for our headquarters. We will build the building, keep it up, and turn it back to the government when we finish our work among the tribes."

John had heard of Townsend's amazing ways with government leaders in Mexico and Peru. Still he watched astounded as the president telephoned his minister of education. "I'm sending Townsend and his assistant over to your office," he announced directly. "They need land to build a headquarters for their linguists."

"Come on, John," the older translator whispered, "let's strike while the iron's hot." They went straight to the office of the Minister of Education, and within minutes had his pledge. As they left, Townsend turned to John and said simply, "The rest is up to you."

John followed through and soon signed an agreement to accept a choice lot near downtown Guatemala City.

A few days after the Indian Congress closed, John went to see the Minister of Finance for duty exemptions on equipment coming into the country. At this time the capital was alive with rumors of revolutionary plots. He was ushered into the Minister's office and directed to a seat near his desk. Suddenly the official lifted his head. Fear froze on his face as he pressed a button. An instant later two guards raced into the room.

"Get that man," he shouted, pointing to John. "He's carrying a time bomb!"

16. *A Dream Fulfilled*

As THE GUARDS searched him, John lifted his hands in protest. "No! No! I don't have a bomb. The tick is in my heart.

"Please pardon me for not explaining before," John said to the amazed official. Then he described the operation and how the ticking resulted from the click of the ball rising and falling in the artificial valve.

The official dismissed the guards and turned back to John. "Senor Beekman, you will excuse me for feeling, as you North Americans say, jittery. But this is not an easy time with so many bombs exploding in the capital. Now, where were those papers you wanted me to sign for the duty exemption?"

President Ydigoras had not become aware of the ticking heart when John and Cameron Townsend first visited his office, but he heard about the incident in the finance minister's office. The next time he saw John, he laughed and said, "Here is the American who scared my minister of finance."

One afternoon Elaine returned from the doctor's office and dropped a bomb of her own. "It's due next February," she said casually.

John looked up from a report he was preparing. "What's due?"

Elaine laughed. "A new chip off the old Beekman block."

Now John was alert. "That's, that's wonderful," he stammered.

A few days later John declared, "We couldn't have timed this better. In August we'll go to Berea and see how the Chol work is doing. The next month we'll go on to the States for a short furlough and the Wycliffe biennial conference. Then you can stay and have the baby in Pennsylvania."

As planned, John turned his duties temporarily over to Clarence

Church, the newly elected Associate Director for the Guatemalan Branch, and they drove to the M.A.F. base at Ixtapa. Hatch flew them into Berea where Vi Warkentin, a former co-worker among the Chols, was waiting. She and a new missionary nurse, Ruby Scott, had been teaching literacy classes in the villages. "They all want to be able to read the New Testament when it is published," Vi said excitedly. "When will it be ready?"

John replied in an impatient tone, "We keep getting promises from the printer in Mexico City. The Chols have waited long enough. I'm going to try to get it out of the log jam."

After a few days in Berea and conferences with the Reformed Church missionaries about the progress of the Bible school, the Beekmans went on to Mexico City. John called on the Bible Society representatives and begged them to persuade the printer to give priority to the Chol New Testament. After a few days, the printer replied through the Bible Society that he would do the best he could.

John and Elaine left Mexico feeling quite discouraged. They knew that eventually the printer would get to the New Testament that had been translated four years before, but they kept thinking of the Chol preachers and teachers who needed it so desperately.

The biennial Wycliffe Corporation conference convened in Sulphur Springs, Arkansas, in September. John gave his director's report of the work in Guatemala. He rejoiced to see three new couples appointed for tribes in Guatemala and Honduras.

Then they drove on to New Jersey for a visit with John's folks. While there, John took the commuter train to Manhattan and conferred with publication officials at the American Bible Society's headquarters. They, too, were concerned and agreed to use the Mexico printer's print-outs and print by offset the Chol New Testament in New York.[1]

John and Elaine spent the Christmas holidays in Clearfield with her folks. While there, they consulted a gynecologist who gave an optimistic report on her RH problem. With this in hand, John flew back to Guatemala.

Baby Gary arrived on January 23. He was so yellow, the floor nurse teased Elaine about stopping in Hong Kong. The doctor

[1]Commercial printers are no longer used in Mexico for Wycliffe translations. Wycliffe has its own presses. The American Bible Society, the World Home Bible League, and the International Bible Society pay printing costs for portions and New Testaments published in Mexico on Wycliffe presses.

quickly realized the problem: antibodies that had passed from Elaine into the baby were destroying his blood cells.

The hospital issued an emergency call for a donor with RH negative blood. The brother of Elaine's closest girl friend and matron of honor at her wedding answered the call. He did not learn the identity of the baby until after giving blood.

Elaine sent a telegram to John who was in Guatemala directing the Branch's business conference. The transfusion had been successful, and there was no urgent need for him to come.

Early in April Elaine and the children met John in Mitla where he had come to direct the second annual Translation Workshop. Here he saw Gary for the first time.

"How's your heart?" Elaine asked immediately.

John grinned. "Can't you hear it?" He did admit to having had "a few angina pains," but assured Elaine this was "nothing for a new mother to worry about."

They celebrated Good Friday in the City of the Dead in a heart-touching Communion service with Christian Indians from twelve different tribes and fifteen translators. The Easter sunrise service, held out on a rolling, cactus-dotted hillside, was just as memorable. Elaine wrote home, "We had a foretaste of the day when some from every tribe and nation shall gather around the Throne to sing His praises."

The Workshop ended on a high note a few days after Easter. The American Bible Society representative, who had been a visiting lecturer, reported to Dr. Ben Elson, "Each of the translators who attended is now doing much better work than would otherwise be possible. The quality of work has especially improved and this will speed up publication."

The Beekmans reached Berea just before the shipment of Chol New Testaments arrived from New York. John grabbed one of the sturdily bound books from the M.A.F. plane and clasped it to his chest. "To hold this Book is the thrill of a lifetime," he exulted. "I can hardly wait for the Chols to get it."

Dedication ceremonies took place in three Chol villages on July 1, 2, 3 with the Aulies, Beekmans, Reformed Church missionaries (including the newly arrived Henry Stegengas), dozens of Chol preachers and elders, and numerous other dignitaries present.

The first dedication was in the packed Carranza church building with the overflow crowd looking through windows. A Chol elder led a prayer of consecration. The church treasurer read John 17:1-9 and 14-17. Then three Chols gave testimonies. One held up the red-bound Testament and said, "I helped with the translation of this Book. I learned to read it. I preached portions of it in villages. Now that we have it all in one volume, let us continue to read and study it and preach it to those who still do not believe."

Then Lopez de Lara, secretary of the American Bible Society for Mexico spoke, centering his message around Hebrews 1:1: "God, who at sundry times and in divers manners spake in time past unto the father by the prophets."

"Now," the speaker declared, "God speaks through the New Testament in Chol."

John's thoughts drifted back ten years to when the village of Carranza had been totally pagan. Eighteen-year-old Mateo, one of his faithful language helpers, had entered the village with a phonograph on his back to proclaim the Gospel. He was met by three wild-eyed men waving sharp machetes and loaded shotguns. Undaunted, Mateo returned again and again until a strong church was established. John looked across an aisle. There — listening intently to the speakers in the dedication service — sat the three men who had threatened to kill Mateo. John wished that the young evangelist could be in the service, but that was impossible. Mateo had died of rheumatic fever and tuberculosis two years before.

That evening John and the missionaries slept on the hard benches in the church. Next morning two M.A.F. pilots, Hatch and Windsor Vick, began shuttling them to Jerusalem for a repeat of the dedication service before a fresh crowd of Chols. The village was one of many in Chol country that had been given Bible names by Chol colonists who had secured new land through the government's program. "God gave us courage to go and get the land, Brother Kwan," a lean elder told John. "We're no longer afraid of the ranchers. The land is good. We're growing our own coffee now. My last crop paid for a galvanized tin roof on my house. Now we need not be so afraid of fire."

John blinked back tears of joy as he thought of what the new economy was beginning to mean. Chol fathers could build decent houses, buy clothes for their women and children, afford medicine when needed, and support their churches with tithes and offerings. The Word of God was setting the Chols free.

The dedication circuit moved on to Tumbala for the third ceremony. Elaine took the place of John who became weary and returned to Berea. Over 600 Chols attended in the historic village where the fire that provided excuses for the tragic imprisonments, had occurred. Elaine rejoined John and the children in Berea. As they packed for Guatemala, John said, "If the Lord provides a director for the Guatemalan Branch, we'll be coming back next year to the Chols for good."

Elaine sighed. "I hope so, John. This moving back and forth gets tiresome after five years. And, anyway, I feel that our home is among the Chols."

"Me, too," Judy said, hugging her dog that they were leaving behind.

They arrived back in Guatemala City in time to celebrate their thirteenth wedding anniversary in a new rented house, nicely furnished and made ready by the Wycliffe group. They quickly enrolled Judy (fifth grade) and Tommy (kindergarten) in the brand new Maya School, opened for English-speaking children living in the country.

They had hardly unpacked when the Mission's Executive Committee convened in their living room. John conserved his strength during the three-day meeting by presiding from a reclining lawn chair.

Everybody wanted to know about John's heart. His stock reply came, "Ticking along. How's yours?" More than once this line opened the door to a conversation with government officials about the spiritual heart.

However, a U.S. AID (Agency for International Development) official bristled with suspicion when John entered his office. "You're carrying a hidden tape recorder," he shouted, "and are trying to record our conversation for wrong purposes."

"No," John replied. "I can explain the ticking." When he did, the diplomat apologized and warmed up to a spirit of helpfulness.

On October 10, Elaine greeted John with "happy anniversary." John looked perplexed and she explained, "Five years ago on October 10 you got the valve. That was on a Tuesday and today is Tuesday."

John remembered, "That's right, and the doctor promised me five more years. Then tomorrow I'll begin living on the Lord's time. You can start calling me Methuselah."

John began "living on the Lord's time" by checking the Carib Gospel of Luke with Ilah Fleming and Lil Howland. Because the so-called "Black Caribs" were the only non-Mayan tribe in Guatemala, he had been interested in them since his arrival.

They were a mixture of Africans and Arawak Indians from off the South American coast where a slave trading vessel had shipwrecked centuries before. Columbus' men had fought with the Arawaks when the great discoverer landed on the island of Hispaniola (shared today by Haiti and the Dominican Republic). A millennium before then, the Arawaks had probably migrated to Hispanola and other West Indies islands from the South American continent.

Early in November John and Elaine spent a weekend in a Black Carib fishing town where the two girls worked. The town of Livingston lay on the tip of a peninsula, an hour and a half by boat from Port Barrios, the stopping place for land travel.

"If I didn't know better, I'd think we were in an African coastal town," Elaine said as they walked along a sandy street. Jet-black children with thick lips, wide nostrils, and kinky hair danced circles around them, hoping to sell a few trinkets. Dark Carib mothers peered from the doorways of tar-paper huts.

John was intrigued with the speech of the Caribs who were such a contrast to the Asiatic looking Chols. He detected English, French, Spanish, and Carib words among their chatter. From talking to Ilah and Lil, he knew that the French words had seeped into the Carib vocabulary during times of French rule, and the English and Spanish had come from their neighbors who spoke these languages. Before that, the Carib language had resulted from blending an unknown African dialect with the ancient Arawak tongue. Another ancient residual John noticed in Black Carib speech, was a dual male and female way of speaking some words. Apparently at one time the men had spoken a different language from the women to maintain a superior male status.

Saturday, they swam, loafed on the beach, and acquired good tans. Tommy and Judy had the time of their lives building sand castles and wading in the friendly surf. They stayed overnight with Ilah and Lil, and on Sunday worshiped with about a dozen new Carib believers. That afternoon they took the boat back to Port Barrios from where they drove home to Guatemala City.

Tuesday evening the translators in Guatemala City held an election party. They relaxed, enjoyed coffee and doughnuts, and sat close to the short wave radio until the results showed John F. Kennedy to be the new president. Occasionally the noise of a bomb explosion could be heard in the distance.

Communist agitation and terrorist attacks brought the small country close to all-out civil war. President Ydigoras decreed a nine o'clock curfew and forbade meetings of more than four people. The restrictions threatened to torpedo a three-day translator's conference scheduled for the following week. Not anxious to disobey the law, John hurried to the ministry of defense to ask special permission for the conference to be held. This was granted.

The following Saturday, old friends Drs. Eugene Nida and William Wonderly flew in for the conference. John greeted them cordially. Nida and Wonderly both made remarks about John's heart. John told them about the incident with the minister of finance and joked, "Don't get too close to me. One of these terrorists could shoot me for a bomb."

Dr. Juan Rosales, head of the Guatemalan Indian Institute, telephoned John during the first day of the conference. He had an appointment set up with President Ydigoras for Wednesday evening at six and could John come? "The President," Dr. Rosales said, "is very concerned about helping the Indians."

John was in the presidential palace at the time appointed. "You look very tired, Mr. President," he told the harassed leader.

Ydigoras managed a smile. "It isn't easy trying to hold this country together in such difficult times."

The three men moved into earnest talk about ways to help the Indians. All knew that the Indians, who comprised sixty per cent of Guatemala's population, were for the most part desperately poor and ripe for Communist agitation. Communism would lose its appeal only when their standard of living and literacy could be raised. Dr. Rosales told the president about immediate plans to print primers for the Quiche Indians in their own language. "Mr. President," he explained, "it is necessary that the Indians learn to read and write in their own language before they can make the transition to Spanish." John gave a brief report of translation work and added, "Our goal is to give the tools of education to every tribesman, including the most important tool of all, the New Testament."

"I'm glad to hear these reports," the haggard chief executive said. "I haven't received much good news lately."

"We are working for a spiritual revolution among the Indians," John declared. "We believe that knowledge of the Christian Scriptures will set the Indians free from vice and superstition and put them on the road to first class citizenship."

"Good. Good," the president exclaimed. "I am Catholic and you are Protestant," he said to John, "but as long as my government stands, it will continue to back your service to Guatemala's Indians."

The conference had lasted for over an hour. John was touched by the president's concern for the Indians. Upon leaving he said, "We will pray for you, Mr. President, during this time of crisis."

President Ydigoras[2] extended his hand. "To know that I have your prayers will be a great comfort."

As his Christmas present for the children, John built a tree house in the front yard of their Guatemala City residence. After Christmas he flew by Pan American jet to Mexico City for a Wycliffe literacy conference. While there he received news that his father was critically ill with cancer of the bladder. He telephoned Elaine and took the first flight to New York.

Tom Beekman's blue eyes twinkled below his thinning gray hair, and he managed a wan smile when John entered the hospital room. When John embraced him, he said, "I can hear your heart ticking, son. It sounds great."

During the next two weeks, father and son became re-acquainted. John carried a record player to the room and played hymns. They read Scripture and talked about past times.

Tom Beekman was still hanging on to life when John said good-by. Both men tried to display good spirits. They were, as Bella Beekman commented, "both alike in that they don't complain."

"I'll be praying that your heart will keep ticking, son," Tom whispered.

"And Elaine and I will be praying for you, Dad. Good-by now, until we meet again."

Tom Beekman lifted one hand a few inches above the covers.

[2]President Miguel Ydigoras held power until 1963, when he was forced to flee the country during a state of siege. The new provisional president suspended the constitution and prohibited all political activities. Democratic elections were held in 1966, and a new constitution was adopted. However, Castro-supported terrorist activity still continues in the rural areas where Wycliffe Translators are serving.

"Yes, until we meet again."

Within three months John's father was dead. His funeral was held on his and Bella's forty-fifth wedding anniversary.

John got back to Guatemala City in time for Gary's first birthday party. He laughed and romped and ate angel food cake until his sides ached.

That night he went to bed with a sore throat and chest cold. The next evening his heart went into a fast staccato beat. Fearful of an impending attack, Elaine awoke a translator who was also a nurse. They checked a medical book and learned that the irregular beat could be caused by unusual deep breathing or cough. They gave John the suggested remedy, phenobarbital, and in a few minutes his heart seemed to be better. However, after the problem recurred, John flew to Mexico City and consulted Dr. Sodi-Pallares. The specialist prescribed foods high in potassium and potassium tablets. These continue to keep the beat regular.

A long awaited letter came from Wycliffe's home office in Santa Ana, California, assuring a $10,000.00 loan for the Guatemala Branch to build a headquarters on the land given by the government. "Wonderful!" John exclaimed when he read the letter. "Now we can return to the Chols with a clear conscience."

At John's urging, the Guatemalan Branch members met to elect a new director. They chose Dr. Marvin Mayers, the translator among the Pocomchi Indians.

John then began transferring duties to Dr. Mayers and made plans to leave for Chol country as soon as Judy's school was out.

In April, before leaving in June, John addressed a conference of Guatemalan educators about the importance of helping the Indians become literate in their own languages. "Imagine how difficult it would be for a child from a Spanish-speaking home to become literate in a school where only English was spoken," he said. "It's just as difficult for an Indian child to learn to read with comprehension in a Spanish-speaking school. Spanish to him is a foreign language which he must learn to speak and understand before he can read and write it with comprehension. But he can become literate in his native language by learning to read and write it. Then he is better prepared to learn to read and write a second language. We want the Indians to learn the national language," John assured the educators.

"That's why our Bible translations are printed in bilingual form with the Spanish text underneath the Indian text."[3]

When John finished, a distinguished looking Indian teacher stood up. "All that Senor Beekman said is so. As a young man I spoke only the Cakchiquel dialect. Then Senor Townsend came and asked me to help translate the New Testament into Cakchiquel. Through reading the Cakchiquel New Testament and then the Spanish equivalent, I came to read and understand Spanish. Today I am a trained teacher in a Spanish school."

John had never met the man and did not know he was in the audience. When he thanked him for the testimony, the Indian retorted, "I am the one who should thank you and Mr. Townsend. Because of translation work, I am a teacher today."

There was so much to do before departure that the days seemed to fly by. Arrangements were made for Judy to attend a boarding school for missionary children operated by the Central American Mission in Huehuetenango, about 100 miles from Guatemala City. They decided this would be better than sending her further away to the United States.

Then something happened to change their plans again. The Wycliffe Board appointed John to the newly created position of Translation Coordinator. This meant he would be fulltime director of translation work for all Wycliffe personnel, not just those in Mexico.

[3]For years, Texas schools have had difficulty teaching children from Spanish-speaking homes to read English. But last year the U.S. Office of Education published (and reprinted in *Reader's Digest*) the story of a dramatic breakthrough by a young teacher. Her method: Teaching the "Tex-Mex" children Spanish before introducing them to English. However, long before this, the Wycliffe Bible Translators began using the bilingual method to help minority groups become literate in the national language. For example, the Agaruna tribe of Peru now has 80 Wycliffe trained bilingual teachers.

17. *Arms Around the World*

THE DECISION TO accept the Board's new appointment was harder for John and Elaine than the assignment to Guatemala had been. They had understood from the beginning that the Guatemalan directorship was only temporary until a new director could be named, but to become Translation Coordinator for all of Wycliffe's work around the world meant a permanent change of direction. They would have to give up their dreams of serving in the Chol Bible School and give full time to helping their fellow translators.

"You are the man best prepared for this job," a board member had told John. "You have lived in a tribe and helped prepare an approved translation. You have had administration experience in Guatemala. And, most important, you have already developed a proven workshop program that helps translators do faster and better work. Now and in the years ahead, hundreds of translators from tribes in many countries will need the type of guidance that you have given the Mexico translators at Mitla."

John and Elaine knew the Board had prayed and given the appointment careful thought. They had decided to accept on the conviction that as long as John lived, he should give his strength to whatever counted the most. "If God can use me in helping translators speed His Word to unreached tribes, then I want to serve," John said.

When the Beekmans reached Mexico, John was like a college president with plenty of eager students, but no campus, office, or classrooms, and no funds for building. A permanent translation center was needed for year-round work.

"We'll pray, believe, and look," Dr. Ben Elson said. A prayer appeal for the center went to almost 1400 Wycliffe missionaries in ten countries and to friends of Wycliffe in the United States, Canada, Australia, and Europe. In keeping with Wycliffe's policy,[1] no funds were solicited.

Suddenly translators in the Mezquital valley of central Mexico learned that a colony of Christian Otomi Indians needed to sell some land to pay a debt. It was a choice level site on the outskirts of historic Ixmiquilpan, market center for the Otomis, off the highway between Mexico City and Laredo. The climate was ideal, averaging about 75 degrees the year round, and the 5,400 feet elevation would not be hard on John's heart.

Wycliffe members in Mexico gave from their own personal allowances to purchase the land, and construction of the first duplex sandstone and slate apartment began under the supervision of a translator with building experience.

By October, 1961, fourteen translator apartments, eight smaller living units for Indian helpers, a small elementary school, and a study building with a lecture hall and twenty private study cubicles were nearing completion. More than half of the $70,000.00 cost came from Wycliffe members, the remainder from friends in the United States, Canada, and Mexico.

Twenty-eight translators and eleven Indians from as many tribes arrived in October to begin a three-month workshop. The work followed the pattern set at Mitla: Lectures on translation principles, personal guidance and verse-by-verse checking by consultants, actual translation with native speakers — all coordinated by the man with the ticking heart who enjoyed nothing better than tackling a tough translation problem.

As anticipated, the speed-up in translation was amazing. One translator, fresh from his jungle hut, testified, "Back in the tribe with Indians in and out all day every day, I was fortunate to finish a chapter each month. Here where I can work on nothing but translation, I am averaging two chapters a week."

By Christmas, when the first Ixmiquilpan Workshop ended, John had a stack of inquiry letters to explain the program and qualifications for participation. The latter included conversational ability in the tribal language, recommendation by the branch director, and accompaniment by a native speaker from the tribe.

John planned for two translation workshops and one linguistic

[1]Wycliffe Members may not directly solicit funds for personal support or field projects.

workshop each year. The latter was for younger workers, not ready for actual translation work and needing guidance in analyzing the difficult tribal languages. Dr. Robert Longacre was appointed to coordinate this workshop which was scheduled to run from January through March.

Early in January, the aging Plymouth carried John and Elaine back to Chiapas. Hatch flew them into Berea where they completed arrangements to sell the "tin" house to the new Reformed Church missionaries, Hank and Charmagne Stegenga.

The continuing advance among the Chols was gratifying. Hank and Al DeVoogd had 27 students in the Bible School. Wilbur and Evelyn Aulie were moving ahead on translation of selected Old Testament books. Iris Mills, who had recently become the wife of a colleague, Dr. Alan Wares, was testing new literacy materials intended for Chol teachers. Vi Warkentin and Ruby Scott, the newest worker among the Chols, were adapting the Chol New Testament from the Tumbala dialect to the Tila dialect which was spoken by 25,000 unreached Chols.

"The dialects have many similarities," Vi told John and Elaine, "but there are some important differences. The Chol Tumbala word for love means 'eat' in the Tila dialect. Someone wanted to know why God would send His Son to eat people. 'Warm' in the Tumbala dialect means 'intoxicated' to these people. 'God is faithful' in Tumbala means to Tila speakers 'God is walking down the trail.' "

News spread quickly through Chol country that their beloved "Brother Kwan and Sister Elena" had returned for a visit. A stream of old friends began arriving from Amado Nervo and other distant villages. Some carried well-marked copies of the Chol New Testament.

The Beekmans learned that several new Chol villages bearing Bible names had sprung up on land secured through the government's ejido system and populated mainly by Christians. The name of one village, "Egypt," puzzled John. He inquired and was told, "A government official named it. Not many Christians live there."

Regretfully and in tears, John and Elaine said good-by to their Chol friends. As the plane soared into the air above Berea and the new Bible school buildings, they looked back and glimpsed a sea of hands waving. Hatch, too, was touched and said, "They really get to you, don't they?"

Elaine, still wiping away tears, said, "They're the sweetest and the most grateful people in the world."

A special donation arrived for a new car to replace the old Plymouth. They bought a new Rambler American and gave the Plymouth to another couple. The new owners promptly christened it "First John."

Life slowly became more routine at Ixmiquilpan with the opening of the spring Workshop. Miss Lulu Reber, a veteran Wycliffe member, was assigned to be John's secretary. His office was in the study building, only 150 feet from the Beekman's three-bedroom apartment.

Elaine did typing and translated portions of the Chol New Testament back into English. John felt that such "back translations" would give other translators examples of types of restructuring needed to make translations intelligible. Besides mothering the two boys, Elaine cheerfully acted as hostess for visitors who came to conference with John and frequently remained for a meal. Some of the Indian guests could hardly sign their names in the guest books. Christian leaders from the states, scientists, government officials, and other missionaries often wrote comments. Dr. Harold Ockenga, pastor of Boston's famed Park Street Church, wrote after a tour of Workshop activities, "Yours is the greatest work in the world."

As Easter week approached, John and Elaine became anxious to see Judy who was due home from Guatemala for spring vacation. They had arranged for missionary friends to put her on the Pan American plane to Mexico City.

They arrived at the Mexico City airport before Judy's plane was due. Elaine was visibly nervous. "I'm not happy about this, John," she said. "Judy is too young to be on a plane by herself."

John touched her shoulder. "Don't worry. After all the Lord has done for us, don't you think He'll take care of our little girl?"

Elaine sighed. "I guess I just don't have enough faith. Sometimes I think the toughest part of being a missionary mother is having your child away at school."

Just then the flight's arrival was announced. They moved as close as possible to the door leading to customs and watched through the glass door.

In what seemed an hour but was actually only a few minutes later, Elaine caught sight of her tall daughter. "There she is," she squealed. "I'd know that blond head anywhere."

"She's going through customs like a professional," John noted with evident pride. "Hey, that's Bill Wonderly of the Bible Society behind her. They must have come up together."

Soon Judy came racing into her parents' arms. Dr. Wonderly walked behind her and greeted John and Elaine cordially.

"It just happened that my trip coincided with Judy's flight," he said. "I think she was glad to see me."

"No, Bill," Elaine interrupted. "It didn't just happen. God planned it that way."

The whole family was together for a happy ten days. John built a 30-foot rope swing beside an existing tree house for the children and took the first swing himself. "My husband," Elaine declared to a translator's wife, "will never grow up."

On Saturday, John took the children exploring along the banks of the swift Tula River that ran near the Translation Center. They discovered a mysterious cave that opened into the river and could be reached only by wading through water. They decided to adopt the cave as a secret place for family camp-outs when John needed to get away from work.

One afternoon they accepted a swimming invitation from Mexican friends who owned a desert resort that featured two oval blue pools and hot mineral water baths. Elaine taught Judy the side stroke, and they found that Tommy could swim underwater like a fish. After a half hour in a hot bath, John felt wonderfully relaxed.

As they were leaving, the owner called, "Come back anytime."

John thanked him and said, "We'll be back."

Both heart and reason moved John to delegate responsibilities. Dr. Sodi-Pallares insisted he should work less than eight hours a day (not even that when he felt tired), and take regular afternoon naps. Occasional angina pains and shortness of breath kept him aware that his life hung by a thread.

Reason suggested that it was not feasible for all translators to come to Ixmiquilpan from such far away countries as the Philippines, Vietnam, and Nigeria. But a few could come for consultant training and return to direct workshops in their own countries. With the consultants — three or four for a twelve-language workshop — John shared the lectures and delegated most of the checking.

The consultants made weekly progress reports of each translator's work. John intervened only to give special counsel or to resolve a conflict.

He tried to prevent problems of human relations from arising by briefing the consultants on the fine points of getting along with their translators. The translators were invited to sit in on the briefing held at the beginning of a workshop. "This is like bringing the kids to the principal's staff meeting," one translator said. "It gives me a good feeling to know that nothing will be said behind my back."

"We're going to put everything out front," John told the group which included men with seminary and Ph.D. degrees. "By knowing what is expected of consultants, you translators can better understand them. Let us remember that we are colleagues, not superiors and inferiors."

· Then John presented some Dale Carnegie specifics for consultants: "(1)) Don't be the big-boss type and try to apply pressure. Put the translator at ease; (2) Don't lay down ultimatums – 'You produce, or we won't approve your work.' If the translator fails to produce an acceptable translation, it is a reflection on the consultant; (3) Don't prejudge the translation on your impression of his ability; (4) Don't insist on a single rigid standard for publication. (Translators have different personalities, educational backgrounds, languages to master, and tribal circumstances. We are not here to produce master-pieces of translation art, but to produce God's Word in an intelligible form for the Indians who need salvation and guidance *now.*); (5) Show sincere interest and honest appreciation of the translator's work; (6) Talk about your own mistakes before pointing out the translator's; (7) Suggest improvements or corrections, but never insist or argue that they be incorporated into the manuscript; (8) Deliberately bypass some errors until a more judicious time. (You discourage and confuse the translator by pointing out a bundle of errors in early checking); (9) Ask questions rather than give orders. ('Would switching the order of these two phrases lighten the com-munication load?' is better than the more direct, 'Switch these phrases and the sentence will make more sense.'); (10) Let the translator save face; (11) Give a choice of alternate translations; (12) Let the translator discover his own mistakes ('Do you see anything in this verse that could be improved?' is better than, 'Correct this mis-take, please.'); (13) Never ridicule; (14) Use humor; (15) Praise every improvement, even the slightest."

There were times for play and good humor. Although John couldn't play volleyball, he cheered from the sidelines. At parties and talent shows he laughed as much as anyone, even when the joke was on him.

A group of translators devised their own poetic rejoinder to John and the consultants. It was sung to the tune of the Mexican birthday song, *Las Mananitas.*

> "Here's an ode to the consultants
> Who've been heckling us each day
> And we hope that our insultants
> Have profited from their stay.
>
> Now we're dreaming similes
> Metaphor, hyperbole
> Third person editorials
> Its meaning pray thee tell me.
>
> Greek genitives are oozing
> From the pages of our draft
> Arndt and Gingrich[2] help confuse us
> So you can have the last laugh.
>
> Here's a toast to Johnny Beekman
> Who keeps ticking on each day
> Tough-locks-to-rough-box Stewart[3]
> Here's a Hip Hip Hurray!
>
> But one thing will we remember
> From the conference this year
> Watch your figures, O translators,
> Or you'll be out on your ear."

The work load piled up while John's heart ticked on. Elaine tried not to be bossy, but often found a firm word necessary to keep him on doctor's orders. "What a guy and how I love him," she confided to a friend. "I only wish I could help him more."

Not even in his dreams could John escape from translation. One night, after a discussion on idioms in which John cited "kick the bucket" as an idiom for death on the U.S. western frontier, he dreamed that he was the central character at a hanging. He was standing on a bucket with hands tied and a rope reaching up to a tree limb was tied to his neck. A mob was yelling, "Kick the bucket!" When someone did, he swung around and caught the limb with his feet and hung there until he gnawed through the rope, dropped to the ground, and escaped.

John felt a special concern for the tribal informants who came

[2]The title of a Greek lexicon and standard reference for translators.
[3]This line was inspired by a response from Consultant Don Stewart to John Beekman's request: "Give me a translation for, 'You will bring my white hairs down to the grave.'" Stewart replied, jokingly, "Tough locks to rough box."

with the translators to Ixmiquilpan. It was the trip of a lifetime for most of them. Some had never seen an automobile before. Some came from tightly-knit tribal societies where they had to get permission from the tribal elders to leave. Married informants usually brought their families.

The informant kitchen and bedroom apartments were modestly furnished with old beds and small gas cook stoves. Still, they were havens of luxury for tribesmen who had always slept and cooked on the ground. When one Indian couple first saw their quarters, the man asked incredulously, "Is this really for us?" When assured that it was, the two knelt before the door and thanked God for such luxury.

Back in the tribe, fear of reprisals from evil spirits and warnings from the elders often kept an informant from divulging the inner culture and beliefs of his people, but once involved in the fellowship at Ixmiquilpan the native speaker began to open up.

For example, Ninu of the Chatino tribe of south central Mexico disclosed for the first time to Translator Bill Upson the number, rank, and sex of the Chatino deities; the names and activities of the evil spirits; and what conduct and attitudes are considered good and which are thought sinful. "My people believe that a person does not have a spirit until after he dies," Ninu said. "While he is living he has a heart which becomes a spirit upon death."

Ninu also told his translator that the word "holy" could be used to modify an idol, a household god, the witch doctor, an altar, a lion, the sea which has caused a flood and disaster, a sacred mushroom, and several other things. The translator and his consultant deduced that holy had two main components of meanings for Chatinos. It referred to persons purported to hold supernatural powers, and to objects which, if not properly respected, would bring evil upon one.

With this and other information, they agreed that they could not use the Chatino words for "holy" and "spirit" in defining the third person of the Trinity. Their approved translation for Holy Spirit became "God's perfect heart" (referring primarily to the life principle of one who is living).

At the end of the workshop, Ninu told the translator, "I want to become a Christian." The next day when he made his prayer in the name of Jesus, he said, "Help the translator to find the right words so that I can learn more and my relatives will also know Jesus."

Conversions of language helpers were recorded in every workshop.

The first Ixmiquilpan convert was a Mixteco Indian who returned home and won fifteen of his relatives.

Frequently such conversions were triggered by contact with Christians from other tribes. As John pointed out to a U. S. visitor, "The unsaved Indian finds his main social outlet at a workshop in the fellowship and meetings of Indian Christians from other tribes. He sees their joy and devotion to the task of translating the New Testament. The accumulative effect of this brings him to the point where he can no longer resist the work of the Spirit leading to conversion."

With the completion of each workshop at Ixmiquilpan, more translators came to believe Cameron Townsend's goal of putting the Scriptures in every tribal tongue could be reached before the year 2,000.[4] Computers were rented and borrowed to build tribal dictionaries, indexes for lexicons, and to do typesetting. Under John's initiative and direction, selected translators and consultants began work on a series of condensed commentaries for translators, composed of the most helpful materials from a variety of regular commentaries. "Translators," he explained, "don't need lengthy discussions on doctrinal matters, homiletical and devotional applications, and discussions of lengthy textual problems. They need to know what the words of Scripture mean, how the phrases and clauses connect, and the purpose of each paragraph."

In November, 1962, two distinguished visitors from Moody arrived at Ixmiquilpan: Dean Maxwell Coder and Alumni Secretary Rev. Lawrence Pearson. Elaine treated them to a leg of lamb while they asked dozens of questions about John's work. After visits with several consultants and translators, they left. "I hope they give a good report of our work to their students," John said. "We could use some more Moody-trained translators."

Nothing more was heard about the visit until January 9 when Elaine opened a letter from the newly elected alumni secretary, Rev. James E. Draper. She raced to the garage where John was doing some auto repairs. "You have been selected as the Moody Alumnus of the Year," she shouted.

John's eyes widened. "What? Let me see the letter."

A moment later he exclaimed, "Well, I never expected that. And

4Wycliffe's goal is to recruit 7,250 workers by 1985 for service in 2,200 language or minority groups. Allowing additional years to do the translation task in each group, the membership believes their God-given assignment (Luke 15:4-6) can be completed before A.D. 2,000.

they want me to come up and get an award during Founders' Week. I can't get away now. You go."

Elaine was all fire and determination. "You're going, too; the letter says they will send plane tickets for both of us."

On Tuesday evening, February 5, John and Elaine and her parents sat at the front of the Moody Memorial Church. At the designated time, James Draper said, "Every year since 1951, the Executive Committee of the Alumni Association has given a trophy to a Moody graduate for outstanding Christian character, Christian service, and loyalty to the Word of God.

"Now I know you're all wondering who it is," he continued. "Well, see if you can guess before I give the name. He was born on December 2, 1918 in Midland Park, New Jersey . . . ."

The crowd of over 1,000 alumni listened quietly as the alumni secretary continued with biographical details. Finally he said, "Perhaps you've guessed by now that I've been talking about John Beekman, Class of '46, and Translation Coordinator for the Wycliffe Bible Translators. He's here with his wife, Elaine, also a Moody alumnus. Come up here, John and Elaine, and say a word to us."

A moment later, John stood before the microphones. The tick from his heart could be clearly heard over the auditorium public address system and throughout the Chicago area over radio station WMBI. He gave a short greeting and briefly explained what made his heart tick. Then he said, "We'll be returning to Mexico shortly. If God leads you, come and help us complete the job of putting the New Testament into every tribal language on earth."

John and Elaine flew back to Ixmiquilpan to prepare for the spring workshop. Twenty-one translators were due to arrive from Mexico, and consultants-in-training from Brazil, Ecuador, and Vietnam.

One month from the date John received the Moody award, David Blood, the translator from Vietnam, received chilling news by radio-telephone. Vietnam translators Gaspar Makil and Elwood Jacobsen had been killed the day before by the Viet Cong at a roadblock 66 miles northeast of Saigon. The terrorists had attacked without provocation, and also killed one of Makil's four-month-old twins.[5]

John heard the report and his eyes filled with tears. When he

[5]Forty-eight Wycliffe members continue to serve in Vietnam, with many working in hazardous areas on 17 of 37 tribal tongues native to South Vietnam. Not one has chosen to leave because of danger. In February, 1968, Henry Blood (David Blood's brother), was taken captive by the Viet Cong. He also trained as a consultant under John Beekman at Ixmiquilpan.

composed himself, he said, "Wycliffe has its first martyrs, but God has a purpose in their deaths."

David Blood later recalled that Gaspar Makil had written before going to Vietnam: "We cannot tell what awaits us, but we do know the Lord is with us. He has commissioned us into the ministry. In a real sense, this work of Bible translation is not our work, but the Lord's."

In January, 1964, John wrote to a pastor friend, "Each tick of my heart symbolizes to me, and those who know me, the wonderful grace of our Lord."

By March he was feeling exhausted and short of breath at the end of each day. He left the workshop in progress and drove into Mexico City for rest and a checkup. Dr. Sodi-Pallares' report was not encouraging. "The first operation gives only partial correction. Your heart is wearing out from the backwash of blood. You should have this corrected with a new valve."

From Mexico City, John flew to Washington to see Dr. Hufnagel. The surgeon said frankly, "An operation is needed, but the risk would be too great. We would have to make an incision through the sternum to insert the newer type valve, and another around your side to remove the old valve. All you can do now is stay on a salt-free diet, continue with digitalis and work only when you are not tired."

He returned to Ixmiquilpan and wrote to his family in New Jersey:

> I receive a lot of advice on my heart condition. Like, 'Retire. You've done enough in the Lord's service. Don't kill yourself with work.' I don't listen to this kind of advice, although I imagine that after I'm dead, some will say I brought on my death by overworking. As long as I'm here, I want to use whatever strength I have to be of some service in His work. When we think of the greatness and tenderness of God's love toward us, can we doubt its constancy and final efficacy on our behalf? With Paul I believe that neither death nor anything else in all creation will be able to separate us from the love of God in Christ Jesus our Lord.

Four more years have passed. John's 1967 report to the Wycliffe Biennial Conference showed that during the past two years 327 translators working in 231 different languages received consultation help. "It was once felt that 20 years of service was required to produce a tribal New Testament," John declared. "Now with trained consultants, computers, and other special helps, we think the job can be done in half that time. This means that many more translators will be able to move on to other tribes. Other translators may choose to remain and assist the native churches."

As John spoke to the delegates, Cameron Townsend — 70 years old and looking forward in faith to linguistic surveys behind the Iron Curtain — sat enthralled. He whispered to a translator, "Listen, John's heart isn't tick-tocking any more. It's speaking and saying, 'Praise God! Praise God!'"

The Beekmans lived in the midst of danger during their three years in Guatemala. Yet despite continuing terrorism and bombings, President Ydigoras (shown above) gave time to talk about the needs of the country's 60% Indian population. In 1967 the 50th anniversary of W. Cameron Townsend's coming to Guatemala for translation work was celebrated by high officials in Guatemala City.

Wycliffe's Translation Center at Ixmiquilpan directed by John Beekman and headquarters for training translation specialists in countries from Viet Nam to Nigeria. The Center includes modest duplex apartments for visiting translators, home for the Beekman family, housing for native informants, elementary school, and a study building with lecture hall and 20 private study cubicles.

Translators arrive with Indian informants (extreme right) for a three-month workshop at Ixmiquilpan. Here, away from tribal distractions, they work in an ideal setting.

John and Consultant-in-training Henry Blood from South Vietnam discuss a translator's manuscript. Translator Blood and his family were later captured by the Viet Cong during the Communist's recent February offensive against population centers. His wife and children were later released, but he remains in Communist hands.

Top left: Translator Neil Nellis (Sierra Juarez Zapoteco tribe of south central Mexico) works with his native informant in study cubicle. *Top right:* Manuel Arenas, informant for Translator Herman Aschmann among the Totonacs, points to his tribe among a section of the tribal listings where Wycliffe has work in Mexico (see map for complete listing). Manuel holds a Master's Degree, speaks four languages, is now building a Bible school among his people. *Below:* John and Elaine Beekman as they appeared shortly after their 20th wedding anniversary.

Tommy Beekman snaps the football to his brother Gary beside their home at Ixmiquilpan. *Right:* John and the boys on a weekend vacation in Cuernavaca, Mexico.

The Beekman family as they now appear: Elaine, Tommy (11 and in 5th grade), John, Gary (7 and in 2nd grade), Judy (17 and a senior at Ben Lippen Christian High School in North Carolina).

Epilogue   *The Speaking Heart*

HATCH POINTED THE nose of the yellow M.A.F. Cessna toward the fleecy clouds and began to climb. I looked back at the jagged brown scar that marked the canyon we had just crossed. "Greyhound wouldn't have a dog's chance down here," the veteran pilot quipped. "You either walk or fly."

We topped the mountain and leveled off over a narrow green valley. "That's Beekman country down there," Hatch said. "Looks pretty from up here, but don't let it deceive you. The trail goes up and down and around through dense jungle and across vine bridges that Tarzan wouldn't cross. How John ever made it with that heart of his is a mystery known only to God."

Fifteen minutes later Hatch set down at Berea. By the time he had taxied to a stop just above the "tin house," a flock of Chols had gathered. One little girl with sparkling brown eyes was named Elena in honor of Elaine. A moment later Hank Stegenga, lean and dark-haired, came striding up. We exchanged greetings, and I asked if he would show me around.

We walked along the strip to a field of tall, healthy corn. "We planted this as a model crop to show what could be done," the Reformed Church missionary said. "Note that the stalks are spaced equal distances apart. The Chols are learning they can get a better crop with less seed."

He pointed to a low spot ahead. "We're growing rice there. And over there we've got watermelons, honeydews, and cantalopes — all new crops for Chol country. We're trying to put some variety in their diet."

We walked back toward the cluster of buildings. Hank pointed to a tractor under a shed. "It was flown in piece by piece. Another first. We use it in the Bible school crops."

He showed me goats, rabbits, chickens, turkeys. "You can just about grow and raise anything down here," he said. "It's an agricultural paradise with good rich land and plenty of water and vegetation."

As we walked toward the stone classroom building, I could see young men inside working at desks. Hank pointed to them in pride. "We hope these fellows will go back to their villages and be preachers, teachers, and agricultural experts."

The dormitory was next. I looked in amazement at the double-tiered pole beds. "Do they sleep there?"

Hank nodded. "They stretch a blanket over the sticks and go right off to dreamland."

The clinic building was at the bottom of the hill. A Chol in white coat leaned over a gap-toothed man in an old dentist's chair. "That's Pedro Sanchez. He and another Chol fellow can pull teeth, give shots, do just about anything."

At the tin house, Charmagne Stegenga was waiting with cold Cokes. As we sipped, Hank counted almost 9,000 Chols in 70 congregations as baptized believers with students from the Bible school serving about 50 of the churches. "The Chol population is up to 60 or 70,000 now," he estimated. "At least half of these speak the Tila dialect in which Vi Warkentin and Ruby Scott work."

A half hour's flight from Berea, Hatch put down at the flatland village of Chivalito. Vi and Ruby welcomed us into their small frame house that fronted the weedy landing strip and backed up to the one-room school where they held literacy classes for Chols of all ages. In getting acquainted, I learned that Ruby and I had attended the New Orleans Baptist Theological Seminary at the same time. "You were the seminary nurse," I ventured in a burst of memory.

"That's right. I probably shot you a few times. It's a small world, isn't it?"

I nodded and looked around at Ruby and Vi's world — a scraggly collection of thatch and pole huts with bright-eyed naked children peering from doorways. "The people were quite unfriendly when we arrived," Vi said, "but they're warming up. There's a small congregation of believers here led by a teenage pastor. We anticipate that more Chols who speak this dialect will become Christians as we revise the New Testament."

Because darkness was already creeping across the valley, Hatch and I decided to spend the night in this village. We fared quite well with mosquito netting and air mattresses in the school house.

Next morning Vi flew with us to Amado Nervo to interpret for me. As Hatch skillfully maneuvered the Cessna through mountain passes and over green peaks, she pointed out villages below where strong congregations existed. I noticed that many of the houses had galvanized sheet roofs. "Used to be that only *ladinos* could afford these roofs," Hatch said. "Now the Chols are joining the affluent society. This is another fringe benefit of the Gospel."

Hatch dropped into another gorge and over a shimmering waterfall. "Around the bend is Amado Nervo," he said. A moment later, he turned right over the rushing river and gave his familiar call, "Tighten your cinch and hang onto your saddle horn. We're coming in."

We hit the strip that begins at the edge of the canyon wall and rolled up the steep incline to the village school. As Hatch helped Vi out, he asked, "Where's the welcoming party?"

He needn't have asked. The M.A.F. pilot had hardly staked the plane down when Chols began swarming toward us from all sides. As my eyes adjusted to the surroundings, I realized that the thatch-roofed huts were all around us and on all sides of the bowl.

Everyone wanted news about "Brother Kwan's heart." When Vi assured them that the heart was ticking happily along, waves of smiles flashed from the crowd. I noticed that many were smiling through their tears. One woman seemed to speak for them all when she said to Vi, "Brother Kwan and Sister Elena were such good friends. How they helped us."

Vi's stack of literacy books were quickly snapped up at less than cost price. Needing change, she asked the church treasurer for it.

He solemnly shook his head. "Sister, we have no money in the treasury. We gave it all to the widows and orphans."

I asked to see the spot where the Beekmans' house had stood. Hatch pointed toward the L-shaped church and began climbing the hill. I got in step with him while an entourage of what seemed to be the whole village followed behind.

The house had been built about 100 feet below the church. All that remained was the smooth cement floor, which still is used for outdoor fiestas.

Hatch, Vi, and I stood on the cement foundation while about 200 chattering, friendly Chols milled around us. As I looked at the happy people, the thought struck that we were standing on a symbol of the Beekmans' ministry. They, like the upper structure of the house, had left beautiful Amado Nervo and Chol country, but the foundation of Scripture and faith in Christ which they had helped lay, remained. On this the Chols were building their own forms and structures that would make the native church indigenous, self-supporting, and strong enough to withstand any opposition.

A few days later my family spent a happy weekend at Ixmiquilpan with the Beekmans. John talked frankly about his heart. "Dr. Sodi-Pallares says I now have the heart of an 80-year-old man. He and other doctors believe I am too weak to stand surgery. From a medical standpoint, my only hope may be an artificial heart. (This was spoken before the first human heart transplant in South Africa.) I just live from day to day and put my life in God's hands. He knows best."

Judy, a tall, willowy blonde and a senior at Ben Lippen High School in North Carolina, had just arrived to begin summer vacation with her family. John suggested we go swimming.

Four adults and six children piled into the Rambler American station wagon that had replaced the old Plymouth. As we rode along the highway to the warm springs resort, John suggested a Gospel chorus.

"What's one of your favorites?" I asked John.

"My Lord Knows the Way," he replied.

And so we sang with John's husky baritone rising above Elaine's clear soprano,

> "My Lord knows the way through the wilderness,
> And all I have to do is follow,
> Strength for today
> Is mine always,
> And all that I need for tomorrow.
> My Lord knows the way through the wilderness
> And all I have to do is follow."

The chorus ended and for an instant there was quiet while the children caught their breath. I could not hear John's heart ticking above the engine, but I imagined it was saying, "Amen!"

Sources and Appreciations

ON MY FIRST of eight trips to Mexico (including two summers' residence with my family), I talked to Ethel Wallis, translator to the Mesquital Otomis and author of the best-selling *The Dayuma Story* and other missionary documentaries. "You've got to meet John Beekman," she insisted. "You'll want to do a story about him."

After meeting John, listening to him tick, taping an interview for a broadcast over the 400-station *Master Control* network, and researching an article, I knew that here was a book.

So began the interviews that took me to Chiapas, back and forth from Mexico City to Ixmiquilpan several times, and to John's home in Midland Park, New Jersey. Everyone, it seemed, had a story about the "missionary with the ticking heart."

One Ph.D. colleague of John's described him as "a true genius whose abilities are harnessed to the will of God." A Ph.D. consultant whom John trained said, "John comes nearer to perfection than anybody I know." She recalled a time when John had apologized to her for speaking sharply.

A veteran translator spoke for many others when he said, "John taught me and many others to translate idiomatically. That may be his greatest accomplishment."

Another said, "John is the best fence mender I know. You can hardly feel resentful or angry when you hear that ticking heart of his while he's trying to settle a misunderstanding. You don't dare get him worked up."

And Elaine, the calm mother and hostess at Ixmiquilpan, who never seems to lose her cool, told me, "Other than my conversion, the best thing that ever happened to me was marrying John Beekman."

To John and Elaine I express primary appreciation. They gave me permission to do the book and consented to uncounted hours of interviews. They also made available their personal files (my major source material) containing hundreds of carbons of personal letters written over a 21-year-period.

I next thank their Wycliffe colleagues. W. Cameron Townsend and Dr. Ben Elson, General and Executive Directors of Wycliffe worldwide respectively, provided information and encouraged me to do the book. Dale Kietzman, Director of Extension, and Dr. Frank Robbins, the new director of the Mexican branch were good sources and kind friends.

I thank the Beekmans' co-workers who have served or are still serving among the Chols: Wilbur and Evelyn Aulie, Mrs. Alan Wares (Iris Mills), and Misses Viola Warkentin and Ruby Scott. A thrilling book could be written about the Aulies who continue to serve among the Chols. It was Evelyn Aulie (then Woodward), who first analyzed the Chol Tumbala dialect, did the first Scripture translation, and translated the first hymns. Like John and Elaine, she and Wilbur have served bravely and valiantly, counting it a privilege to suffer in the work of Christ. (For that matter, a book should be published about the service of Marianna Slocum and Florence Gerdel among the Tzeltals, neighbors to the Chols, where there are now more than 15,000 believers.)

Dozens of other Wycliffe members helped, especially the headquarters staff in Mexico City where my family lived for two summers, and various translators who attended workshops at Ixmiquilpan. A feature writer could easily spend a year at Ixmiquilpan doing personality profiles on the spiritual adventurers who come there from the most remote parts of the world.

M.A.F.'s "Hatch" Hatcher and Red Brown (radio technician and operator) were extremely helpful. After flying with Hatch and hearing from missionaries about the dangers of flying with bush pilots, I came to appreciate the contribution of missionary aviation. An adventure book for boys should be written about Hatch who said, "We fly the most valuable cargo in the world — missionaries. We're only here to help them serve more efficiently." Since arriving in Chiapas in 1949, he has made 25,000 landings, marred by only one that was "precautionary." An average of two Mexican pilots have been killed each year in the rugged mountains. He is the only pilot still flying among those who were ferrying cargo and people in 1949.[1] Naturally his favorite Scripture is Psalm 121:8: "The Lord shall preserve thy going out and thy coming in." His motto: "We trust the Lord and take nothing for granted." You believe this when you watch him check his plane before every take-off.

Most of the pictures shown in this book come from the Beekman file or were taken by me. The archaeological photos were furnished by the Mexican Tourist Bureau. A few were taken by Wycliffe photographer Paul Smith.

Several members of the Reformed Mission in Mexico contributed information. I note Dr. John Kempers, who now teaches in the Mexico City Presbyterian Seminary, and the Henry Stegengas who serve at Berea. (Three new missionary couples, specialists in agriculture, literacy, and youth, have just come to the Chol field.) In addition, my wife and I enjoyed an interesting visit in Mexico City with Rev. Leonard Ingram, the pioneer missionary to Chiapas.

I talked with a number of Mexican leaders to get their opinions of Wycliffe's work. A Methodist layman and businessman said bluntly, "The denominational missions could learn some lessons from Wycliffe about working with nationals." Lic. Adolfo Lopez Mateos, president of Mexico from 1958-64, called Wycliffe's General Director Townsend, "a great ambassador." There is no doubt that Wycliffe is the best-known and loved mission inside Mexico and has contributed immeasurably to the growth of the national evangelical church.

Certainly, I must not neglect to express appreciation to John Beekman's mother, his sister Jean, and brother-in-law Pete, and old friends in Midland Park, New Jersey who shared memories of John's childhood. Unfortunately, Richard Beekman, John's brother and now the president of the Ridgewood City Bank, was out of town during my visit to New Jersey.

A final expression of appreciation goes to my wife, Marty, who was in on many of the interviews and helped edit the manuscript. While in Mexico we often enjoyed fellowship with the Beekmans in the home, swimming, and picnicking. Apart from author-subject relationships, we count them as dear friends.

A sage has opinioned that all life is meeting. If this be true, then our lives are infinitely richer for knowing Elaine and John and their illustrious colleagues who follow literally our Lord's command to "preach the Gospel to *every* creature." *If only one person should*

[1]*Editor's Note*: Just before publication, Hatch was appointed field director of M.A.F.'s work in Spanish-speaking Latin America.

read this book and find God leading him to join the Wycliffe team, then this book has been more than worthwhile.

Translation and linguistic work in progress

1. SERI – Edward and Becky Moser
2. YAQUI – John and Mary Jane Dedrick
3. MAYO – Howard and Beth Collard
4. RECOROIBO TARAHUMARA – Donald and Esther Burgess
5. SAMACHIQUE TARAHUMARA – Kenneth and Martha Hilton
6. NORTHERN TEPEHUAN – Burt and Marvel Bascom
7. SOUTHERN TEPEHUAN – Brete and Louise Hart
8. CORA – Amby and Mary Jo McMahon
9. HUICHOL – Joseph and Barbara Grimes
10. CHICHIMECA PAME – Lorna Gibson, Norma Smith
11. HUASTEC – Ray and Kay Larsen
12. HUASTECA AZTEC – Mary Ann Thomas
13. MEZQUITAL OTOMI – Nancy Lanier, Donald and Isabel Sinclair, Ethel Wallis
14. EASTERN OTOMI – Artemisa Echegoyen, Vola Griste, Viola Reimer, Katherine Voigtlander
15. TEPEHUA – Bethel Bower and Dorothy Herzog
16. NORTHERN TOTONAC – Ruth Bishop, Ella Button, Aileen Reid
17. TENANGO OTOMI – Richard and Faith Blight
18. NORTHERN PUEBLA AZTEC – Earl and Gertrude Brockway
19. LOWLAND TOTONAC – Herman and Elizabeth Aschmann
20. HIGHLAND TOTONAC – Herman and Elizabeth Aschmann, Margaret Wendell
21. SIERRA AZTEC – Dow and Lois Robinson
22. STATE OF MEXICO OTOMI – Henrietta Andrews, Doris Bartholomew
23. MAZAHUA – Patricia Hamric, Hazel Spotts, Donald and Shirley Stewart
24. TARASCAN – Julia and Phyllis Burpee, Max and Elizabeth Lathrop, Mary Smith
25. MICHOACAN AZTEC – Richard Beller, William Sischo
26. TETELCINGO AZTEC – Forrest and Jean Brewer
27. EASTERN POPOLOCA – Alice Beebe, Marjorie Kalstrom
28. WESTERN POPOLOCA – Ann Williams
29. ACATLAN MIXTEC – Kent and Mary Lou Wistrand
30. GUERRERO MIXTEC – Edward and Joyce Overholt
31. AYUTLA MIXTEC – Leo and Barbara Pankratz
32. AMUZGO – Amy Bauernschmidt, Marjorie Buck, Cloyd and Ruth Stewart
33. LOWLAND MIXTEC – Henry and Barbara Bradley
34. TATALTEPEC CHATINO – Leslie and Kitty Pride
35. YAITEPEC CHATINO – William and Jessamine Upson
36. EASTERN MIXTEC – John and Margaret Daly
37. HIGHLAND MIXTEC – Georgia Hunter, Kenneth and Evelyn Pike, Betty Stoudt
38. SAN ESTEBAN ATATLAHUACA MIXTEC – Ruth Mary Alexander, Cora Mak
39. COPALA TRIQUE – Bruce and Barbara Hollenbach
40. CHICAHUAXTLA TRIQUE – Robert and Gwendolyn Longacre
41. OCOTEPEC MIXTEC – Ruth Mary Alexander, Cora Mak
42. SAN PEDRO MOLINOS MIXTEC – Georgia Hunter, Betty Stoudt
43. NOCHIXTLAN MIXTEC – Audrey Johnson, Joy Oram
44. HUAJUAPAN MIXTEC – John and Marian Cowan
45. APOALA MIXTEC – Larry and Linda Jordan
46. HIGHLAND MAZATEC – George and Florence Cowan, Ruth Cruikshank, Eunice Pike
47. COATZOSPAN MIXTEC – Priscilla Small, Janet Turner

48. LOWLAND MAZATEC – Paul and Marion Kirk
49. OJTLAN CHINANTEC – Paul and Dorothy Smith
50. TEUTILA CUICATEC – Richard and Ruth Anderson
51. USILA CHINANTEC – Leonard and Marlene Skinner
52. PALANTLA CHINANTEC – Alfred and Patsy Anderson, William and Grace Merrifield
53. TEPEUXILA CUICATEC – Marjorie Davis, Lillian Webb
54. SOCHIAPAN CHINANTEC – William and Shirley Rogers
55. OZUMACIN CHINANTEC – Evelyn Krotzer
56. HIGHLAND CHINANTEC – Richard and Laura Mae Gardner, Frank and Ethel Robbins
57. SIERRA JUAREZ ZAPOTEC – Neil and Jane Nellis
58. RINCON ZAPOTEC – Robert and Katherine Earl
59. LALANA CHINANTEC – Calvin and Carolyn Rensch
60. ETLA ZAPOTEC – Dorothy Wright
61. TABAA ZAPOTEC – Robert and Katherine Earl
62. CHOAPAN ZAPOTEC – Larry and Rosemary Lyman
63. VILLA ALTA ZAPOTEC – Inez Butler, Otis and Mary Leal, Ramona Millar
64. NORTHERN MIXE – John and Gwendolyn Crawford, Joanne North, Linnie Parman, Alvin and Louise Schoenhals
65. TLAHUITOLTEPEC MIXE – Donald and Shirley Lyon
66. JUQUILA MIXE – Walter and Vera Miller
67. CAMOTLAN MIXE – Walter and Vera Miller
68. OCOTLAN ZAPOTEC – Donald and Anne Olson
69. MIAHUATLAN ZAPOTEC – Manis and Jane Ruegsegger
70. CHONTAL OF OAXACA – Viola Waterhouse
71. HUAVE – Glenn and Emily Stairs, Milton and Clara Warkentin
72. ISTHMUS ZAPOTEC – John and Jean Alsop, Virginia Embrey, Laurine Kolderup, Velma Pickett
73. SOUTHERN MIXE – Searle and Hilda Hoogshagen
74. EASTERN MIXE – Norman Nordell
75. SAYULA POPOLUCA – Lawrence and Nancy Clark
76. SIERRA POPOLUCA – John and Royce Lind
77. ISTHMUS AZTEC – Carl and Marilyn Wolgemuth
78. CHONTAL OF TABASCO – Charlotte Hunt, Kathryn Keller, Jim and Mary Walker

79. SANTA MAGDALENA ZOQUE –
80. OCOTEPEC ZOQUE – Robert an
81. COPAINALA ZOQUE – Roy and
82. SAN ANDRES TZOTZIL – Colin
83. CHAMULA TZOTZIL – Kenneth
84. CHENALO TZOTZIL – Kenneth
85. HUIXTEC TZOTZIL – Marion Ce
86. HIGHLAND TZELTAL – Robert Crawford, David and Je
87. CHOL – Wilbur and Evelyn Aulie
88. TILA CHOL – Ruby Scott, Viola
89. LOWLAND TZELTAL – Egbert a and Rae Gifford, Ronal Mary Morgan
90. LACANDON – Philip and Mary B
91. TOJOLABAL – Julia Supple